BAKAR BANK OF THE ORIENT BANKAMERICA FOUNDATION ALVIN H. BAUM, JR. MR.
EN MR. AND MRS. JOHNSON S. BOGART THE BOTHIN FOUN... ...AM
...WN AND BROOK BYERS FRANK A. CAMPINI FOUNDATION LAU... ...ON
...H YUNG CHANG ANNA CHAVEZ AND RICHARD FINEO MR. AN... ...EN
...ENS ALLIANCE-SAN FRANCISCO LODGE THE CHRONICLE PUB... ...ANK
...ENEE DORSEY COLEMAN AND DR. ARTHUR COLEMAN ARTHUR J. COLLINGSWORTH AND
...TER AND GREG MCINTYRE S. H. COWELL FOUNDATION COW HOLLOW FOUNDATION
...MRS. RALPH K. DAVIES CARLOTA AND RAYMOND DEL PORTILLO JACQUELINE AND BEN
...S DOYLE REBECCA S. DRAPER MR. AND MRS. JAMES M. EDGAR ESPRIT FOUNDATION
...LD AND KYLE ANDERSON FILIPINO CULTURAL CENTER FOUNDATION MR. AND MRS.
...WILLIAM S. FISHER FLEISHHACKER FOUNDATION CASSANDRA M. FLIPPER AND WILLIAM
...ENDS OF THE SAN FRANCISCO PUBLIC LIBRARY DONNA WICKHAM FURTH THE GAP
... AND MRS. ADAM P. GEBALLE ALISON F. GEBALLE SHELLEY AND GORDON GEBALLE DR.
...NGER MR. AND MRS. FRED GELLERT, JR. IRA AND LEONORE GERSHWIN PHILANTHROPIC
...GILMORE FOUNDATION LISA AND DOUGLAS GOLDMAN RICHARD & RHODA GOLDMAN
...D EVELYN & WALTER HAAS JR. FUND MIRIAM AND PETER HAAS FUND WALTER AND ELISE
...CY B. HAMON THE LUKE B. HANCOCK FOUNDATION HANDLERY HOTELS, INC. JAMES
...N WHITE & MCAULIFFE CHRIS AND WARREN HELLMAN CLARENCE E. HELLER FOUNDA-
...E HERBST FOUNDATION MR. AND MRS. STANLEY HERZSTEIN HISPANIC CHAMBER OF
...J HUME FOUNDATION MRS. JOHN JAY IDE THE INDUS GROUP, INC. THE INDUSTRIAL
...N MRS. DOUGLAS JOHNSON DORRWIN BUCK JONES MARTHA AND PROCTOR JONES
...LANIE M. KILDUFF MR. AND MRS. JERROLD KINGSLEY MRS. NANCY J. KINGSLEY LAUREN
...JR. MARIAN S. KOBAYASHI ROSALYN AND KARLSON KOO KORET FOUNDATION MRS.
...E FOUNDATION DR. AND MRS. JULIUS R. KREVANS CLARA LAAN AND CHARLES J. CHUN
...ZARUS DR. CARRIE E. LEE TATWINA AND RICHARD LEE JEAN M. LEGARE WALTER LEISS
...ORIAL FUND MATT LOWMAN LOUIS R. LURIE FOUNDATION MRS. WILLIAM F. LUTTGENS
...DATION, INC. MCKESSON FOUNDATION, INC. CAROLE AND ROBERT MCNEIL MERRILL
...MITSUI & CO. (USA), INC. ROBERT M. MOORE DEE MOSBACHER AND NANETTE GARTRELL
...WAILAN NG AND DR. RAYMOND SHUNGWING NG MR. AND MRS. RUDOLF NOTHENBERG
...S. GEORGE OTTO PACIFIC BELL PACIFIC GAS & ELECTRIC COMPANY PACIFIC TELESIS
...N II LISA AND JOHN PRITZKER PUBLIC RESOURCE FOUNDATION DR. ALMA RIBBS THE
...ICHARD RODRIGUEZ LOUISE AND CLAUDE ROSENBERG, JR. GERALD ROSENSTEIN BOB
...CLUB THE SAN FRANCISCO FOUNDATION ROBERT W. SASS RICHARD F. SCHEY ALLEN
...RLES SCHWAB & CO., INC. GAIL SENECA DR. ALBERT SHUMATE JO SCHUMAN SILVER AND
...S. CARL W. STERN, JR. MRS. CARL W. STERN MRS. HARLEY C. STEVENS MISS MARY LOUISE
...G AND DINNER FAMILIES CHARLOTTE MAILLIARD SWIG AND MELVIN M. SWIG THE MAE
...MRS. WASHINGTON SYCIP KATHRYN TAYLOR AND TOM STEYER JAMES THIGPEN JANICE
...RUE NORTH FOUNDATION KENNETH A. TURNER UNION BANK USL CAPITAL DANIEL
...N WALTER CARRIE L. WALTHOUR SALLY WARD AND WEST SHELL TERRANCE K. WATANABE
...ARGO BANK MR. AND MRS. FREDERICK W. WHITRIDGE BRAYTON WILBUR FOUNDATION
...TER-GILLETTE DIANA AND WALTER WONG MR. AND MRS. FRED G. WOO

A Free Library
in this City

"Whereas, We, the citizens of San Francisco, here assembled, believe that the dissemination of education among people is the only safeguard to republican liberty and government, and believing the establishment of public libraries to be the best and cheapest means of educating the people therefore; Resolved, That we do most heartily approve of the project about to be inaugurated for the establishment of

A Free Library in this City

and do pledge to the same our hearty and united support."

CITIZENS' PROCLAMATION, DASHAWAY HALL, AUGUST 1877

THE ILLUSTRATED HISTORY OF THE SAN FRANCISCO PUBLIC LIBRARY

PETER BOOTH WILEY

WELDON OWEN

To Marjorie Stern, whose vision and energy helped bring the new main library—and this book—into being.

Produced and published by Weldon Owen Inc.
814 Montgomery Street, San Francisco, CA 94133, USA

A member of the Weldon Owen Group of Companies
San Francisco • Sydney • London

in association with

The Library Foundation of San Francisco
The San Francisco Public Library, Civic Center, San Francisco, CA 94102, USA

Proceeds from the sales of this book benefit the Main Campaign of
The Library Foundation.

Weldon Owen
President   John Owen
Publisher   Roger Smoothy
Managing Editor   Laurie Wertz
Copy Editor   Judith Dunham

Art Director   John Bull
Book Designer   Elizabeth Marken
Production Director   Stephanie Sherman
Production Coordinator   Tarji Mickelson
Picture Researcher   Lindsay Kefauver
Project Photographer   Andrew McKinney
Artwork Coordinator   Sharon Smith
Jacket Illustrator   Boris Lyubner

Literary Editor   Isabel Allende

Editorial Advisory Board   Marjorie G. Stern, Carol Field, James H. Clark

Library Foundation
Board of Directors   Steven Coulter
Board of Directors   Marjorie G. Stern
Executive Director   Sherry Thomas
Director of Development   Tricia Foster
Director of Annual Giving   Beatrice Burgess
Special Events Manager   Ruth Ann Gonzales
Development Assistant   Charles Williams

First edition published simultaneously with the public dedication
of the New Main San Francisco Public Library, April 1996

Library of Congress Cataloging-in-Publication Data
Wiley, Peter Booth.
    A free library in this city: the illustrated history of the San Francisco
  Public Library / Peter Booth Wiley.
      p.   cm.
    Includes bibliographical references and index.
    ISBN 1-875137-05-X. — ISBN 1-875137-04-1 (trade pbk.)
    1. San Francisco Public Library—History. 2. Public libraries—
  California—San Francisco—History—19th century.   I. Title.
  Z733.S22W55   1996
  027.4794'61—dc20   95-49935
                        CIP

Manufactured by Mandarin Offset, Hong Kong
Printed in China

*Page 2: Grove Street facade of the new main branch of the San Francisco
    Public Library, with City Hall in background*
Right: Larkin Street side of the new library

Contents

Where Spirits Dwell

FOREWORD BY ISABEL ALLENDE

This book is a gift to the city of San Francisco and an homage to the spirits that live in the public library. If you have ever been in the building, you know what I am talking about. It is full of presences; the air vibrates with memories, secret voices, and stories. Everything that has ever happened, is happening, or will happen in this city and its surroundings is contained between those walls, as if the library was a vault where the essence of San Francisco is preserved forever from the erosion of time and the dust of oblivion.

I grew up in my grandfather's large and somber house in Chile, at the south of the south of the world. I had an uncle who looked like Rodolpho Valentino: dark eyes, greased black hair, handsome Spanish features. He bought books by the thousands and cherished them like holy relics. He always wore a coat, even in the summer, with big pockets to hide the volumes he stole from public libraries, bookstores, and the homes of his friends because he believed that literature belonged to humanity in general and to him in particular. His bedroom was covered from floor to ceiling with bookshelves and at the center he had a cot and a reading lamp. Hundreds of volumes piled up on the floor and reproduced themselves mysteriously, slowly invading the rest of the house like a voracious flora, in the midst of which I wandered, with my mind and my senses agitated by indiscriminate readings. This magnificent uncle convinced me that in the stillness of the night the characters left the pages and mingled freely. They strolled from room to room: heroes and villains, maidens and courtesans, warriors and pirates, angels and demons, all busy with their literary adventures and overwhelming passions. Then one of those catastrophic Chilean earthquakes hit in the middle of the night. We heard a terrible noise, as if a train had crushed my uncle's room. We tried to open the door, but it was stuck. The shelves had fallen on the bed and my uncle was buried under a mountain of books. In despair, we started to remove them, looking for his cadaver. Finally we found a foot and dragged him out. He was in perfect health and in control of all his faculties, including his sense of humor. He said that because of the earthquake the characters could not find their way back to their own stories and they had to find refuge in just any book, creating great confusion of time, space, and plots. I have always thought that some contemporary literature was born in a cataclysm like that.

That was my first contact with literature and since then it has been just as exciting. Thirty years later, when I became a writer, my uncle's belief was confirmed: my house is full of presences escaped from literature. If this is the case in my home, can you imagine how it is in a library?

When I was asked to contribute to *A Free Library in this City*, the image of all those spirits roaming freely at night in the vast spaces of the new public library started to haunt me. Spirits of the past, of today, of the future; events, people, emotions, and stories—everything is contained there. The library is the mind and soul of this crazy and wonderful city. In the name of the literary spirits that now have a new home, and of the readers of all ages, and the bookworms, and the authors who research and write in the building, I want to thank those who have made this book possible. Welcome to the main library, my friends. . . .

ISABEL ALLENDE
Literary Editor, *A Free Library in this City*

CHRONOLOGY

Important dates and events in the history of the San Francisco Public Library

1877
Residents of San Francisco hold a meeting at Dashaway Hall, initiated by Andrew S. Hallidie, to advocate the funding and establishment of a free public library.

1878
Governor William Irwin signs the Rogers Act, instituting a property tax to raise library funds and creating a board of library trustees.

1879
First city librarian, Albert Hart, is hired.

First San Francisco Public Library opens on the second floor of Pacific Hall on Bush Street.

1888
Library moves to the Larkin Street wing of City Hall.

1888–89
First three branches are opened, in the Mission, in North Beach, and on Potrero Hill.

1893
Library relocates within City Hall to the third floor of the McAllister Street wing.

1901
The foundation established by Andrew J. Carnegie gives $750,000 to the city to help fund a new main library and several branches.

1903
San Francisco voters pass a bond issue to supplement the Carnegie bequest.

Chicago architect Daniel Burnham, leader of the City Beautiful movement, begins to design a master plan for San Francisco, including a Civic Center with a new library building.

1906
Daniel Burnham presents his final plan for the city's redesign, but shortly afterward earthquake and fire destroy much of the city, including City Hall and the main library and its collection. Of the six branches opened in the decades before the earthquake, two are destroyed.

1907
Temporary main library is built at Hayes and Franklin streets.

1909
The city begins to raise funds and consider plans for a new Civic Center.

1914
Temporary main library reaches capacity.

Architect George W. Kelham's design for a new main library—the first building to be constructed specifically for the library—is chosen for a Civic Center location, the block bound by Larkin, McAllister, Hyde, and Fulton streets.

Carnegie Foundation funds are earmarked for the building of branch libraries in the Richmond, the Mission, the Sunset, Noe Valley, and Golden Gate Valley.

1915
Ground is broken for the main library.

1916
Cornerstone for the main library is laid—ten years after the devastating earthquake of 1906.

1917
Main library is dedicated and opens to the public.

1920
Main library begins to acquire rare books and the works of San Francisco's fine printers and binders, a collection that in 1927 is named for Max J. Kuhl.

1921
Carnegie Foundation funds are used to finance branches in North Beach and on Sacramento Street.

1929
Business branch opens in the Russ Building in the financial district.

1943
Main library building reaches capacity.

1947
Nat Schmulowitz donates collection of humor books and magazines to main library.

1948
Voters turn down bond issue to fund eighteen branches and an addition to the main library.

1949
Citizens concerned about future of library meet to form the first, short-lived Friends of the San Francisco Library.

1952
Series of articles in the *San Francisco Chronicle* criticizes library.

1957
Hale Champion's series in the *San Francisco Chronicle* negatively critiques the library's operation and services.

1958
Emerson Greenaway, an eminent librarian, delivers a report recommending additional city funding, improvements to the main library, and hiring of trained staff.

1959
Mayor George Christopher creates the Committee of Fifty, a group of prominent cultural and business leaders, to build support for the library.

1960
San Franciscans for a Better Library, a citizens' group, is formed.

1961
Prominent residents meet to form another library support group, the San Francisco Library League.

1962
The Committee of Fifty, San Franciscans for a Better Library, and the San Francisco Library League join forces under a new name—Friends of the San Francisco Public Library.

Main library begins to organize its collection into departments, including Literature, Philosophy, and Religion; Art and Music; and History, Travel, and Biography.

1963
Richard Harrison, local calligrapher and collector of calligraphy, gives his collection to the library.

1964
The Friends holds its first annual book sale, raising $4,000 to purchase rare materials for the library.

Main library establishes a collection of material on local history, later named the San Francisco History Room.

1965
Robert Grabhorn's collection of 1,500 rare books becomes part of the main library's Special Collections.

1967
Bay Area Reference Center opens and for twenty-one years shares information and resources with the other library systems in northern California, and enhances the services of the San Francisco main library.

1969
San Francisco librarians form the Librarians' Guild, which soon replaces the Library Staff Association.

1970
Librarians' Guild supports the four-day citywide strike of public employees.

1972
Keep Libraries Alive! forms to protest the closing of branches to meet the cuts in the city's budget for the library system.

1974
Library commission, the Friends of the Library, Keep Libraries Alive!, and other citizen groups fight successfully to retain Marshall Square as the site of a new main library.

1978
Passage of Proposition 13, rolling back property taxes, deleteriously impacts the city's ability to fund the library and other public institutions.

1982
Report by Lowell Martin recommending consolidation of branches catalyzes public support for the branches.

1985
Friends of the Library offers to work with Mayor Dianne Feinstein on the completion of the Civic Center, including use of Marshall Square for a new library.

1986
Task force is created by Mayor Feinstein to complete the design of the Civic Center.

Report by Becker and Hayes/Omni-Group criticizes Old Main and calls for building a new library in Marshall Square.

Friends of the Library inaugurates a private fund-raising campaign for the New Main.

Library Foundation of San Francisco is established to support a New Main.

1987
Second study by Becker and Hayes/Omni-Group underscores the use of Marshall Square for a new library. Another study, by Skidmore Owings Merrill, recommends that the Old Main be used for a museum.

Mayor calls for a new main library in Marshall Square as part of a Civic Center master plan.

1988
Voters in San Francisco approve Proposition A, a city bond measure of $109.5 million to build a new 376,000-square-foot library and renovate branch libraries. A state bond measure, also approved, provides additional funds.

1989
Pei Cobb Freed & Partners of New York and Simon Martin-Vegue Winkelstein Moris of San Francisco are hired by the library commission as architects for the New Main.

1991
Library Foundation officially announces its campaign for the New Main.

1992
Groundbreaking ceremony is held in Marshall Square.

Special Gifts campaign is launched to seek funds from various local constituencies (affinity groups) for particular collections and capital gifts.

1994
Topping-out ceremony marks the completion of the framing for the new building.

Library Foundation reaches $30 million fund-raising goal and keeps going.

1995
New Main is completed. By the end of the year, Library Foundation has raised $35 million.

1996
New San Francisco Public Library opens.

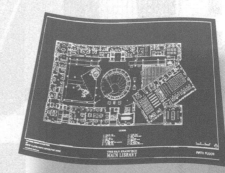

CHAPTER ONE

FROM FRONTIER TOWN TO CULTURAL CAPITAL

❖

San Francisco Realizes its Dream

For aeons the western shores of San Francisco Bay had been the chosen wintering place of prehistoric people who gathered there to fish and to hunt among the sand dunes intermingled with thick woods that ran gently and ever more steeply westward. The oldest known visitor came to stay, leaving her thigh bone to be discovered by a

Preceding pages: San Francisco in 1851, shown in a chromolithograph by Francis Samuel Marryat. Ships brought forty-niners to the gold diggings and were often abandoned, converted into buildings, or left to rot on the mudflats. Yerba Buena Island is in the background.

Mission Plank Road, shown here in 1856, was built in 1850 to connect the waterfront city with the settlement around Mission Dolores. Twin Peaks rise to the left, with Lonely Mountain and the heights of Buena Vista Park on the right. Along Market and Mission streets there were numerous high sand dunes with swampy areas in between.

construction worker excavating a site adjacent to that now occupied by the new main library. This human remnant has been carbon-dated to around 3000 B.C.

Drawn as well to the bay front, a later generation of settlers established Yerba Buena, as San Francisco of the early 1800s was called. The village was little more than a collection of shacks and adobes. A trail wound through the dunes and dense patches of scrub connecting Yerba Buena to the Mission Dolores, founded in 1776 by Spanish friars. "We mounted speedily and commenced our route through a dense thicket, where the path was narrow, and where the trees so intersected their branches, as to endanger our heads as we rode," Alfred Robinson wrote in 1828 about a journey that took him past what would become the Civic Center. He had come to California to trade and ended up marrying into a prominent Hispanic family. "Thus we went on," Robinson continued, "sometimes crossing little valleys, where the fox-like coyote prowled, and sometimes rising sandy eminences, where a glimpse was had of the neighboring bay. Through the woods resounded the wolf's howl, and the heavy track of the grizzly bear lay printed in our course. At length through an opening in the woods, we saw the Mission of Dolores."

When a boomtown sprang up seemingly overnight along the bay after the Gold Rush of 1849, the *ayuntamiento*, or town council, chose the same lonely

sand dunes for the Yerba Buena Cemetery. The cemetery, located on the site where the old main library now stands, quickly filled with the remains of paupers and many a young man who came to seek his fortune but died unknown. "It lies in a hollow among miserable sandhills, which are scantily covered with stunted trees, and tufted weeds . . . among the most dreary and melancholy spots that surround the city," wrote a trio of early historians. To the south of the cemetery, the Mission Plank Road Company in 1850 built a forty-foot-wide wooden toll road so that wagons and carriages could cross the marshy ground to the mission. Thus Mission Street, one of San Francisco's major arteries, was born.

As the city pushed westward from San Francisco Bay and the population raced forward at an astounding rate—57,000 in 1860, 150,000 in 1870, 234,000 in 1880—the golden dunes and unhappy graves disappeared beneath city streets while homes, stores, and apartment buildings brought the clamor of the ebullient young city with them. In 1871 construction began on a new City Hall near the intersection of Market and Hyde streets, two blocks from the present City Hall; it would take more than twenty-five years to complete. Soon the unfinished City Hall, an ugly and incongruous amalgam of architectural styles known to local wags as "the ruin" and "the cyclops," towered over a neighborhood studded with empty, sandy lots. These lots, particularly those south of City Hall, became the province of street agitators who spoke to the gathered crowds from rickety wooden platforms.

THE FIRST FREE LIBRARY

In August 1877, in the midst of a recession and the turmoil of anti-Chinese riots that began with a round of speechifying at the sandlots near City Hall, San Franciscans decided that it was time to build a public library. One generation after the East Coast's first literary renaissance—the renaissance of Emerson, Hawthorne, Melville, Poe, Thoreau, and Whitman—San Francisco was already a writers' town. The gold rush, which had attracted a well-educated crowd, inspired its chroniclers, and the city, wide, open, and brimming with youthful energy, became an important stopover for itinerant young souls. Some even came to stay. Mark Twain, Bret Harte, Ambrose Bierce, Joaquin Miller, and Ina Coolbrith were among the best-known talents that fed a prodigious and delightful array of journals and newspapers with names such as the *Golden Era, Alta California, Argonaut,* and *Wasp.*

In 1879 the San Francisco Free Public Library was opened in Pacific Hall on Bush Street between Kearny and Dupont (later Grant) streets. It had so few books that there were no borrowing privileges for several years, but in less than a decade the library outgrew its space. It was little wonder that this first public library, despite its shaky beginnings, became an overnight success. In 1888

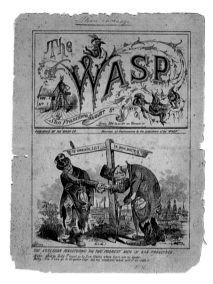

The first issue of the Wasp, *August 5, 1876. Edited by Ambrose Bierce, the journal featured color cartoons and social satire written in a style that was exuberantly and personally venomous. When Oscar Wilde came to town to lecture in 1882, he was described as the "sovereign of insufferables," a "dunghill he-hen," and the "littlest and looniest of a brotherhood of simpletons." And that was only the beginning!*

the library moved to the Larkin Street wing of the unfinished City Hall. In 1893 it moved again, this time to the more spacious and elegant McAllister Street wing of City Hall, where it filled the top floor.

By this time San Francisco's civic leaders, many of them sons of the forty-niners who had patched together vast fortunes in the space of one generation, had developed greater ambitions for their young city. San Francisco lives "to be the capital of an empire," wrote James Duval Phelan in the July 1896 *Overland Monthly,* "and to foster the arts of peace; to yield for her citizens the fruits of a civilization, riper and better than those which gladdened the Athenian heart and fulfilled the Roman's boast—'to be Roman was greater than to be a King.'" Phelan, banker, patron of the arts, and politician who would later serve as mayor of the city and United States senator, spoke of the "arts of peace," but it was war, war with Spain in 1898 and the seizure of the Philippines, the United States' first colony, that led San Franciscans to view the Pacific Basin as their new dominion.

To these more polished and culturally aspiring men of the world, much about San Francisco was, frankly, an embarrassment. City politics was dominated by a rough crowd of demagogues and party bosses who drew their support from the alleys, boardinghouses, modest homes, saloons, and dives that graced the waterfront, the area south of Market Street, and other working-class districts. Parsimony reigned supreme in the province of public spending. City Hall, its construction funded from year to year, was finally completed in 1898, but architecturally was hardly the centerpiece of a great city whose earnest boosters wished to compare it with Athens, Paris, and Rome. If San Francisco was to retain its place as the foremost American city on the shores of the Pacific, it would have to do something ambitious to overcome its tawdry reputation and make its mark in the world.

Led by James Phelan, a group of civic leaders turned to Daniel Burnham, the pioneering Chicago architect who was at the forefront of the ambitious City Beautiful urban planning movement. Burnham devised a vast plan for San Francisco modeled after Baron Georges-Eugène Haussmann's plans for Paris. At the heart of the Burnham plan was a new Civic Center, a constellation of public buildings, including a new public library, that would truly be worthy of a metropolis that aspired to be ranked among the great cities of the ancient world and modern Europe.

FIRE AND REBIRTH

On April 17, 1906, Burnham presented his plan to the public. The next day the face of San Francisco was changed forever: the heart of the city was laid waste by the earthquake and fire of 1906. Up in smoke and ashes went the collection at the

Opposite page: The City Hall that was built between 1871 and 1898 and destroyed in the 1906 earthquake. A sprawling agglomerate of various architectural styles, it epitomized the corruption and architectural bad taste of a frontier city. It also housed the main library at different times in two different wings. The Pioneer Monument sits in Marshall Square, in the foreground, which became the site of the main library opened in 1996.

main library, leaving 25,000 volumes at two book depositories and the four branch libraries that survived. A nightmare, yes, but also an incredible opportunity: the city could be rebuilt along the lines of the Burnham plan and with it a new modern library. Yet that was not to be. The business community demanded that the city be rebuilt quickly. There was no time for plans, not even time to rebuild many structures according to the new earthquake-inspired construction code.

A new Civic Center was built, but only after a pause of nearly a decade while the city recovered both from the earthquake and from an unsightly bribery scandal that sent the mayor to jail and a number of supervisors into disgrace. First came the Nourse Civic Auditorium (later named the Bill Graham Civic Auditorium) in 1915, then that same year a new City Hall, a Beaux Arts masterpiece with a dome taller than that of the Capitol in Washington, D.C. Two years later, the new public library opened its doors.

The library was a noble structure, conservatively designed in the Italian Renaissance style to harmonize with the rest of the Civic Center. The building, which seemed to provide reasonable space for expansion, had arched Roman windows, a sweeping center staircase, and a large atrium at the head of the stairs. Its capacity: 500,000 volumes, a remarkable number at a time when the total library collection was 191,960 volumes.

The library was built at the beginning of an expansive era in San Francisco politics under Mayor James Rolph Jr. (1912–30). The city built the first municipal railroad system in the country. A vast fantasy city was erected along the bay to house the Panama-Pacific International Exposition of 1915. Water was brought to San Francisco via a 150-mile-long aqueduct from the newly completed Hetch Hetchy Reservoir in the Sierra Nevada. The library benefited from this expansiveness: ten new branch libraries were completed in the decade after the opening of the main library, bringing the total number of branches throughout the city to fifteen. But the library never became a significant cultural institution like the opera.

The Great Depression brought unprecedented use of the library and a threat to halve its budget. Five more branches were built, two with federal funds. Through the war years the

The main library designed by George W. Kelham and built in 1917 as part of the city's new Civic Center. Its exterior, like the facades of the new City Hall and civic auditorium, evoked Beaux Arts Paris, but its internal layout turned out to be less than ideal. It took the city more than half a century after this building reached capacity in 1943 to construct a new main library.

library kept up appearances. The book collection was good, not excellent, and a small number of wealthy patrons established special collections. Branch construction continued, with eight more buildings erected between 1945 and 1963.

Little notice was taken in 1943 when the main library reached capacity. Soon, however, the very grandeur of the library—its high-ceilinged reading rooms, sweeping staircase, and lavish atrium—was seen as its biggest problem. Only half of the building's space was usable. Gradually, due to lack of funding, library services began to deteriorate. Retired staff who worked through those years describe a sleepy atmosphere where untrained employees, many of them close relatives of powerful figures in city government, served the reading public.

The main reading room of the old main library in 1925, which evokes the grand reading rooms of great European libraries. The beamed ceilings were meant to resemble those of an Italian Renaissance palazzo. The space will become an exhibit hall in the new Asian Art Museum.

LITERARY RENAISSANCE

Sad times at the public library became a matter of public record when *San Francisco Chronicle* reporter Hale Champion blasted the library in 1957 as a disgrace. "There are so many things that have been wrong for so many years that the San Francisco library system is nationally ill-famed," he wrote. And this in a cultured city renowned for its ballet, symphony, and opera.

The city seemed to respond quickly. Mayor George Christopher appointed a commission of prominent citizens. Emerson Greenaway, a librarian of national stature from Philadelphia, was hired to study the situation. He recommended a number of reforms in the administration of the library and the delivery of library services, but not a new library. In 1960 William R. Holman, a dynamic young city librarian, was hired, and the next year the Friends of the Library was reorganized with the intent of setting standards and making the library a first-class institution. But the years dragged by. Innumerable studies were conducted, from the early 1960s to the early 1980s. All reached the same conclusion: a new library must be built.

For a time during the first administration of Mayor Joseph Alioto (1967–71), the mayor appeared to be leading the charge for a new library, but again nothing happened. Civic leaders were focused on what were deemed more pressing matters. Billions of dollars poured into the city, literally transforming the skyline—funds for new freeways, for the Bay Area Rapid Transit system, for a new convention center, for block after block of new high-rises. A new symphony hall was constructed, but not before its backers unsuccessfully attempted to preempt

Story hour at a branch library. Starting in 1888, the library began opening branch libraries. There are now twenty-six branches, a large number for a city the size of San Francisco. In a city increasingly defined in terms of distinctive neighborhoods, a branch library came to be seen as a vital part of each community.

the Marshall Square site one block south of the main library, which had been previously promised for a new library. Library budgets inched upward slowly and painfully, but hardly at a pace to keep up with the reading public's needs.

The themes played upon by civic leaders in the 1960s and 1970s were remarkably the same as those trumpeted earlier by James Phelan and his associates. San Francisco must uphold its place against Los Angeles as the premier city of the Pacific Basin. It must have a thriving downtown business district and port, an elaborate convention center, and attractions for tourists, or it will become a provincial backwater.

Meanwhile San Francisco grew more literary than ever. Over the years many a well-known writer had claimed the city as his or her home, whether permanent or temporary. Among the greats were Jack London, John Steinbeck, Dashiell Hammett, William Saroyan, and Kathryn Forbes. Wallace Stegner taught at nearby Stanford University. Oscar Lewis, George Stewart, and Irving Stone made major contributions to Western history from here. The post–World War II years spawned the San Francisco renaissance, whose writers, the beatniks, graced the bars and coffeehouses of North Beach. In time the beatniks gave way to the hippies, and the literary world, once fused with the jazz world, found new companions in the world of rock and roll. Like a tide that never seemed to ebb, the literary currents rolled on. Prominent women writers and poets such as Kay Boyle, Tillie Olsen, Diane DiPrima, and Jade Snow Wong foreshadowed the later emergence of Amy Tan, Maxine Hong Kingston, Isabel Allende, and Alice Walker. A realm that was for many years predominantly male and white had fractured and reconstituted itself into a glorious array of themes, colors, and sexual preoccupations. At the same time, the city became known for its fine bookstores and emerged as the hub of a thriving publishing industry second only to New York.

THE COMMUNITY RESPONDS

The Friends of the San Francisco Public Library, led for the most part by what started out as a group of civic-minded and determined young people, kept the torch burning for a new library. Using the Friends as their base, Margaret Mayer, Mary Louise Stong, and Marjorie Stern—known collectively as the "three Ms"—worked year in and year out with hundreds of other volunteers, but with little or no assistance from the political establishment, to build a constituency that would support a new library. In 1988, thirty-one years after the *Chronicle*'s exposé, a bond measure finally went on the ballot to provide funding for the construction of a new main library and rehabilitation of five branches. An astounding 78 percent of the voters cast ballots in favor of the measure. With $109.5 million in the bank, construction on a new library finally began in 1992.

From the time when San Franciscans began to see themselves as builders of a great city in the tradition of the ancient world and Europe, a library was central to their plans. Every great metropolis dating back to the first city-states of Sumeria had its civic center, and every great city had its library. Libraries were fundamental to the accumulation of human knowledge, and nineteenth-century San Francisco was determined to be at the forefront of urban progress. Fittingly, a century later, the idea for a new main library was brought to the public by a highly organized citizens' movement that, after triumphing at the ballot box, went on to organize a successful campaign to raise $35 million to furnish the new library, enhance its existing book collections, start new information centers, and bring the library into the electronic future. With the opening of the New Main in April 1996, San Francisco was ready to lay proper claim once again to a heritage that stretched back to the earliest days of urban life and the written word.

The Grove Street facade of the new main library. The exterior was designed in two distinctive styles, one in the spirit of the Beaux Arts Civic Center, the other in a modern idiom that harmonizes with the glass-and-steel structures on Market Street.

CHAPTER TWO

RECORDING THE HUMAN EXPERIENCE

Ancient Libraries

The Bible tells of the great cities of Aram-naharaim, the land that lies between the two rivers, the Tigris and the Euphrates. These were the cities of Mesopotamia (modern-day Iraq), one of the regions of the world where writing first developed. It was in this fertile valley that humans pioneered irrigated agriculture, built the first great metropolises, ringed them with enormous walls,

Preceding pages: The marketplace in Athens in the third and fourth centuries B.C. during the height of the city's intellectual ascendancy. According to a Roman historian, there was a public library in Athens until the collection was carried away by Xerxes in 480 B.C.

Map of the fertile Tigris and Euphrates river valley (now part of Iraq), where the Sumerians developed writing around 3100 B.C. and the first libraries were built.

and within these walls constructed monumental palaces and houses of worship, while pushing their trade routes from the Mediterranean Sea to the Indus River Valley and perhaps beyond. Here humans began to keep a written record of their economic transactions, of their history, and of their gods. Here, too, humans first wrote a code of law, compiled the first genealogies, and combined the stories of the heroic deeds of their ancestors with the flights of their imagination and committed them to a written form. In all, some half-million documents describe the life of this ancient world. The act of writing was the beginning of history, an act of accumulated memory, the codification of a unique civilization. To facilitate that accumulation and build a better world, the Sumerians, the first city builders of Mesopotamia, constructed the first libraries.

In time little was left of this ancient world beyond scattered bricks, some covered with strange writings that came to be known as cuneiform, and numerous mounds dispersed across the dry and desolate landscape. So little was left that the existence of the great empires of Assyria and Babylonia was very much doubted, and the Sumerians were unknown. As the French and British pressed their imperial ambitions upon the ancient lands of Mesopotamia in the early nineteenth century, young adventurers, the forerunners of modern archaeologists, came to dig in these strange mounds, for here, supposedly, lay hidden the fabled cities of the Old Testament, cities such as Nimrud, Erech, Nineveh, and Babylon. When Austen Henry Layard and Paul Émile Botta, two of the most celebrated

early archaeologists, cut into these barren tumuli beginning in 1842, by wonderful happenstance they quickly found the remains of Nimrud and Nineveh. They unearthed massive walls, detailed reliefs, and enormous statues of winged beasts with human heads. These figures rose up from the sandy soil, said the Muslims who did the digging, like so many demons from the netherworld.

In one of his digs at Nineveh, Layard made a discovery that would have a far greater impact on our understanding of Mesopotamia than any of his spectacular finds. Tunneling within the great mound of the ancient city, he came across two rooms filled to the ceiling with cuneiform tablets. "We cannot overstate their value," he wrote. "They will furnish us with materials for the complete decipherment of the cuneiform character, for restoring the language and history of Assyria, and for inquiring into the customs, science, and, we may perhaps even add, literature, of its people."

Layard could not have been more correct. This was part of the library of Ashurbanipal (668–627 B.C.), the ruthless transvestite warrior king known for his military exploits, including the subjugation of Egypt, and also for his fascination with learning. Soon after, the strange writings inscribed in clay with a three-sided stylus were deciphered. This written record pointed backward and downward, following the path of the archaeologist through layer upon layer, past the early years of Assyria to the fourth millennium B.C., when the Sumerians built the first cities of Mesopotamia.

Below: A nineteenth-century view of the site of Nineveh, the great Assyrian city. The circular mound above the tower on the right is the remains of the palace where Ashurbanipal's library was discovered by Austen Henry Layard in 1850. Layard (above), shown dressed as a Bakhtiyari tribesman, was one of the great archaeological adventurers.

This bronze statue located adjacent to the old San Francisco Main Library depicts how Ashurbanipal, founder of one of the greatest libraries in the ancient world, might have looked.

EARLY WRITING AND RECORD KEEPING

Among the most important Sumerian cities were Ur (Abraham was a Chaldean from Ur), Uruk (the Erech of the Old Testament), and Eridu (regarded by the Sumerians as the oldest city in the world). Part of a world of city-states, each was ruled by a single monarch and a priestly caste who worshiped many gods but built temples to their principal deities. Uruk in 2700 B.C. was a city of 50,000 spread over 1,100 acres with seventy-six out-lying villages. The city was surrounded, according to the *Epic of Gilgamesh,* by a six-mile-long wall made of burnt brick that shone "with the brilliance of copper" in the bright sun.

It was in the Red Temple at Uruk that the earliest signs of writing—mankind's first symbolic language, dating to about 3100 B.C.—were found. On these clay tablets, scribes had written lists of local products that were most likely controlled and traded by the temple's priests. Engaged in far-flung trade in grains, timber, copper, ivory, and precious and semiprecious stones, the rulers of Uruk needed to keep records of their extensive trans-actions and other daily activities. For this reason they also needed an archive, the first collection of written records. Approximately 80 percent of the tablets and fragments of tablets found throughout Mesopotamia were linked to the particulars of daily life: lists of possessions, regulations for communal life, receipts, loan documents, marriage and dowry agreements, wills, apprenticeship contracts, price indices.

There were other documents—documents that revealed a culture in full flower, a complex urban society that shared much with later urban soci-eties and our own. Preserved in the collection were accounts of what to us are myths, but to the Sumerians and their successors were the sum of their the-ology: descriptions of the supernatural hierarchy; hymns, prayers, and divi-nations of dreams; celebrations of particular rulers; royal annals and other historical works; recipes; encyclopedias; bilingual and trilingual dictionaries; scientific documents including treatises on mathematics, astronomy, and law (the Code of Hammurabi); technical formulas for the production of glass, perfumes, dyes, and beverages; diplomatic correspondence, international treaties, and reports from spies; and some of the earliest masterpieces of world literature, such as the *Poem of Creation* and *Epic of Gilgamesh.*

From the extent of these collections of clay tablets inscribed in the third and second millennia B.C. and from their location often within temple walls, we can deduce that numerous libraries existed in the early Mesopotamian city-states. For Hammurabi, the great Babylonian king who ruled from 1792 to 1750 B.C., to have written his famous code, which is really a treatise on exemplary laws, there must have been an ample collection of sources available to his scholars and scribes.

By the end of the third millennium B.C., the Sumerians had passed into history, taking with them their spoken language but leaving behind their written language and their vast literary, religious, and scientific heritage to form the basis of Greek and later civilizations. Other peoples moved into the Fertile Crescent—Akkadians, Semites, Assyrians—intermarried, and built their own urban civilizations. In time, we come to the first descriptions of libraries.

Sargon II (722–705 B.C.), one of Mesopotamia's foremost warrior kings, fought far and wide from Egypt to the mountains of Azerbaijan to maintain his sway over the Assyrian Empire. Not satisfied with the glories of his capital city at Kalakh (Nimrud), he built a second city near Nineveh and named it Dur Sharrukin (now Khorsabad). Within it he constructed an enormous palace and temple complex with a main gate flanked by two winged bulls with human heads. In this palace Sargon put together a library whose main treasure was a list of kings stretching back to 2000 B.C. and the reign of the original Sargon.

It was the legacy of Sargon's great-grandson, Ashurbanipal, to have built the first truly renowned library of the ancient world. Thought to have had a scholarly upbringing, Ashurbanipal personally supervised the collection of 25,000 tablets for his library, employing a staff of scribes and scholars to search out and copy the known written documents of the extensive lands over which he held sway. At the entrance to each room was a kind of subject catalogue or bibliography written on tablets.

Sumerian cuneiform, like this specimen from about 2900 B.C., bears the characteristic wedge-shaped impressions made in soft clay with a stylus. The development of cuneiform, the earliest form of writing, marked the transition from pictograms to letters.

According to an ancient papyrus, Egyptian scribes did not produce pyramids, stelae, or children as their legacy. Rather, they "made as heirs for themselves the writings and books of instruction which they had compiled."

FROM HIEROGLYPHS TO HOUSES OF BOOKS

Today we, like many peoples of the ancient world, look to the Sumerians, a people unknown until the last century, for our cultural antecedents. Writing, we now know, developed almost simultaneously in disparate parts of the classical world—in Sumeria, in the Indus River Valley, and in pharaonic Egypt, another civilization spawned in a fertile river valley. The Egyptians employed a pictographic form of writing

known as hieroglyphics, the earliest known examples of which appear on the walls of tombs and temples dating to 3100 B.C. and are thought perhaps to have derived from Sumerian pictographs.

As in Sumeria, the earliest libraries or archives in Egypt, from the third millennium B.C., are connected with the temples and palaces of the great dynastic leaders. Variously called Houses of Sacred Writings or Archives of the Ancestors, these were also institutions where scribes were trained and apparently served a general educational function. Early Egyptian libraries contained mainly religious scriptures, but eventually the collections grew and included scrolls on mathematics, medicine, and astronomy. One of the most impressive medical collections was found in the Temple of Thoth, the god of wisdom, at Hermopolis. The scribe-priest was called Keeper of the Sacred Books and his female assistant, Lady of Letters, Mistress of the House of Books.

Egyptian literature flourished repeatedly, producing particularly outstanding works during the Twelfth Dynasty (1991–1786 B.C.) and the New Kingdom (1550–1070 B.C.). Egyptians wrote in many forms, including collections of maxims, funerary writings (*The Book of the Dead*), dream interpretations, works of magic, historical romances, poetry, and novels (*The Story of Sinuhe* is regarded as one of the classics of the ancient world). Literacy appears for the most part to have been restricted to the elite and their retainers. But excavations at the site of a village of workers engaged on a construction project for Ramses II (1299–1232 B.C.) revealed papyrus scraps and other writing materials covered with bills, work reports, accounts of lawsuits, letters, and even literature, indicating that literacy may have been more widespread.

Ultimately the land of the pharaohs was overwhelmed by outsiders, first by the Hittites, who sacked Thebes in 661 B.C., then by the Persians, and finally by the Greeks, who under Alexander the Great conquered Egypt in 332 B.C. It was on Egyptian soil that Alexander's successor, the Greek pharaoh Ptolemy Soter, established the greatest library of the ancient world.

In this papyrus from The Book of the Dead, *dated 1250 B.C., the scribe Ani makes an offering to Ra, the falcon-headed sun god. In Egypt, hieroglyphic writing progressed from rough symbols to an art form.*

Inset: According to myth, Thoth, the ibis-headed god of wisdom, taught the Egyptians how to write.

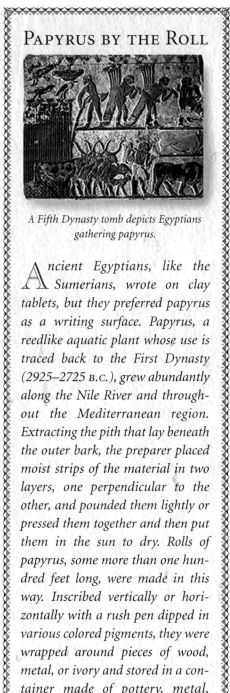

PAPYRUS BY THE ROLL

A Fifth Dynasty tomb depicts Egyptians gathering papyrus.

Ancient Egyptians, like the Sumerians, wrote on clay tablets, but they preferred papyrus as a writing surface. Papyrus, a reedlike aquatic plant whose use is traced back to the First Dynasty (2925–2725 B.C.), grew abundantly along the Nile River and throughout the Mediterranean region. Extracting the pith that lay beneath the outer bark, the preparer placed moist strips of the material in two layers, one perpendicular to the other, and pounded them lightly or pressed them together and then put them in the sun to dry. Rolls of papyrus, some more than one hundred feet long, were made in this way. Inscribed vertically or horizontally with a rush pen dipped in various colored pigments, they were wrapped around pieces of wood, metal, or ivory and stored in a container made of pottery, metal, ivory, or leather.

Expanding the Frontiers of Knowledge

In his School of Athens *(1508–11), Raphael portrayed Aristotle, center right, in conversation with Plato. Aristotle and his followers built an impressive research library at the Athens Lyceum. Preservation of his works became an important task for great libraries over the centuries.*

Greece, and particularly Athens, between the days of Solon (who became chief magistrate in 594 B.C.) and the death (in 336 B.C.) of Philip II of Macedon, Alexander's father, produced one of those quantum leaps in human knowledge that appears astonishing in retrospect. Consider the greatness of the achievement of Athens alone. In drama there were Aeschylus, Sophocles, Euripides, and Aristophanes; in history, Herodotus and Thucydides; and in philosophy, Socrates, Plato, and Aristotle, to name the most prominent Athenians. Greeks pushed the frontiers of human thought forward, introducing theoretical analysis and speculative thinking in a way that was unknown in other parts of the ancient world. The Sumerians excelled in astronomy, and the Egyptians in mathematics, but whereas the Egyptians left little more than lists of mathematical formulas, the Greeks subjected mathematics to formal analysis.

Ironically, little is known about the libraries of ancient Greece because Greek and Roman writers made only occasional references to specific collections. What is clear is that the works of a philosopher like Aristotle or a historian like Herodotus presuppose access to a large body of written works from around the known world. Herodotus was the first historian to emphasize the importance of using written records, and Aristotle and his collaborators compiled and culled enormous amounts of information for their seminal works in biology (*Historia animalium,* or *History of Animals*), geology, meteorology, chemistry, and psychology (*De anima,* or *On the Soul,* and *De parva naturali,* or *On the Senses and Their Objects*). Thus the collection of information centered in libraries took on new meaning in ancient Greece.

Mosaic depicting the school of Plato. Originally a disciple of Socrates, Plato made an enormous contribution to the development of philosophy through his famous dialogues and works such as The Republic.

A second-century Roman author wrote of Peisistratus, the tyrant who ruled Athens three times between 561 B.C. and his death in 527 B.C. and established the city's first library when he gave his personal collection to the city and opened it to the public. This would be consistent with the claim that Peisistratus appointed a commission to write down the works of Homer and sponsored the first Dionysian Festival in Athens, which played an important role in the evolution of Greek drama. Peisistratus's collection was supposedly added to over the years until Xerxes carried it off after he captured and sacked Athens in 480 B.C.

The Athenians were a literate and well-educated people, more literate than any Westerners before the twentieth century, although literacy was confined to perhaps 15 percent of the population. Athens was an international city, an open community with a large foreign population, the democratic headquarters of an Aegean empire. It provided a high standard of living for many of its citizens and a degree of leisure that permitted its culture to flourish. The locus of city life was the agora, or marketplace, which lay in the shadow of the Temple of Hephaestus, the god of fire.

Gathered around this civic center were market stalls, offices of the archon (chief magistrate), a council house, an archive, an arsenal, and a mint. But to date no city library has been found in Athens.

Ptolemy Soter, who grew up with Alexander the Great and ruled Egypt after his death in 323 B.C., founded the great library at Alexandria.

THE FIRST UNIVERSAL LIBRARY

The effort to acquire Aristotle's library, housed at the Lyceum in Athens, where he taught, and preserve his works was a major factor in the development of the library at Alexandria. To deal with his obstreperous son, Alexander, Philip II of Macedon asked Aristotle to become his son's tutor. Aristotle took on the task, instructing Alexander and a group of his companions including Ptolemy, who would later rule Egypt and found the great library. Upon the assassination of Philip of Macedon in 336 B.C., Alexander proved to be an eager successor of enormous skill and ambition. After accomplishing the final subjugation of the Greek city-states, he marched into Asia Minor to wreak vengeance upon the Greeks' historic enemies, the

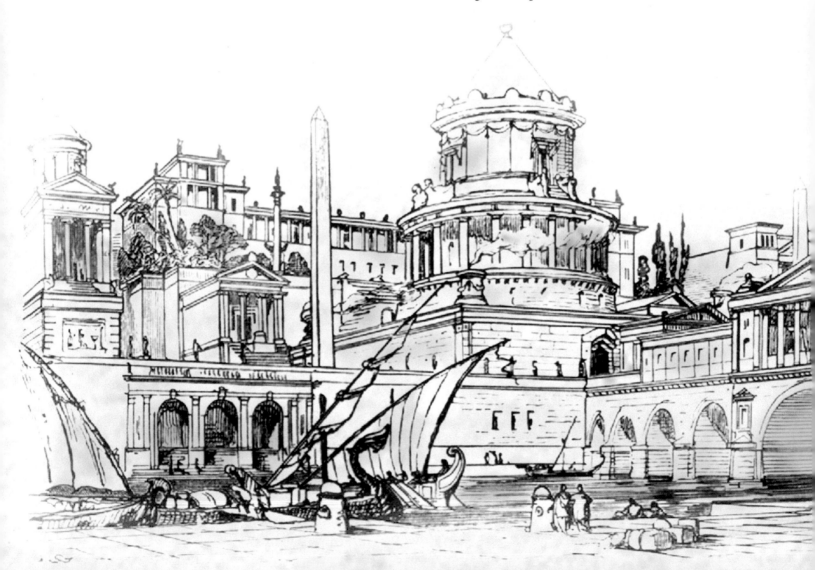

Persians. Alexander then seized the seaport of Phoenician Tyre and entered Egypt, where he had himself proclaimed pharaoh. Eager to supplant Tyre with a Greek-controlled trading center, Alexander personally laid out the city of Alexandria. His location proved astute: Alexandria was to flourish as the principal city in the eastern Mediterranean for centuries.

Alexander's achievements as the conqueror of a world that stretched from Greece to the steppes of Asia and the fertile plains of the Indus River Valley were greater than those of any military figure of antiquity. More than a military genius, Alexander was also an avid reader, a student of medicine and biology, who took a troop of surveyors, botanists, and zoologists along with him on his conquests. Much of the information they gathered found its way into Aristotle's hands for use in his scientific works. These scholars also brought back with them new knowledge of Indian mathematics and astronomy.

Upon Alexander's death in 323 B.C., his empire quickly shattered into three kingdoms ruled by his leading generals, among them his childhood

Eratosthenes (270–194 B.C.), Greek poet, mathematician, and geographer, was the second librarian at Alexandria. One of his achievements was to devise a method to measure the circumference of the earth.

Alexandria, imagined in a nineteenth-century pen-and-ink drawing. The city founded by Alexander in 332 B.C. became the most important scholarly center in the Mediterranean world because of its library.

A nineteenth-century German engraving shows scholars at work in the hall of the great library at Alexandria, known as the Cage of the Muses. The library, because of its impact on scholarship, became the model of a universal library.

companion Ptolemy, who became Ptolemy Soter, the new Egyptian pharaoh. In building up Alexander's city, Ptolemy returned to his scholarly roots in Greece. He asked Demetrius of Phaleron, the deposed ruler of Athens and a student of Aristotle, to assemble a museum and a library—really a complex of lecture halls, study rooms, cloisters, gardens, and an astronomical observatory known as the Museion—within the walls of Ptolemy's fortified palace, the Brucheion, near the waterfront. Ptolemy and Demetrius decided that they needed to collect 500,000 scrolls if they were going to gather together in one spot "the books of all the peoples of the world." To accomplish this, Ptolemy wrote a letter "to all the sovereigns and governors on earth" asking them to send him every conceivable type of writing. At the same time, agents were dispatched to acquire or borrow collections that they either deposited in the library or copied and returned to their owners. Other scribes went to work copying scrolls borrowed from ships that called at the port. Some estimates put the total number of scrolls in the collection during Alexandria's finest hours at 700,000. It is thought that Demetrius or a successor acquired Aristotle's library from the Lyceum, but not his original works, which disappeared for a time and then were taken to Rome.

The Alexandrian library and its offspring, the so-called Daughter Library, or Serapeion, located in the same city at the Temple of Serapis, became the intellectual centers of the Mediterranean world. Greek scholars worked on a new edition of Homer. An Egyptian scholar was hired to collect and translate local works into Greek and write a history of Egypt. Two million lines of Zoroastrian verse from Iran were also translated into Greek. Here, too, Euclid worked on his *Elements of Geometry,* and Archimedes developed his principles of mechanics.

Many elements of the modern library—catalogues, the trained librarian, open shelf and other storage systems, even the central distribution desk—are associated with the achievements at Alexandria. The Alexandrian catalogue, which filled 120 scrolls, was known as the Pinakes. *The Lists of Those Who Distinguished Themselves in All Branches of Learning and Their Writings,* the catalogue's full title, was organized by subject—drama (perhaps comic and tragic), law, philosophy, history, oratory, medicine, mathematics, natural science, and miscellanea—and became the standard for future great libraries.

For many years it was thought that the Alexandrian library was destroyed by Julius Caesar (100–44 B.C.) while he was Cleopatra's lover and became embroiled in her conflict with her brother, Ptolemy XII. When Caesar torched Ptolemy's fleet, he inadvertently destroyed 40,000 scrolls stored in a warehouse adjacent to the waterfront in Alexandria and destined for Rome. It was Roman emperor Aurelian who sacked the Brucheion in A.D. 272, destroying most of the library. The Daughter Library was burned in A.D. 391 during an antipagan riot led by a Christian bishop. "The history of the libraries of antiquity often ends in flames," wrote classical scholar Lucien Canfora of the sad destruction of the libraries of Alexandria.

BY THE SWORD AND BY THE BOOK

During the Golden Age of Athens, the peoples of Italy, at least those outside the Greek colonies of southern Italy and Sicily, were viewed by the Greeks as little more than barbarians. Not until the late fourth and early third centuries B.C. did Greek culture begin to have a significant impact upon Rome, which by that time had been a city for two centuries or more. Nevertheless, early Roman literature and library collecting were definitely influenced by the Greeks. Papyrus scrolls were found in the coffins of early Romans, and according to one account, a mission was sent to Athens in the fifth century B.C. to bring back the laws of Solon, in which certain democratic practices were codified.

Marcus Tullius Cicero reading, in a detail from a fifteenth-century Italian fresco by Vincenzo Foppa. Cicero, who epitomized the Roman scholar-statesman, considered his library to be the "soul" of his house.

The earliest known Roman "libraries" held collections of historical records and laws, such as the *Annales Pontificum (Records of the Priests)*, which consisted of eighty scrolls and was kept in the official residence of the chief priest, or Pontifex Maximus. These libraries were private collections, a number of the best known having been seized by Roman generals on their forays abroad. One such collection was taken from Macedonia in 168 B.C. by Paulus Aemilius, who thought books more precious than the booty his troops stripped from the royal palace. Cornelius Sulla brought Aristotle's original works to Rome after he torched Athens in 86 B.C. The collection had been kept by one of Aristotle's students, buried by a family member, thereby damaging many of the scrolls, and then exhumed and taken to Rome. Sulla passed the collection on to his son, in whose house Cicero reported seeing it. Sulla's son was forced to sell his father's library to pay his debts, and thereafter Aristotle's collection disappeared.

There were numerous private collectors before the era of public libraries in Rome. The library room—described by Cicero as the "soul" of his house—soon became a standard fixture in every wealthy Roman's home.

Scholars working in a library in ancient Rome. This eighteenth-century engraving creates the impression that bound books were widespread. The scroll was more common than the codex, an early form of book that was developed in the first century B.C. but was not widely used until three centuries later.

When Imperial Rome staggered under the weight of conspicuous consumption during the height of the empire, the philosopher and writer Seneca (c. 4 B.C.–A.D. 65) deplored the ostentatious display of books: "What is the use of having countless books and libraries, whose titles their owners can scarcely read through in a whole lifetime?" He concluded that "a library is considered as essential an adornment of a house as a bathroom."

Influenced by his stay in Alexandria, Julius Caesar was the first Roman statesman to consider collecting books on a large scale and opening his library to the public. Marcus Terentius Varro, whom Caesar enlisted to carry out his plans, wrote what may be the first treatise on libraries, *De bibliothecis*, which did not survive. Caesar's plans were not carried out until after his death, when Asinius Pollio, the wealthy conqueror of Dalmatia, founded Rome's first public library in 37 B.C. by bringing together a number of collections, including parts of Caesar's and Sulla's.

Successive Roman emperors, beginning with Augustus (63 B.C.–A.D. 14), who built a library in the Temple of Apollo on the Palatine Hill and a second in the Porticus Octaviae, made library building part of their civic responsibility. Augustus's library on the Palatine Hill housed both Greek and Latin collections—a common practice in Roman libraries—and was supplemented by the emperors Tiberius and Caligula. This library survived for hundreds of years and was one of Rome's two major libraries.

In A.D. 114 Trajan built Rome's finest library and public record office, the Bibliotheca Ulpiana, to which he gave his family name (Ulpia). This library was housed in two rectangular structures, one for Greek works, the other for Roman writings and archives, that stood at the north end of the spectacular forum on either side of Trajan's Column. Decorated with the busts of the greatest writers of the Greek and Roman worlds, the Bibliotheca Ulpiana was built around a private collection of 30,000 scrolls and ranks with the great libraries of the ancient world. Despite the grandness of its design and its collection, Trajan's library, like other ancient libraries, was quite small. Each of the two rooms measured only sixty by forty-six feet. Trajan's Column, which can be seen today, bears the inscription "Ense et Style," meaning roughly "By the sword and by the book." The spirals that encircle it are thought to represent scrolls commemorating his victories and his commitment to the extension of Roman culture. In the fourth century the Bibliotheca Ulpiana was moved, apparently temporarily, to more sumptuous quarters at the Baths of Diocletian, where it adjoined a theater and lecture hall and thus may have established a standard for library luxuriance that was never again equaled.

According to a fourth-century Roman survey, the city had twenty-eight libraries that had become sufficiently institutionalized to be overseen by librarians who were imperial administrators. Clerical work was undertaken by slaves. The best-known Roman librarian was Suetonius, who supervised the city's library system under the rule of Emperor Hadrian in the second century.

The conquest of the Mediterranean world by Roman legions led to the establishment of libraries in other major cities. Hadrian ordered that a library be built in Athens. Spacious and beautifully designed, it included reading and lecture rooms and a central "circulation desk" where scrolls could be delivered to readers. Other libraries were built or rebuilt at Pergamum (in modern-day Turkey), where a library had been established in the second century B.C. to compete with Alexandria; Ephesus (also in Turkey); and Timgad (in North Africa). The gift of a library to a provincial center was considered a particularly noteworthy form of charity in Imperial Rome. Pliny the Younger gave a sum of one million sesterces to his hometown, Novum Comum, for a library.

Augustus built the Bibliotheca Palatina, an early public library and one of Rome's most important and long-lasting libraries, on the Palatine Hill.

Greco-Roman poetess from a Pompeian fresco.

A PUBLISHING EMPIRE

By the first century A.D., Rome surpassed Alexandria as the center of the international publishing trade. Previously, books were copied by hand mostly one at a time or in very limited numbers. The Romans began to mass-produce books by using slaves to copy them, a practice that kept prices low and books accessible. Roman publishers sought out manuscripts, advanced funds to authors, and developed a sophisticated distribution system. There was no copyright, however, and there are indications that publishers pocketed all profits rather than paying royalties. A typical bookstore stood either in a market or adjacent to one of the major forums. The pillars outside the store were covered with notices calling attention to new books. Public readings and regular appearances by authors were other methods used to publicize their work.

In the earliest Chinese writing, characters were inscribed in bone with a sharp instrument. Oracle bones such as this one dating from the Shang dynasty (1500 B.C.) were used for divination.

This scroll of the Diamond Sutra, *dated A.D. 868 and showing Buddha, is thought to be the oldest printed book-length work. On the last page the printer wrote that he "reverently made this for blessings to his parents, for universal distribution."*

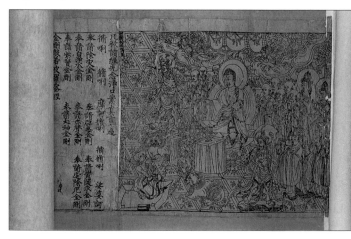

Although the Greeks, and later the Romans, viewed the world beyond the Mediterranean as the home of barbarians, they were eager for information about these remote lands. Scholars accompanying Alexander brought back reports of the peoples to the east in the Indus River Valley and modern-day Afghanistan. In Imperial Rome little was known of the world beyond where the Roman legions had marched, with one fascinating exception. Pliny the Younger wrote that silk, which we now know came from China, was imported by the Romans in the form of skeins of thread and silk yardage. Reports as far back as sixth century B.C. in Greece told of a silk-producing land known as Seres—this at a time when trade already passed along what would later become known as the Silk Road, which stretched from northern China across interior Asia into the Middle East. As this trade led to other forms of communication, each civilization impacted the other.

CHINA AND ITS WORLD OF BOOKS

In 138 B.C. the Emperor Han Wu Ti sent one of his courtiers, Zhang Qien, on a diplomatic mission to the West. Zhang Qien, despite prolonged captivity at the hands of a hostile tribe, made his way to Bactria—the Alexandrian name for a country that is now part of Afghanistan—where he heard reports of extensive trade among lands to the west of China. China had established direct contact with the Persian world, the bridge between East and West. By the first century B.C. there was regular trade between China and the Mediterranean world. It would take years, however, before the West received news of significant inventions in the East. According to one estimate, more than half the books published prior to the nineteenth century would be written in Chinese characters, and China would bring forth a remarkable number of inventions, among them paper and printing.

China until the late Middle Ages was very much a world unto itself, with its own writing, literature, and libraries. The earliest signs of Chinese writing are inscriptions found on bronze vessels and oracle bones from the Shang dynasty (1765–1122 B.C.). These lists of questions and answers asked of diviners by individual Chinese are in archaic but clearly recognizable Chinese characters.

The Chou dynasty (1122–255 B.C.) saw the emergence of a centralized bureaucratic state and with it the creation of archives by scribes using wooden blocks to print individual characters on bamboo strips. The growth of a monarchy exercising power through a bureaucracy also coincided with the rise of philosophical schools, notably one founded by Confucius (551–478 B.C.), whose writings would have a profound influence on the development of China, Japan, and Korea down to the present.

There are indications that the rise of philosophical speculation during this golden age coincided with the construction of an imperial library or archive in China's capital city of Loyang. According to tradition, the philosopher Lao-tzu, whose dates are unknown and identity is even questioned, was the librarian. The imperial library was built up by successive Chou emperors until Shih Huang Ti, the first Ch'in emperor and the unifier of China, swept them aside in 221 B.C. This gradual accumulation of knowledge was interrupted in 213 B.C., when Shih Huang Ti is said to have heard an after-dinner speech recommending that he emulate the emperors of the previous dynasty. Styling himself the First Emperor, he took the remarks as an insult and in response ordered that all books throughout his domain, with the exception of those on medicine, witchcraft, and farming, be brought to the capital and burned. All those who resisted were to be branded on the face and sent to work on the Great Wall. The wall was constructed during Shih Huang Ti's reign with considerable loss of life—hundreds of intellectuals perished. This disaster was the first of innumerable instances of the destruction of Chinese libraries by fire and sword over the next two millennia.

In this detail from a scroll painting, sixth-century Chinese scholars assemble the best literary works for the education of the emperor's son.

The establishment of the Han dynasty (206 B.C. –A.D. 220) brought peace and stability for a time to a newly unified China as the country entered a period of political reorganization, technological innovation, and literary expression. Three imperial libraries were established. Books were brought out of hiding while scholars worked to replace those destroyed. Emperor Hsiao Ho started an imperial archive, where catalogues listed the works of Chinese authors. All of this was to no avail: much of the work went up in smoke when the Han capital at Ch'ang-an was burned by rebels in A.D. 24.

The Han emperors oversaw the creation of a large and sophisticated civil service whose members were nurtured through study of the *Shih Ching (Book of Poetry)*, *Shu Ching (Book of History)*, and *I Ching (Book of Changes)* and engaged in extensive record keeping, including the compilation of annual calendars and two

Early Chinese papermaking. Paper was invented in China in the second century B.C., but was not introduced into Europe for another six hundred years. Printing on paper led to a quantum leap in the number of books available.

Opposite page: Detail from an official history of the Wei dynasty compiled by Wei Shou during the sixth century and printed in 1144. By the sixth century, calligraphy was regarded by many literati as China's highest art form.

annual censuses. Chinese script was reformed, and the first Chinese dictionary, compiled·about A.D. 100, explained the meaning and variant forms of 9,000 characters. New libraries were built, most notably a central library established by Emperor Wu in the third century, which survived for almost two centuries before its destruction by fire in 554.

Repeatedly throughout Chinese history, books were teased out of private collections by offering rewards for them. At times this practice proved counterproductive, as it encouraged a large number of forgeries. Libraries were often collected by one dynasty in order to prepare an official history of the previous one and to record significant present events. Libraries were greatly restricted in their use and served, with very few exceptions, the needs of the emperor, his officials, and selected scholars until the founding of public libraries at the beginning of the twentieth century.

The development in ancient China that ultimately would have an enormous impact on books and libraries was the invention of paper during the Han dynasty. Before this time the Chinese wrote on silk, wood, and bamboo. The oldest samples of paper made from hemp fiber date from 140 to 87 B.C., but at first it was used for clothing, wrapping, lacquerware, and personal hygiene. Paper was made by pouring a solution of disintegrated plant fibers onto a woven mat, later into a box or mold. This permitted the water to drain, leaving a layer of dried sediment, which was then peeled away. According to a number of accounts, Ching-Chung, a eunuch attached to the imperial court, demonstrated the process of papermaking to Emperor Ha-ti in A.D. 105, and thereafter paper was in widespread use. The oldest sample of paper with writing was found in the ruins of a Chinese watchtower and is dated A.D. 110.

China and the West in ancient times were still worlds apart, despite the beginnings of trade. The invention of paper, for example, would not affect the production of books outside of China for another six centuries.

The Legacy of Ancient Civilizations

In retrospect, the accomplishments of the great urban societies of the ancient world, both East and West, were startling and prodigious. Humans mastered language probably 100,000 years ago. But it was only after a long oral tradition and in very contemporary times—5,000 years ago—that mankind developed a written language. Not surprisingly, the appearance of written language and the consequent need to store information in libraries coincided with the emergence of city-states and the opening of extensive trade routes that more than likely linked much of Europe, the Middle East, and Asia. The increasing complexity of society—the need to keep track of trade, scientific and pseudo-scientific information, and the written demands of a society based on custom and then law—led to the establishment of the first library-archives in Sumeria. No longer was it possible to store such an enormous amount of information in the human memory and then to use it reliably or pass it on to another.

With Ptolemy's establishment of the library at Alexandria, librarians for the first time aspired to universalism, by attempting to collect knowledge from the known world. Rome marked a second peak in the development of libraries. Here, in a highly sophisticated urban society, many people collected books, publishing flourished, and public libraries became a civic responsibility. Literacy and therefore library use during classical times were restricted to a small percentage of the population, despite the evolution of the library from serving as the personal collection of an individual, such as Ashurbanipal, to functioning as a civic institution. Even the greatest of the ancient libraries, with the exception of Alexandria, were quite small.

Despite the mighty efforts of the librarians of Alexandria, Rome, and the Chinese imperial court to preserve and then extend the intellectual legacy of the ancient world, much of it was swept away in the West in the wake of the collapse of the Roman Empire and in the East in repeated conflagrations. It is estimated, for instance, that Aeschylus, Sophocles, Euripides, and Aristophanes wrote more than three hundred plays, only forty-six of which are extant. Almost the entire corpus of Greek lyric poetry, such as the works of Sappho, has disappeared, along with numerous works by authors such as Aristotle, Plato, and Cicero. The loss of original works by the great writers of Greece and Rome is also due to the unfortunate habit of destroying originals after copies were made. Those works that exist today are based on copies often made centuries later.

China, too, suffered terrible losses in its written heritage. But the continuity of a single culture within an area whose boundaries were more or less established in the Han dynasty—along with the development of printing and the consequent large print runs for books—meant that enormous amounts of information were saved.

As the centuries passed into the so-called Christian era, China would thrive both culturally and technologically, inventing printing with movable type, for example, in the eleventh century, four centuries before a similar invention in the West. Europe, despite its backwardness, remained tied by tenuous links of trade to more advanced centers of culture, such as Byzantium and the new world of Islam. These regions would reintroduce Europe to the lost heritage of ancient cultures and pass on the tradition of great libraries.

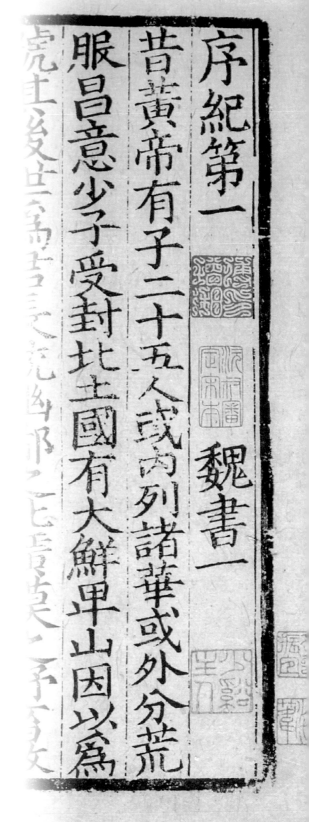

CHAPTER THREE

AN ACCUMULATION OF RICHES

❖

The Beginnings of the Modern Library

Rome did not fall overnight. Staggering under the weight of its bureaucracy and an army that could not forestall the barbarian hordes sweeping down from the north, the empire lurched through fifty years of anarchy, from A.D. 235 to 284. Revived by Diocletian, who reigned from 284 to 306, the empire was divided

Map of Constantinople in the sixteenth century after it was absorbed by the Ottoman Empire. With the decline of Rome, Constantinople, founded in 326, became the capital of a new Christian empire and an important center of learning and libraries.

Preceding pages: Interior of the library at the University of Leyden in the Netherlands in 1610. Books were more plentiful after the invention of the printing press in the fifteenth century, and university libraries took on a greater role in their preservation.

between the sons of the Christian emperor Theodosius I and then was sacked for three days by Visigoths in 410 on its way to its final demise.

The fate of the great public libraries of Rome after the fall of the empire is largely unknown. Relying as they did on imperial patronage, these libraries could only have suffered during the gradual decline of the city and its eventual abandonment by the Western emperors. Since most Roman libraries were connected with temples, they must have been dealt a near-fatal blow when Theodosius I enacted a series of laws in 391 that forbade sacrifices, worship of pagan gods, and visiting temples for worship. The libraries of Rome undoubtedly suffered further damage during the pillage by the Visigoths. Even before then, the fourth-century historian Ammianus Marcellinus wrote that "the libraries were closed like tombs." Boethius, the Roman scholar who lived in the afterglow of Imperial Rome and worked hard to preserve the classics of the ancient world, expressed his "fear that many things which are now known soon will not be." And he was right.

With the decline of Rome and the West, the cultural center of gravity shifted eastward, where the cities of the Eastern Empire led by Constantinople continued to prosper. Constantine I converted to Christianity in 312 and, spear in hand, paced out the plan for the walls of Constantinople, the New Rome, in 326, much as Alexander had with Alexandria. He or his son founded an imperial library in the portico of the imperial palace sometime between 330 and 336. Almost a century later, Theodosius II, a serious scholar and scribe in his own right, founded another library in conjunction with Constantinople's Academy, a school for the study of philosophy staffed by Greek and Latin teachers. The third important library in Constantinople was the library of the patriarch, the head of the Eastern Orthodox church.

Little is known about the collection that must have been one of Constantinople's most significant. These were the law books assembled by Justinian I, Byzantine emperor from 527 to 565, so that scholars could compile the 2,000-volume Justinian Code, which would have a profound impact on the future of civil law in the Western world. Not all of Justinian's contributions were positive, however. In 529 he closed the Academy at Athens, the last center of Greek learning that remained outside the control of the Byzantine emperors. By the fifth century the imperial library of Constantinople had grown to an estimated 120,000 volumes, making it the largest in Europe, but in 477 it was torched during an uprising.

Despite the growing orthodoxy of Eastern Catholicism, great emphasis was put on education in both the classics and church writings in the early years of the Byzantine Empire—at least until the reign of Leo the

Isaurian. Attacking idol worship, Leo abolished the Academy in Constantinople in 727, introducing an era of anti-intellectualism that did not bode well for the city's libraries. After a dark century, the Academy was rebuilt, and the imperial family, beginning with the new dynasty marked by the reign of Basil I (867–886), took the lead in encouraging scholarship.

The imperial family's interest in scholarship ebbed and flowed with the generations. Whatever the intellectual temperament of the successive emperors, Constantinople enjoyed a lively book trade, and libraries, whether patronized or ignored, managed to retain large numbers of books and their accumulated knowledge. Byzantium, however, was not known for scholarly innovation: it was a transmitter of knowledge from the ancient world. "The value of Byzantine culture," library historian James Westfall Thompson wrote in his study *Medieval Libraries*, "lies not so much in its own contributions as in its preservation of Greek, even Roman, thought and literature. Without the faithful and laborious copying of Byzantine scribes it is probable that many Graeco-Roman classics would have been lost."

On the way to the Holy Land in 1204, Christian crusaders attacked Constantinople, then the capital of a rival Christian empire, in search of loot and relics. Perceived to have little value, many books were destroyed during the subsequent fire and pilfering.

Sadly, many of the classics were lost. Photius, tutor to the children of Basil I, compiled his massive *Myriobiblion* after plowing through the imperial library and putting together his own impressive private collection. In this work he describes the writings of various scholars of the classical world, such as Memnon, Conon, Arrian, and Diodorus Siculus. Today these authors' works are known only by their titles.

Ultimately the most dangerous enemies of the great imperial and private libraries of the Byzantine world were rival Christians from the West. In 1204, during the Fourth Crusade, these Christian zealots were diverted from their intended targets in Egypt and the Holy Land to Constantinople, where German, French, and Flemish crusaders attacked and sacked the city,

Page from a sixteenth-century Koran. Muslims, required to read and understand the Koran, are known as "people of the book." During Europe's Dark Ages, the Muslim world was ablaze with learning.

torching it three times. Nicetas, a Greek historian who witnessed the conflagration, described "ignorant and utterly illiterate barbarians" parading through the streets with priceless manuscripts impaled on their spears.

Ironically, the sack of Constantinople—and the earlier plundering of Tripoli and its libraries in 1109 and the libraries of a number of Greek monasteries by crusaders—is thought to have triggered a new Mediterranean book trade that brought priceless works to the West. Years later many of these books turned up in the libraries of Florence, Rome, Athens, Oxford, and Moscow.

KNOWLEDGE TRAVELS EAST TO WEST

More important than the impact of the nefarious activities of the crusaders on the Mediterranean book trade was the rise of Islam. Islamic civilization permitted the consolidation and extension of the great intellectual achievements of the classical and early Christian worlds, particularly in the sciences and mathematics. It also encouraged the mingling of these achievements with ideas and inventions brought from India and China, and finally the large-scale introduction of this knowledge into Europe, which by the twelfth century was more receptive to learning. The followers of Muhammad (570–632) built the great libraries of the Middle Ages, and without them Europe might have had a very different cultural heritage.

Muhammad himself could neither read nor write. But within a century after his death, his followers had spread a new religion based on the study of one book, the Koran, from China to the Pyrenees. Muhammad turned to his Jewish and Christian prisoners of war, offering them freedom in exchange for teaching his followers to read. "To know the Koran and its teaching became the duty of all Moslems, and hence literacy became all-important and schools began to be organized," wrote library historian Michael Harris.

The Muslim world forged its ties to the ancient cultures of the Mediterranean via Persia. Persians had reclaimed the throne after ousting the country's Parthian rulers in 226 and, in the years before Muhammad, embraced Greek science and philosophy. The Persian court became the home in exile of hundreds of Hellenized Syrians persecuted by the Byzantines. These Nestorian Christians translated the Greek classics into Persian. Among these translators were scholars from the Academy at Athens closed by Justinian. The Arabs conquered Persia in 634 and in time absorbed Greco-Persian culture and its love of books. By 750 what remained of the Greek classics had been translated into Arabic. According to Harris, Aristotle was so widely read that Muslim scholars wrote hundreds of books about him.

The first great libraries of Islam were established in Damascus in the seventh century during the Omayyad dynasty, when the immediate followers of Muhammad were extending their rule East and West. But it was Baghdad, the capital city of the Abbasid caliphs who seized power in 750, that became the center of the Islamic book world. Writing had returned to the place of its origins: the ruins of ancient Sumeria lay beneath the new palaces, universities, and libraries of the Abbasids.

Baghdad under the Abbasids became, according to a tenth-century Persian geographer, "a city of scholars and great riches." Some 4,000 years after the Sumerians built the first cities, Abdulah al-Mansur, the second Abbasid caliph, laid out Baghdad as a great walled circle, two miles across, centered on the royal mosque. Harun al-Rashid, the caliph of the *Arabian Nights,* a lover of learning and, according to a contemporary, the owner of 120 camel-loads of books, established one of Baghdad's first libraries, employing scholars to translate Persian works into Arabic. His son, al-Mamun, caliph from 813 to 833, became one of the great patrons of Islamic learning. He established the House

This Istanbul library was among the many Muslim libraries responsible for preserving the intellectual heritage of Greece and Rome and then passing it on to Europe starting in the twelfth century.

Public library in Hulwan, Egypt, depicted in a thirteenth-century manuscript. Public libraries were common in the Islamic world beginning in the ninth century.

of Wisdom, which was similar to a modern university, with an extensive library drawn in part from Greek scientific and philosophical works that he acquired from a ruler of the Byzantine Empire. Al-Mamun claimed that Aristotle appeared to him in a dream and spoke to him about the importance of reason. Indeed, al-Mamun is associated with the Mu'tazili thinkers, who, influenced by Greek philosophy and Aristotle in particular, sought to reconcile God and reason and taught that mankind was subject to free will.

Baghdad at the height of Abbasid rule had some thirty-six libraries, and all of the major cities of Persia built their own libraries, both private and public. The library in Mosul, which was founded in the tenth century by the poet Ibn Hamdan, was open to all scholars, who, if they were poor, were given free paper. The famous House of Science, established by the Fatimid caliphs in Cairo in the eleventh century, was also open to the public. To facilitate copying, patrons were provided with paper, pens, and ink.

The demand for books fueled the Middle Eastern book trade. Baghdad's bookselling area, which lay to the south of the city, was made up of hundreds of bookstores, and in every city bookstores opened near mosques and other centers of learning. The enormous publishing enterprise undertaken in Islam was enhanced by the arrival of paper from China.

Baghdad became, as its founder had predicted, "a marketplace for the world," the center of a complex of trade routes that linked Asia with the Mediterranean. As early as the eighth century, Middle Eastern traders—Arabs, Jews, and Persians—established direct contact with the imperial court in China. Inevitably, paper made its way to Baghdad, having moved out of China into Eastern Turkestan and Tibet and along the Silk Road to Samarkand (now in Uzbekistan) by the seventh century. In 794 Chinese craftsmen set up a paper mill in Baghdad, and from then until the fifteenth century, the Arab world remained a major supplier of paper to the European market.

Monasteries Illuminate the Middle Ages

Given the expansiveness and enormous cultural vitality of Islam, it was only a matter of time before the cosmopolitan book trade of the Middle East impacted Europe. While Islamic civilization flourished and began almost simultaneously to fragment into separate dynasties, Europe struggled in isolation, its small monastic libraries maintaining tenuous links between rudimentary centers of learning. The origins of the monastery are unclear. But it is clear from studies of the Dead Sea Scrolls—which may have been part of a monastic library stocked with books rescued from Jerusalem when it was threatened by the Romans—that the practice of setting up self-contained religious communities dates at least to the time of Christ. Some of the earliest Christian monasteries have been found in Egypt. With these monasteries began an emphasis on reading and copying books. By the fourth century, monasteries were being established in Europe, particularly around Rome.

Magnus Aurelius Cassiodorus, minister of state and secretary to Theodoric the Great, Ostrogothic ruler of Italy from 493 to 526, wanted to establish a great Christian university and library in Rome modeled on Alexandria's. His plans went up in flames when Justinian I conquered Italy after besieging Rome in 546, perhaps causing the final destruction of the Bibliotheca Ulpiana built in the second century by Trajan. After retiring from public life a wealthy man, Cassiodorus founded a monastery on one of his estates at Vivarium (now Squillace) in southern Italy and laid out rules for the handling and copying of books. He is credited with establishing the monastic regimen, which combined physical labor with reading and copying in the monastery rooms called scriptoria. It was his contemporary, St. Benedict, who through the spread of the Benedictine order across western Europe had a more profound impact on the painfully slow re-creation of libraries.

Spain and Sicily were the most important bridges between the learned Muslim civilization and book-starved Europe. Works in Arabic, including Aristotle's, were translated into Latin in monastery rooms called scriptoria. This scriptorium at the monastery in Tavara, Spain, appears in a thirteenth-century illuminated manuscript.

PETR̄

St. Benedict's views, however, were not particularly enlightened; he was more interested in the discipline of copying manuscripts—what Cassiodorus called "fighting the Devil by pen and ink"—than in the scholarly pursuit of learning, which he felt could be dangerously distracting.

Itinerant Irish monks, described by a contemporary as traveling the countryside with shaved heads and painted eyelids, triggered the successive waves of missionary work that played a major role in spreading monastic principles into the heartland of Europe. Catholicism came to Ireland from the Roman part of England in the fifth century, either brought by St. Patrick, who was probably English, or spread by him. Seeking isolation among foreigners, the Irish missionaries first crossed into England in the sixth century. The communities that they established spawned the next wave of religious work, which took men like St. Columba to Europe, where he and his twelve followers founded monasteries between 590 and 614 at Luxeuil, Fontenay, and Annegray in France and Bobbio in northern Italy.

Gall, one of the followers of St. Columba, established a monastic cell in the mountains south of Lake Constantine in Switzerland. Eventually, the monastery joined the Benedictine order and in the ninth century became one of the most important religious centers in central Europe. The monks, despite the shortage of good vellum, began to copy manuscripts in the eighth century on whatever vellum they could find, some yellowed and full of holes, some with earlier writings erased and written over. Through an exchange of manuscripts with other monasteries, the monks of St. Gall monastery ever so slowly built up their collection. By the ninth century it included over three hundred volumes, a sizable and diverse collection for its time and place: works of Virgil; the earliest manuscript of a death song by Bede, England's first historian, in Anglo-Saxon; a Latin-German word list; and manuscripts from Italy, which proved later to have fragments of plays by Terence, the Roman playwright, under later copying. But how pathetic the collection was compared with even a modest private library in Baghdad.

Europe in the Middle Ages was, according to historian Norman F. Cantor, "an underdeveloped, thinly populated, intensely rural society." Roads were terrible. Most of the population never moved more than ten miles from where they born. Violence and famine were ever present, and life expectancy hovered around thirty years. In the absence of urban centers and a large-scale book trade, all of which had disappeared with the Romans, monasteries served in their place as cultural centers. Itinerant monks and scholars forged the links between monasteries and the growing number of

Illuminated manuscripts are windows into the Middle Ages. Monks preserved not only the classics of the ancient world but also the writings of the first church fathers such as St. Augustine. An art form of their own, the illustrations reveal more about medieval life than written documents of the time.

Opposite page: Twelfth-century portrait of Gregory the Great (540–604) dictating to his scribe Peter. Pope Gregory shaped early church doctrine and was a strong supporter of the Benedictine order, which made reading and copying manuscripts a central part of its religious regimen.

cathedral libraries, which eventually became associated with urban centers and fledgling universities, such as the University of Paris in the twelfth century. Churchmen treasured and copied the works of the early church fathers, particularly St. Augustine (354–430), wrote commentaries on the Bible and the early saints, and began to write local histories.

The embers of knowledge were fanned to a healthy glow for a time at the court of Charlemagne, who ruled from 768 to 814. His interest in educational reform led to the establishment of schools at the cathedrals and monasteries within his empire. St. Gall was one of the monasteries that benefited from Charlemagne's patronage. Charlemagne also encouraged scholars from England, Italy, and Spain to come to the impressive library at his court at Aachen. His emphasis on the revival of Latin led to the preservation and restoration of many of the Latin classics. It also secured the future of education based on a Latin model, which influenced Euro-American pedagogy into the twentieth century. But within a half century of his death, the Carolingian empire was pressed from all sides, and many of the monasteries and cathedrals were plundered by Magyars, Vikings, and Saracens during the two centuries of fragmentation and turmoil that followed the collapse of the empire.

The Rise of Universities and the Unfolding of the Renaissance

In time the intellectual achievements of the Islamic world and the copies of the works of the classical world stored in the libraries of Byzantium would infiltrate Europe, particularly during what has been called the Twelfth Century Renaissance. Spain became an independent Islamic caliphate in 756. Southern Italy remained part of the Byzantine Empire until the eleventh century, and Arabs controlled Sicily during most of the tenth and eleventh. Knowledge moved northward from these centers of learning as illustrated by the travels of one monk, John from the monastery at Gorze in Lorraine. John visited Calabria in 950 and brought back with him a copy of Aristotle's *Categoriae (Categories)*. Returning from a later diplomatic mission to Cordova, the capital city of the Spanish caliphate, he brought with him a horseload of books in Arabic. Historians have demonstrated that this modest collection had

Charlemagne (742–814), shown in this reliquary designed to hold fragments of his skull, was illiterate, but he accumulated an impressive library at his court at Aachen and advocated educational reforms throughout his empire.

Cathedral libraries such as this one at Hereford, England, marked the emergence of large collections of books kept in dedicated library facilities. Starting in the late thirteenth century, books were chained to the shelf, indicating that, though more abundant, they were still rare and had to be secured.

an impact that spread throughout Lorraine over the next century.

Spain was the main conduit by which books and ideas flowed into Europe. Islamic Spain boasted some seventy libraries. The greatest was built in the tenth century in Cordova, an urban center that rivaled Baghdad and Constantinople, by caliph Hakim II. Hakim, an inveterate book collector, dispatched buyers to the book centers of Islam and eventually assembled 400,000 to 600,000 volumes. After Christians recaptured Toledo in 1085, the city became one of the most important intellectual centers in Western Christendom, a gathering place for scholars from the Mediterranean world. At the library, the works of classical Greece were translated from Arabic into Latin and were sent northward into knowledge-hungry Europe. These translations were done by itinerant scholars, like Gerard of Cremona, Arabized Christians called Mozarabs, and local Jews. Gerard's followers noted that he translated seventy-three volumes including works by Aristotle, Ptolemy, Euclid, Galen, and Hippocrates. "Indeed, more of Arabic science in general passed into Western Europe at the hands of Gerard of Cremona than in any other way," concluded Charles Homer Haskins, historian of the Twelfth Century Renaissance.

The accelerated transferral of the accumulated knowledge of the classic world and the Islamic renaissance was fortuitous. After the golden years of the Abbasid caliphate in Baghdad, Islamic scholars became increasingly preoccupied with religious orthodoxy. As with the Romans so it transpired with Islam: outsiders—Christians, Persians, Mongols, and Turks—carved away larger and larger chunks of the empire until what remained of the Islamic heartland came under Turkish rule in the sixteenth century. In Spain conflict within the caliphate and the Christian reconquest took a terrible toll on libraries. Many were destroyed; others were scattered before the winds of war.

The editor-copyist Jean Mielot by Jean Le Tavernier of Bruges, c. 1450. Mielot's copying stand is equipped with holes for pen and inkwell and a clamp to hold the book being copied. On the floor to the left is an armarium for books. The medieval Latin word for library was armarium, indicating the very small size of collections: they fit in a trunk or cabinet.

The Medicis of Florence, beginning with Cosimo (1389–1464), were passionate collectors of books and patrons of the new humanism. Giorgio Vasari, painter and biographer of Renaissance artists, pictured Cosimo seated among artists and philosophers.

Meanwhile the monastic and cathedral libraries in Europe slowly added to their collections. Separate rooms and buildings to house libraries began to be built. Armaria, the small trunks in which books were kept, gave way to cabinets, book presses, and shelves. The public was admitted to some parts of these libraries, and the most popular works were chained to desks. Simultaneously, urban centers began to flourish once again and with them universities, such as Oxford University, the University of Paris, the medical school at Salerno, and the medical and law schools at Bologna, all of which, significantly, were founded in the twelfth century. The monastery and later the cathedral library had played a role in preserving, and in a much more limited way furthering, knowledge and passing it literally from hand to hand throughout Europe.

The new universities would become cosmopolitan centers of active scholarship where the lessons of the past would be analyzed and applied to the present. Irnerius, the first great legal scholar at the University of Bologna, taught students from all over Europe how to analyze the Justinian Code and, more importantly, how to apply this knowledge to contemporary problems. Across Europe, scholars began to test the boundaries of tradition and push for new ways to look at the world. Twelfth-century scholars like Peter Abelard made significant intellectual breakthroughs after studying the growing, though still limited number of classical works available, such as Boethius's fifth-century translations of Aristotle. By the thirteenth century Thomas Aquinas was able to draw on almost all of the works of Aristotle that exist today.

The number of classical works and the quality of the editions subsequently published and collected increased greatly during the Renaissance, thanks to the efforts of dozens of scholars who scoured the monasteries and libraries of Europe and the Mediterranean. Francesco Petrarch (1304–74), the Italian scholar, poet, churchman, and diplomat, was the forerunner of the great Renaissance scholars and a founder of the intellectual movement known as humanism. He polemicized for a new course of studies to be known as *litterae humanae,* or "humane letters," that would emphasize the spiritual value of classical works. With his friend and contemporary Giovanni Boccaccio (1313–75), Petrarch searched the monasteries of Europe for lost classical manuscripts. He decided to give his private library to the city of Venice for public use, a wish that was never carried out.

The book trade in the Mediterranean flourished in the fifteenth century when Italian sea captains brought back impressive collections from the East. When the Turks pressed Constantinople and finally captured it in 1453, many Byzantine scholars fled to city-states like Florence and Venice, taking their precious manuscripts with them. The great book collectors and scholars of the Italian Renaissance—Pico della Mirandola; Vespiano da Bisticci, who owned a manuscript shop and worked for Cosimo de' Medici; and Tommaso Parentucelli, who served as Cosimo's librarian—were staggered by the treasures that came their way as the tides of knowledge once again ran westward.

The book-collecting mania of the humanists laid the foundation for some of the great libraries. Cosimo de' Medici's father owned three books, all of them religious. Cosimo (1389–1464), in contrast, was educated in Greek and Latin and as a young man combed the hills of Italy searching for lost manuscripts in monastery libraries. Using the vast trading system through which the Medicis made their fortune, Cosimo bought books throughout Europe and the Mediterranean and then organized his first library in the Convent of San Marco in Florence. Other family members, including Leo X (Giovanni de' Medici) and his nephew, Clement VII, added to this collection. Clement VII commissioned Michelangelo to build a library within the cloister of San Lorenzo in Florence, which was completed in 1571 and named the Bibliotèca Mediceo-Laurenziana.

The Vatican Library was the greatest of the Renaissance libraries. Tommaso Parentucelli is credited with beginning the revival of the Vatican Library when he became Pope Nicholas V in 1447. Although the Vatican Library flourished for a time, the church could not champion humanism and at the same time order the burning of all books that questioned the pope's

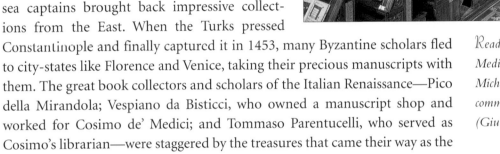

Reading room of the Bibliotèca Mediceo-Laurenziana in Florence. Michelangelo's design for the library was commissioned by Pope Clement VII (Giulio de' Medici, 1478–1534).

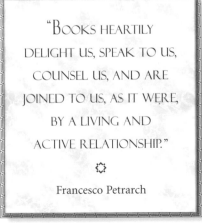

"BOOKS HEARTILY DELIGHT US, SPEAK TO US, COUNSEL US, AND ARE JOINED TO US, AS IT WERE, BY A LIVING AND ACTIVE RELATIONSHIP."

✿

Francesco Petrarch

Pope Sixtus IV, known as a patron of arts and letters and the second founder of the Vatican Library, inspects the library in a mural from the school of Melozzo da Forli. He was also one of the most corrupt of the Renaissance popes. An aggressive political intriguer, he tried to have Lorenzo de' Medici, Cosimo's grandson, assassinated as he attended mass in Florence in 1478.

authority, as it did in 1502. The library was partially destroyed when Rome was sacked by Lutheran soldiers in 1527. A century later the Papacy had its revenge, marching into the German Palatinate and seizing three collections, including one at Heidelberg's public library.

The Vatican Library, however, remained shuttered off from the outside world. Protestants were denied access, and into the nineteenth century even approved scholars had to work in one small room and were not allowed to consult indices or catalogues. In the late nineteenth century under Pope Leo XIII, the library began its present career as a major research library with a vast collection of manuscripts and hundreds of thousands of books.

As the Renaissance unfolded and learning was on the march, the development of university libraries lagged behind. Although bookstores for both the sale and the rental of books proliferated around the new universities, books were still copied by hand, by workers for pay—no longer by monks for the good of their souls—and remained prohibitively expensive. Some teachers had their own private libraries; students shared books and put together "textbooks" consisting of notes taken during lectures. The thirteenth century in particular witnessed great interest in the assembling of compendia of existing knowledge and the writing of textbooks in areas such as cosmology. Eventually the students themselves began to put together their own libraries in separate colleges that became the building blocks of early universities.

University libraries, if they existed at all, were originally quite small. The library at the University of Paris was started when Robert de Sorbon gave his collection of books to the college he endowed in 1253. In 1289 the library held only 1,000 titles. The university's individual college libraries grew, soon numbering fifty, but a central library was not established until the nineteenth century. The main library at Oxford University was begun in the fifteenth century, but suffered horribly, as did all English libraries, during Henry VIII's attack on Catholic ecclesiastical orders and was finally abandoned after further "reforms" mandated by Edward VI. The books were summarized and sold off for their vellum, and most of the furnishings were removed. The library was rebuilt beginning in 1598, when Sir Thomas Bodley provided for its restoration and then successfully encouraged others to donate books.

The Printing Press Ushers in the Modern Era

The shift from hand copying to the printing press is regarded as one of the most significant technological breakthroughs in the history of humankind and, of course, had a major impact on libraries. Printing with movable type was invented in China in the eleventh century. Chinese block printing, already in existence for four hundred years before the invention of movable type, was used in part to meet the demand for clear, detailed imagery and numerous copies of sacred texts inspired by the rapid spread of Buddhism. A craze for card playing, another Chinese invention, may have brought printing to Europe, where the first cards turned up in the fourteenth century. Soon there were enough cardplayers to inspire St. Bernard of Siena in 1423 to urge a crowd gathered at St. Peter's in Rome to go home and burn their playing cards. Blockprints, including block-printed books, printed textiles, and religious images, also began to appear in Europe in the four-teenth century. In the middle of the fifteenth century, Johannes Gutenberg invented

Printing, like paper, was a Chinese invention. It may have been introduced into Europe in part through a craze for playing with woodblock-printed cards, one century before Johannes Gutenberg's printing press.

Right: Johannes Gutenberg, inventor of the printing press and movable type. He is pictured in Joseph Moxon's Mechanick Exercizes *(1683), which is in the rare book collection of the San Francisco Public Library.*

The printing press invented by Gutenberg sometime before 1448. His press resembled the presses used to make wine and paper. The novelty of Gutenberg's process for making movable metallic type demonstrated his real genius and led to a revolution in the making of books.

the form of movable type and printing press in common use into the nineteenth century. The printing press ushered in a new era of cheaper, more accessible books. Scholars estimate that there were anywhere from 10 to 20 million books in Europe in 1500. Previously, the number of hand- and block-printed books could be counted in the thousands.

The invention of printing has been linked to profound shifts in human thought and behavior. The Protestant assault on Catholic tradition, the beginnings (from Copernicus to Newton) of the scientific revolution, and the age of exploration all followed the invention of the printing press and were enhanced by the presence of printed words and images. Although similar to the creative breakthroughs in ancient Athens, the intellectual achievements associated with these events were quantum leaps of a far greater magnitude. The very basis of human knowledge was shifting like mighty tectonic plates. Since the appearance of scribes in ancient Sumeria, the collection of information had been tied to laborious and time-consuming handwork. Tremendous time and energy went into reproducing the products of the human mind. With the rise and fall of civilizations, the recurring cycles of destructive human behavior, and the simple problems of decay, additional energy was also devoted to retrieving the works of the past. Freed from these burdens, humankind once again could push forward, devoting energy to creative thought and invention.

In an aggressively inventive society, libraries took on new meaning and provided the springboard for the next great leaps ahead. Geographers, scientists, mathematicians, philosophers, and the new historians all needed to collect, organize, and then refine the enormous amounts of information assembled during this knowledge explosion. Simple, but significant changes were made in post-

Gutenberg libraries: bibliographies were compiled, book catalogues were organized alphabetically, and books were unchained from desks and placed spine outward on shelves. All of these developments pointed to the problem of managing large quantities of information in a confined space.

The gradual stabilization of nation-states, particularly in England, France, and Spain, permitted the beginnings of what would become national libraries. As Europeans ranged across the seas in their quest for empire, the curiosity aroused by distant lands meant that books were collected far and wide and a new element of internationalism entered literature and influenced library collections. European libraries once more aspired to a kind of universalism, albeit a universalism posited on colonial conquest and increasingly on notions of European cultural superiority. With the invention of the steam printing press in England in 1791 and the resulting flow of numerous cheap books, the new national libraries would eventually be faced with the formidable task of warehousing them.

The Bibliothèque Nationale in Paris, the grande dame of European national libraries, had its humble beginnings when the French captured Naples in 1485 and carried away the library of its king. In 1537 a royal decree established the first law of legal deposit, which required every printer and bookseller to deliver one copy of each new book to the royal library, a practice that would contribute to the growth of many national libraries, including the Library of Congress in the United States. The Bibliothèque Nationale, originally called the Bibliothèque Royale, was really the private library of the Orleans family. It grew gradually until the reign of Louis XIV (1643–1715). His minister, Jean Baptiste Colbert, was said by a contemporary to have forgotten "nothing that is necessary to augment and embellish the library in order to satisfy the generous inclination of his master." Colbert headed an ambitious collecting effort that sent diplomats on book-buying missions to the Middle East, India, and China. During the French Revolution, the Bibliothèque Royale became the Bibliothèque Nationale, its collection enhanced by hundreds of thousands of books confiscated from the Catholic church and aristocracy. Later Napoléon Bonaparte, in the best European tradition, helped himself to the libraries of the countries he invaded and added this bounty to the collection. In the nineteenth century, the Bibliothèque Nationale emerged as one of the foremost libraries in the world, a standard for grand national and municipal libraries from St. Petersburg to New York.

Nineteenth-century Paris became a global atelier, an architectural workshop for the world as well as a model for urban planning. Architect Henri Labrouste was one of the pioneers of the neoclassical style associated with

PORTRAIT OF A COLLECTOR: CHARLES VAN HULTHEM

Charles Van Hulthem served as director of both the Bibliothèque Nationale and the Bibliothèque de Bourgogne after the French Revolution.

"Van Hulthem's taste for books, nourished on the riches of secularized abbeys and distressed aristocracy, had reached the stage of mania. His personal collection of 32,000 volumes, all excellent copies and including many great rarities, filled to overflowing one house in Brussels and another in Ghent. Books were heaped on every table so that there was never room to spread a tablecloth, and stood in piles in the alcove where he slept. He allowed no fire in the house and in cold weather kept himself warm in bed by putting folios on his feet, his favorite for this purpose being Barlaeus's account of Maurice of Nassau's expedition to Brazil. His contemporary, Voisin, records that he would sometimes be found contemplating with infantile pleasure an engraving of a 'fine female torso': this was his sole contact with the opposite sex. 'Carried away by a sudden apoplectic fit, he died on a pile of books like a warrior on the battlefield.'"

Anthony Hobson, *Great Libraries*, 1970

The first Beaux Arts building in Paris was the Bibliothèque Ste. Geneviève, opened in 1851 and designed by Henri Labrouste. He combined an exterior based on classic themes taken from the Renaissance and the ancient world with an interior that was startlingly modern and provided ample light for reading.

the influential École des Beaux-Arts. Labrouste's seminal work appropriately was a library opened in 1851, a new building for the Bibliothèque Ste. Geneviève, the oldest and most prestigious collection at the University of Paris. Labrouste's final work was the remodeling of the Bibliothèque Nationale, finished after his death. For the Bibliothèque Ste. Geneviève, Labrouste poured what he had learned studying the whole range of classical architecture in Italy into a thoroughly modern structure that was fireproof, gaslit, and centrally heated and ventilated. The Bibliothèque Ste. Geneviève incorporated the first use of an exposed iron skeleton in the history of architecture. Its arched windows were designed to provide adequate light for the long double-vaulted reading room that occupied the top floor. In contrast to the neoclassical exterior, the interior is strikingly innovative: in the huge reading room, the iron frame is left exposed as narrow columns that support the vaulted ceiling, and the ceiling is spanned by iron ribs that make a latticework of intricate ornamentation.

Labrouste and his colleagues were building grand *civic* structures, structures for a public whose very nature had been redefined by the American and French revolutions. Integrated into a city altered dramatically by Baron Georges-Eugène Haussmann during the reign of Napoléon III, their buildings provided ideas for urban planners such as Daniel Burnham who brought them to San Francisco and other American cities.

It was to Paris and its libraries that San Franciscans turned repeatedly for inspiration. First, Burnham, the Chicago architect who was a founder of the City Beautiful movement, used Paris and its Beaux Arts architecture as the basis for his famous but unrealized 1905 plan for the reconstruction of San Francisco, which included a new library. The new Civic Center finally built in the decade after the 1906 earthquake was considered the finest and most complete example of Beaux Arts architecture outside of Paris. When George W. Kelham designed San Francisco's main library as an important element of the new Civic Center, he looked for inspiration to Henri Labrouste's Bibliothèque Ste. Geneviève. And it was to Parisian libraries—the Bibliothèque Ste. Geneviève, the Bibliothèque

Nationale, and the high-tech Bibliothèque Publique d'Information, completed in 1995—that librarians Kenneth Dowlin and Kathy Page, architects James Ingo Freed and Cathy Simon, and library commission president Steven Coulter turned in 1990 for inspiration and design ideas for the city's new main library and for information about the high-tech library of the future.

These San Franciscans came from a new library tradition—the tradition of the free public library spawned during the early years of the democratic experiment in the United States. Before the rise of public libraries, libraries had been restricted in their use to those who could read and most often to their owners and patrons and to the scholarly elite that they served. The emphasis on free education in the young republic led quite understandably to the establishment of free libraries open to all.

Main reading room of the Bibliothèque Nationale in Paris. Henri Labrouste, the pioneer architect from the École des Beaux-Arts, remodeled the library at the end of his career.

CHAPTER FOUR

ORIGINS OF "THAT BOOKISH AMBITION"

❖

The Public Library in America

The historian Louis B. Wright suggested that the first European immigrants to America followed the advice of a contemporary who wrote, "Affect not as some do that bookish ambition to be stored with books and have well furnished libraries, yet keep their heads empty of knowledge:

Recognizing the importance of literacy and education, early immigrants to New England owned small collections of books and started some of the first public schools in the colonies. These Pilgrim children head for school carrying hornbooks—readers made of parchment leaves between covers of transparent horn.

Preceding pages: Children gather at the West Church in Boston, which was used as a public library. This watercolor and graphite work, circa 1900, is by Maurice Brazil Prendergast.

to desire to have many books and never to use them is like a child that will have a candle burning by him all the while he is sleeping."

Given the arduous nature of the transatlantic passage and the forbidding challenges of their new lives in the colonies, it is surprising how many of the first settlers, particularly in Massachusetts, brought a few books with them or acquired them soon after their arrival. Fifty-eight of seventy wills drawn up by members of the Plymouth colony between 1620 and 1690 list books in their contents. Decades went by, however, before libraries anywhere near as well furnished as those in Europe could be established. Understandably, early private libraries were practical in nature: books on farming, surveying, medicine, law, and military matters, and encyclopedias, particularly those with basic scientific information. Religious books were a given, the Bible a household furnishing, but the colonists, as children first of Puritanism, then of the Enlightenment, brought or quickly acquired a wide range of books: ancient and contemporary histories, literary, philosophical, and scientific works, and the works of the great writers of the classical world (Aristotle, Thucydides, Homer, Seneca, Virgil, Caesar) in Greek and Latin.

The first colonists were, for the most part, a literate people. Many were brought up in the well-established dissenting and Protestant traditions that emphasized reading as a way to learn God's word as recorded in the Bible. The new arrivals also valued education: public schools were established by law in Massachusetts as early as 1642. Successive waves of immigrants were more varied in their backgrounds. Levels of literacy declined with the importation of slaves, convicts, and indentured servants, most of whom were probably illiterate. Once they were here, education, for those with access to it, was an important means to fulfilling the promise of a new land.

Historians have noted the lack of belles lettres during the colonial period. The press was also constrained by politicians and theologians until the colonialists turned against the mother country. "I thank God," Governor William Berkeley of Virginia said about that colony in 1671, "there are no free schools nor printing, and I hope we shall not have these [for one] hundred years; for learning has brought disobedience, and heresy, and sects into the world, and printing has divulged them, and libels against the best governments." Clergyman and author

Cotton Mather, who owned 4,000 volumes, one of the largest private libraries in the world, wanted children to read "handsomely," but warned that they could "stumble on the Devil's Library, and poison themselves with foolish Romances, or Novels, or Playes, or Songs, or Jests"—a warning that many public librarians with their Puritan background continued to take seriously well into the twentieth century.

Despite these fears, a number of cities, which at first were really nothing more than towns, enjoyed a robust book trade. Boston, for instance, hosted twenty booksellers in 1690. The new settlers were colonial in their mentality, however. For Americans, London was the center of the publishing world and remained so well into the nineteenth century. Thus when the poet Anne Bradstreet sought a publisher for the first literary work written in the colonies, she sent her poems to London in 1650. Although approximately 50,000 books were published in the United States before 1800, the lists of American publishers and booksellers were heavily weighted with British imports or local reprints, many of them pirated by the publishers. This bias endured even when the New England literary renaissance was flourishing in the mid-1800s.

John Harvard was responsible for founding one of the earliest libraries when he died in 1638, leaving his property and four hundred books to be used in building an educational institution. The Harvard library was in no way a public institution and, by modern standards, was quite restrictive in its lending practices even for students. According to the library rules of 1663, no one below a "Senior Sophister" was allowed to borrow books, and no one below "master of Art (unless it be a fellow)" could borrow a book without permission from the president.

There were early efforts to establish public libraries. Captain Robert Keayne, a Boston merchant who died in 1656, left funds for a library for that city. It was housed along with the city government in the Town House, where it was destroyed in the fire of 1747. James Logan, secretary to William Penn, the founder of the Pennsylvania colony, collected a well-balanced library of 3,000 volumes, including classical and modern works and many titles in botany and other natural sciences. Upon his death in 1751, he left this library and his house to the city of Philadelphia. In a more ambitious effort, Dr. Thomas Bray, a British cleric, sought to promote the Church of England through the Society for Promoting Christian Knowledge by sending some 34,000 volumes to the colonies in the early years of the eighteenth century. Bray provided clergymen with libraries of religious books for their exclusive use and then funded more ambitious provincial libraries, also of a mostly religious nature, for general use. The largest of these, 1,095 volumes, was in Annapolis, Maryland; others, particularly the library in Charleston, South Carolina, became the foundation upon which later libraries were built.

An advertisement for a New York bookstore shows a bibliophile and his books. New York and Boston, followed by Philadelphia, were the main centers of bookselling and publishing in nineteenth-century America.

The Golden Age of the Social Library

When Benjamin Franklin moved to Philadelphia, he found a bibliophile's desert. "There was not a good Bookseller's shop in any of the Colonies Southward of Boston. . . . Those who lov'd Reading were oblig'd to send for their Books from England," he wrote. In 1728 Franklin formed a book club and discussion group known as the Junto, which combined tippling with philosophizing, and for a while the members kept their books in a common library. Franklin found this arrangement so useful that he drew up plans for the Library Company of Philadelphia, which became a model for numerous other social libraries. "So few were the Readers at that time in Philadelphia, and the Majority of us so poor," he wrote in his *Autobiography*, "that I was not able with great Industry to find more than Fifty Persons, mostly young tradesmen, willing to pay down for this purpose Forty shillings each, and Ten Shillings per annum." The social or subscription library took many forms, but essentially it was a private organization whose owners held stock and whose users paid an annual subscription fee.

Benjamin Franklin, printer, publisher, inventor, and revolutionary diplomat, helped found the Library Company of Philadelphia, which became the model for early private libraries.

The Boston Athenaeum was the foremost American private library of the early 1800s. The exclusivity of the athenaeum and other private libraries inspired the drive for free public libraries.

Franklin consulted with James Logan, who would later give his library to the city of Philadelphia, about what books to buy. The original order for seventy volumes and a few choice periodicals was uniformly secular, combining practical works, geographies, histories, the classics, and contemporary literature, such as the works of Joseph Addison, the British essayist and poet. A major threat to this library after it was moved to a room in the State House, now Independence Hall, was the proclivity of visiting Native American delegations to build tepee fires indoors.

Franklin's effort represented a larger movement among middling parts of the population, such as tradesmen and mechanics, that reflected the belief in cooperative self-help and autodidacticism, ideas common among young Americans. Library historian Jesse H. Shera has described the early years of the republic (1790–1815) as the golden age of the social library. Legislatures passed laws that made it easier to start such libraries, while booksellers competed for this important part of the book-buying public. In 1802 the *Massachusetts Register* estimated that there were at least one hundred social libraries in that state alone. Many of these libraries were tiny—hardly more than a bookshelf in someone's home—but others went on to become well-known private libraries, such as the American Antiquarian Society, the Boston Athenaeum, and the Massachusetts Historical Society. Although the bulk of the social libraries were of a general nature, specialized social libraries began to emerge—libraries for women, libraries for children, historical libraries, libraries for factory workers, law libraries, medical libraries.

The first social libraries inspired numerous variations, all of which helped to build a book culture during the early years of the republic. Libraries were set up at public schools in many states. Sunday school libraries originated with the practice of awarding a book to a student for good behavior and regular attendance. This practice gave way in the 1820s to establishing small libraries from which spiritual and other books could be borrowed by students and their families. Before these libraries died out at the end of the nineteenth century, 30,000 of them were in operation.

While Sunday school libraries were often established, according to one of their founders, to put books in the hands of those "who otherwise would never have them," in some cities members of the urban gentry assembled private libraries that were modeled after libraries known as athenaeums in England. The Boston Athenaeum, opened in 1807, was the first and best known of these

A crowded Saturday night at the New York Mercantile Library in 1871. Mercantile libraries were set up by clerks who aimed to join the merchant class.

Early publishers were jacks-of-all-trades who printed, published, and sold their works. Traveling book salesmen lived on the road, often following the circuit court from town to town. When necessary, they exchanged their books for goods such as eggs, firewood, and salt fish.

Card summarizing the rules at a nineteenth-century apprentices' library. Among the plethora of early library types, apprentices' libraries generally catered to skilled workers and self-employed craftsmen.

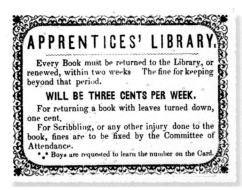

libraries. Founder William Smith Shaw, who served as librarian for sixteen years without a salary, wanted to arouse our "literary men . . . from their stupid lethargy" by creating a reading room that offered books, newspapers, and periodicals. Shaw's effort inspired other athenaeums in New York, Providence, Philadelphia, and more than a dozen other eastern cities and towns. Athenaeums, with their high fees and stock purchase plans, were the most elitist of the early libraries.

Two other variants of the social library, the mechanics' or apprentices' libraries and the mercantile libraries, were founded by particular members of the business community for their own specific purposes. The first of these libraries appear to have been inspired by British efforts to put books into the hands of working people for a nominal fee—one penny a week at the Artisans' Library in Birmingham in 1795. The American versions, first seen in Boston, New York, Portland, and Philadelphia in 1820, were the work of mechanics' mutual assistance societies and small businessmen with an interest in educating young workers. The Apprentices' Library in New York was formed by the General Society of Mechanics and Tradesmen and included an elementary school. It opened on November 25, 1820, with a collection of 4,000 volumes. Three hundred books were borrowed on the first day. In a distinctly idealized description of the library, the *New York Daily Tribune* claimed in 1850 that "when the labor of the day is over, instead of the apprentice scouring the streets, visiting bar-rooms or theatres, mingling with idle vicious companions, he takes his seat in this library with a rich intellectual repast before him."

Mercantile libraries were formed by and for another part of the business community—merchants' clerks who aspired to become businessmen themselves. This is what motivated the group of young clerks who met at New York's Tontine Coffee House on November 9, 1820, to form the Mercantile Library Association. They solicited funding from their employers to set up a library and offer educational programs that would teach clerks how to become like their masters.

One other type of library, the circulating library, flourished in the country's formative years. The circulating library was a purely commercial proposition, a rental library often connected with a bookstore. Unconstrained by the high-mindedness of the social libraries, rental libraries catered to the popular taste for novels, and in this way were a more accurate barometer of nineteenth-century reading habits than their cousins, the social libraries.

Most of the social libraries and many of their variants did not outlast their founders. Limited financing aggravated by frequent recessions and the problem of sustaining voluntary support were the principal problems. After the Civil War, the number of social and school libraries declined precipitously as free public libraries emerged as the most important provider of books to American

MY FIRST LIBRARY

THERE HAVE BEEN MANY SINCE, and many of them memorable and seductive.

Some have been massive, like fortresses around the books. I think of the New York Public at Fifth Avenue and Forty-second Street with its great stone lions alert at either side of the broad entrance steps, standing guard.

A few have swept me into centuries past: the creaking parquet floors, high windows, and graceful balustrades and catwalks of the library of Trinity College, Dublin, transported me into the Age of Reason, and the strange illumination, dark wood, and forbidding systems of the Bibliothèque Nationale in Paris seemed to symbolize the elite and dangerous world of aristocratic France.

A great-great-great-uncle of mine, Richard Hildreth, was known as the "Gray Ghost of the Boston Athenaeum." He wrote a twenty-two-volume history of the United States there in the late 1840s as well as political pamphlets and a popular, abolitionist novel. When I visited the athenaeum a few years ago, I saw that, radical though Hildreth had been, he had enjoyed the privileges of a comfortable club. Perfectly bound books and an art show a couple of times a year. Polished brass. Tea.

But most important was the first library—to me it is as memorable a "first" as only a very few others. The library of the Fountain Valley School of Colorado, a small boarding school to which I was sent when I was twelve, was contained in a room no more than twenty by twenty feet. Its ceiling was relatively high, however, and the shelves were full to the top, reachable by ladder.

A teacher who had assigned us John Steinbeck's *In Dubious Battle* had told me that I might find other books by Steinbeck in the library, and I had entered timidly the first time. I had no habit of reading; in fact reading had been difficult for me. Steinbeck's *Battle* had made a vivid and intelligible picture of the world, and I wanted intelligibility.

The trip from my home in New York to the school had taken two and one-half days by train. I had been frightened when my father had accompanied me to Grand Central Station to meet one of the teachers and a handful of other boys, but I had never been homesick. My parents had recently and confusingly divorced and I was glad of the distance from them. So I began to read and read—almost anything that came to hand in those dark shelves. I can smell the room. I see the librarian pulling out a drawer in the wooden card file. Most important I glimpse parts of the worlds I encountered there—Thomas Wolfe's New York, Pearl Buck's China, and many more.

Blair Fuller

George Ticknor, a Harvard historian, led the campaign to establish a free public library in Boston, which opened in 1854. The founders of the Boston library and its first librarians had a profound impact on the public library movement.

readers. The social libraries, however, had served their purpose, both in the dissemination of books and in the encouragement of learning. In a young and fluid community without antecedents beyond those brought from Europe, Americans in the early years of the republic were passing through an experimental phase into a period of institution building, whether in banking or in the foundation of utopian communities. Social libraries fit the pattern of small-scale, locally controlled experimentation characteristic of a nascent democracy.

THE FIRST FREE PUBLIC LIBRARIES

Looking back to the history of Massachusetts before 1820, Ralph Waldo Emerson wrote that "there was not a book, a speech, a conversation, or a thought in the State." Looking ahead, Emerson was in a less dyspeptic mood: in 1837 he "read with joy some of the auspicious signs of the coming days, as they glimmer already through poetry and art, through philosophy and science, through church and state." The country was indeed in the formative years of a literary renaissance in which Emerson and his fellow New Englanders would play a major role. Another aspect of this new era was the widespread establishment of free public libraries, one of the most significant contributions that the United States made to the world of books.

At least three New England towns can claim the honor of founding the first free public library: Salisbury, Connecticut (1810); Lexington, Massachusetts (1827); and Peterborough, New Hampshire (1833). However, it was the opening of a tax-supported free public library in 1854 in Boston, the republic's literary capital, that, by its example, would have a major national impact. The circumstances of the library's founding were somewhat peculiar.

Nicholas Marie Alexandre Vattemare, a popular French actor and ventriloquist, was promoting the international exchange of books and the creation of grandiose civic structures to house them. At a meeting of the Mercantile Library Association in 1841, he urged a group of enthusiastic young Bostonians to open a public library that would house the books he proposed to import. Vattemare's scheme fit well with plans long espoused by George Ticknor, the high Brahmin who was the self-proclaimed arbiter of the city's social and intellectual life, to consolidate all of Boston's libraries and museums into one public library, museum, and lecture facility. Ticknor was a man of wealth, a former Harvard professor, and a historian of Spanish literature. His cousin was William Davis Ticknor, owner of the Old Corner Book Store and partner in Ticknor & Fields, the publisher of such literary lights as Robert Browning, Thomas De Quincey, Ralph Waldo Emerson, Nathaniel Hawthorne, Oliver Wendell Holmes, Harriet Beecher Stowe, Henry David Thoreau, John Greenleaf Whittier, and Henry Wadsworth Longfellow. George Ticknor's closest associate in the campaign for a public library was Edward Everett, the boy wonder who began his career at the age of nineteen as a Congregationalist minister and went on to be president of Harvard and secretary of state.

Ticknor and Everett's social clique at once disdained and was fascinated by Vattemare, who showered the city with strange literary gifts, including reports on Parisian slaughterhouses and the effects of cholera morbus on the city of Paris, and a "Statistical Map" of the city's sewers. All of these were duly enshrined in City Hall alongside books donated by well-known local authors, while the various participants in the library campaign fought over funding and whether a sacrosanct institution like the Boston Athenaeum should be joined with a library for the plebeian masses. After thirteen years of meetings, posturing, and political intrigue, the Boston Public Library was finally opened in March 1854, in two small, poorly lit, drafty rooms in the Mason Street schoolhouse.

The *Report of the Trustees of the Public Library of the City of Boston, July 1852,* authored in part by George Ticknor, became the Magna Carta of the public library movement, setting the tone for American public libraries for the next half

The wonderfully ornate reading room at the Boston Public Library. The library's architecture was influenced by the Bibliothèque Ste. Geneviève in Paris and in turn influenced the design of other American libraries, including San Francisco's.

Steel baron and philanthropist Andrew Carnegie, shown in a cartoon from 1902, gave nearly $45 million to fund the construction of 1,946 libraries in the United States, including the San Francisco Main Library and six of its branches. Toward the end of his life (below), he visits his native Scotland.

century or more. There were numerous private libraries, particularly in Boston, the report argued, but they did not meet the needs of the populace because they were inaccessible to the multitudes. "It is of paramount importance," the report went on, "that the means of general information should be so diffused that the largest possible number of persons should be induced to read and understand questions of social order, which are constantly presenting themselves, and which we, as a people, are constantly required to decide, and do decide, either ignorantly or wisely." Ticknor agreed with Everett's argument that a public library "would put a finishing hand" to Boston's public educational system. Citizens were educated up to a certain point, but then had no access to books that could further their education.

Early historians of American libraries describe the Boston Public Library as a major achievement for democratic egalitarianism. More recently, historians such as Michael Harris have pointed out that the library's founders were living in an urban climate that very much alarmed them. In their view, American institutions were threatened by a flood of immigrants who "think little of moral and intellectual culture." The Boston library's Standing Committee pointed to the most recent census figures, which indicated that "this influx of ignorance" meant that "the preponderance in our city at least will be largely in their favor." In this situation a public library was needed to teach virtue and respect for social order.

The Boston library report was widely read. With its wealth of practical information about how to set up and run a free circulating library, it became the blueprint for any number of new libraries. The report had its most immediate impact in New England, where thirty-five libraries were opened in the same decade as the Boston library. Then came the economic crisis of 1857 and the Civil War. Still, by 1875 ten states had passed enabling legislation for public libraries, eight major cities had opened municipal libraries, and a total of 2,240 libraries had been established.

PHILANTHROPY ON THE RISE

The next period in library construction was dominated by the philanthropic activities of Andrew Carnegie, the Scottish-born steel baron. Carnegie was a singular individual, a poor immigrant from a radical background who worked his way into an enormous fortune, which left him both ambivalent and defensive about the perquisites of great wealth. Carnegie's father was a damask linen weaver whose skills with a hand loom were undermined by the growth of textile factories in his native Scotland. His father was one of several family members who were vociferous opponents of wealth and privilege and supporters of the Chartist movement, which called for universal manhood suffrage during the turbulent 1840s. Unable to support themselves in Scotland, Andrew's family moved to Pittsburgh, where Carnegie

A Tribute to Andrew Carnegie

❋

The public library saved my life when I was a child. My particular library was the Morrisania branch of the New York Public Library in the South Bronx. It was a refuge and a sanctuary for me. I could go there when things got tough or when somebody was after me, which was often. Many cowards, I think, must spend long hours in the library to avoid the bullies outside. Consequently, they become readers. Some, like myself, even become writers.

Books open doors for people. That's the traditional role of libraries—to expand horizons and to provide information. But libraries can close doors as well. If you are an imperfect child as I was—a liar, a crier, and a coward—you can escape from yourself into your books and find your true persona. I could go anywhere I liked in my books and be any person I chose. My books not only entertained me, but gave me courage and hope.

And they taught me to write. I receive many letters from children who want to write. I tell them "Read!" I tell them to go to the library, pick out their own books, and read. The library is one of the few places kids can really be free. They can choose any of the thousands of books on the shelves, and in reading, they learn the craft of writing. Painlessly, they pick up the tricks of the trade. They learn how to put words together, how to pace, how to highlight, how to beguile.

I need to say a few words in tribute to Andrew Carnegie. I know he made his immense fortune in steel, which means a lot of it must have come from weapons. I suspect he must have had a guilty conscience which prompted him to give away so much of his money to support education, public libraries, and the world peace movement. His money built over 2,500 public libraries, and one of them was my Morrisania branch. So I can't help having a soft spot in my heart for bad, rich, old Andrew Carnegie.

I became an addicted reader as a child, and I'm still an addict. I don't travel anywhere without the security blanket of my books. I go to the library at least once a week for my fix. My neighborhood branch is a Carnegie library, which makes me very happy. I love the old library smells and the creak of old library furniture. I love the shadowy corners and the high windows that shut out the world. But I can happily coexist with a new library building as long as it still serves as a sanctuary for its readers, and as long as it continues to put books free of charge into the hands of children.

Marilyn Sachs

Marilyn Sachs

MATTHEW ARNOLD AT THE BOSTON PUBLIC LIBRARY

*Described by an Anonymous
Staff Member*

❖

"He came in here one day and saw a little barefooted news-boy sitting in one of the best chairs in the reading room, enjoying himself apparently for dear life. The great essayist was completely astounded. 'Do you let barefooted boys in this reading-room?' he asked. 'You would never see such a sight as that in Europe. I do not believe there is a reading-room in all Europe in which that boy, dressed as he is, would enter.' Then Mr. Arnold went over to the boy, engaged him in conversation, and found that he was reading The Life of Washington, and that he was a young gentleman of decidedly anti-British tendencies, and, for his age, remarkably well informed. Mr. Arnold remained talking with the youngster for some time, and, as he came back to our desk, the great Englishman said: 'I do not think I have been so impressed with anything else that I have seen since arriving in this country as I am now with meeting that barefooted boy in this reading-room . . . It is a sight that impresses a European not accustomed to your democratic ways.'"

Library Journal, June 1887

❖

went to work as a bobbin boy in a cotton textile mill at the age of thirteen. To Carnegie, the United States was everything that Britain was not. "We have perfect political Equality . . . no Royal Family . . . No established Church . . . We have the Charter which you have been fighting for years," he wrote his cousin.

Carnegie's considerable intelligence and business skills allowed him to move up the ranks of the local telegraph company into management of the Pennsylvania Railroad and thence to establishment of the Carnegie Steel Company, which he sold to J. P. Morgan for $500 million in 1902. At the age of thirty-three, Carnegie had planned to retire, writing in a year-end memo in 1868, "50,000 per annum. Beyond this never earn . . . but spend the surplus each year for benevelent [sic] purposes . . . the amassing of wealth is one of the worst species of idolatry." He went on, however, to become the overlord of the steel industry, an industry built upon ruthlessness and rapid technological innovation. Carnegie, according to David Brody, historian of the steel industry, "defined the treatment of steelworkers. Long hours, bleak conditions, anti-unionism, flowed alike from the economizing drive that made the American steel industry the wonder of the manufacturing world."

Heir to a radical tradition, Carnegie was not always anti-union. He wrote two magazine articles in 1886 arguing that unions were beneficial to both labor and capital. But this was six years before Henry Clay Frick, his ruthless lieutenant, sent three hundred Pinkerton guards to Carnegie's Homestead, Pennsylvania, mill to break a strike while Carnegie was out of the country. The resulting pitched battle led to the death of three Pinkertons, the occupation of Homestead by 8,000 troops, and the end of unionism in the steel industry until the 1930s.

Carnegie's interest in libraries can be traced to his father's role in founding the Tradesman's Subscription Library in Carnegie's hometown of Dunfermline. Later, Andrew Carnegie, having organized a debating society among his friends at the age of eighteen, was introduced to Colonel John Anderson of Allegheny, Pennsylvania. Anderson opened his personal library on Saturday to Carnegie and other young working men, then expanded his collection and founded the Mechanics' and Apprentices' Library. The annual subscription fee was $2,000; apprentices could use the library free. Carnegie was expected to pay the fee since he was not an apprentice. Instead he started an anonymous letter-writing campaign in the Pittsburgh newspaper, which ultimately led to removal of the fee.

Carnegie first gave funds to build a library in Dunfermline in 1881. By that time he was already an exponent of "scientific philanthropy," describing the man of wealth as "mere trustee and agent for his poorer brethren, bringing to their service his superior wisdom, experience, and ability to administer, doing for them better than they would or could do for themselves." Starting with Allegheny in 1886, Carnegie ultimately gave $44,854,731.25 to build 1,946 libraries in the United States. Another $10 million went for libraries abroad. The impact of his funding was extraordinary: it was estimated that 35 million people a day used his libraries. New York City received $5.2 million for 65 branch libraries. Indiana, Carnegie's largest beneficiary, was blessed with 164 libraries, California with 122.

Carnegie's library philosophy fit nicely with that of the Boston Brahmins and the rest of the first generation of librarians who saw themselves as part of a social and intellectual elite dispensing enlightenment and morality to the less fortunate. Libraries were "the best agency for improving the masses of people, because they give nothing for nothing. They only help those who help themselves." Knowledge gained at libraries, Carnegie explained, made "men not violent revolutionaries, but cautious evolutionists; not destroyers, but careful improvers."

The Homestead Strike, however, haunted Carnegie, and his funds were not always welcomed as they were in Dunfermline, where he was drawn through town in a coach-and-four before a crowd of 8,000. In a widely circulated editorial, the *St. Louis Post Dispatch* called Carnegie a coward and commented that "ten thousand 'Carnegie Public Libraries' would not compensate the country for the direct and indirect evils resulting from the Homestead lockout." Unions in Carnegie's own Pittsburgh opposed his funding of the local library. In Detroit, which was offered a library in 1901, opposition to Carnegie delayed funding until 1911, as it did in San Francisco at roughly the same time.

Carnegie was not the only library philanthropist. John Jacob Astor gave $400,000, an astounding sum in those days, for a public research and reference library that opened in New York in 1854. Leading Bostonians like Edward Everett donated funds, books, and papers to their library, while Enoch Pratt gave $1 million, an even more impressive donation, to found a public library in Baltimore in 1866. The rise of library philanthropy came at a fortuitous time. Major cities lacked the political will and often the authority to raise taxes for institutions like a public library. Hence the state enabling acts, which permitted cities to tax their residents for libraries. In this context, Carnegie's largesse, tied as it was to the recipients' commitment to support libraries that were constructed with his funds, played a role in pushing American cities toward the use of taxes

Carnegie built sixty-five branch libraries in New York City, the first of which was the Yorkville branch, opened in 1902.

Librarians at the Minneapolis Public Library in 1892. Librarianship generally was considered women's work. Head librarians were predominantly male, as were library commissioners and trustees.

In a burst of idealism that began in the early twentieth century, public librarians reached out to serve patrons with such innovations as this book cart at the National Cash Register Company in Dayton, Ohio.

for the construction of municipal facilities. As such, it was part and parcel of the drive toward the reconstruction of American cities, symbolized by the City Beautiful movement that began in the last decade of the nineteenth century.

LIBRARIANS: SOCIAL WORKERS OR MORAL GUARDIANS?

By the turn of the century, the country was well endowed with public libraries. Library building continued well into the 1920s, but the problem became how to define or redefine the role of the public library. The conditions that startled the Boston Brahmins in the mid-1800s—large-scale immigration, crowded slums, and limited educational opportunities for the poor—became the plight of every city, only on a far grander scale, by the beginning of the twentieth century. In this context, librarians, like missionaries in a foreign country, remained committed to their role as educators.

The mission of the first public librarians had been both grandiose and naive. Given the day-to-day reality of working people's lives, the library could neither function as "a people's university," as some early library leaders liked to claim, nor easily reach those with little time or sufficient education to read for pleasure or for knowledge. For many librarians this meant changing the way the library functioned and creating new services that attracted patrons. Open shelves, dating from 1879, were among the first innovations. Later came interlibrary loans. Collections were departmentalized around subjects, such as reference and information, sociology, religion, philosophy, and history. Special collections were developed in industrial arts and for the business community. At first, children under the age of twelve were barred from many of the early libraries—in some cases because library books were thought to distract children from their school work! Starting in 1890, children's rooms became common, and in a number of instances separate children's libraries were opened. Reference services were defined and specialized. Beginning with the East Boston Branch in 1870, branch libraries were built in numerous cities. They were supplemented by deposit stations for small collections of books that were placed in schools, churches, clubs, factories, and stores and delivery stations, usually drugstores, where a patron could pick up a book ordered from the library. Books were circulated by horse and wagon and later by bookmobile.

There were even experiments, particularly in Pittsburgh and Cincinnati, with the placement of small libraries in the homes of poor families, where they were used by a group of children supervised by a library employee. Those who created the home library movement soon assumed the responsibilities of social workers, setting up reading groups for delinquent boys, supervising recreational activities, organizing dramatic and singing societies, and taking children on field trips.

As libraries pushed outward, many of them were transformed into community centers. Sewing and other skills were taught. Art exhibits and folk pageants were organized. English language, citizenship, and other classes were set up for immigrants. Books written in foreign languages were purchased. Library facilities were used by universities to offer extension courses and lectures, and by local organizations ranging from the Boy Scouts to the anarchist union, the Industrial Workers of the World.

The public debate among librarians seemed to emanate from two very different camps. Those who were oriented toward the social work ethos that emerged in major cities at the turn of the century saw themselves as part of a larger movement to ameliorate the conditions of the poor. In an era of trade union militancy and radical politics, others remained more concerned with problems of social order. Patriotism and "right thinking" were the major preoccupations of this group. "Free corn in old Rome bribed a mob and kept it passive. By free books and what goes in them in modern America we mean to erase the mob from existence," proclaimed the American Library Association in a 1910 pamphlet titled "Why Do We Need a Library?" But even among those who saw

The 1920 newspaper story that accompanied this photograph described "a perambulating library by means of which books are carried to the illiterate corners of Evanston, Illinois." The half-ton truck visiting a factory site was an early bookmobile.

The Great Depression of the 1930s eventuated in federal programs, such as the Works Progress Administration, that funded innovative library efforts. In Kentucky, pack-horse librarians brought books to remote areas of the state.

themselves as social workers, a patronizing attitude prevailed. Immigrants lacked culture and morals and needed to be Americanized. Children were all too often dirty little miscreants who needed to be watched (and washed) carefully. In the Cleveland Public Library, for example, a librarian suggested that the names be taken of children who were sent to the washroom so that they "may be singled out and dealt with as their case requires."

Despite the public librarians' continuing commitment to education, most of the books that circulated were hardly educational. Library patrons preferred fiction, much of it popular novels and romances. Studies as early as the 1870s demonstrated that a majority—sometimes an overwhelming majority—of readers chose fiction. This situation posed a problem for librarians, who generally agreed with early library leader William Fletcher when he wrote in 1896 that librarians must "accept and exercise full authority for the moral character and influence of the library." For one group of librarians, the right kind of fiction served an important function: it was the avenue to a higher class of books. Others were chary of all fiction, particularly since young women appeared to be the largest group of readers for this particular genre.

In 1881 the American Library Association, then only five years old, surveyed seventy libraries to find out which authors librarians excluded from their shelves in the selection process. An ALA committee then compiled a list of sixteen questionable authors, ten of whom were women authors who wrote for an exclusively female audience. (Interestingly none of these authors would be familiar to contemporary readers.) Inspired by the ALA, most libraries assembled lists of objectionable books: books that appealed to "lower nature [by] exalting passion," books about the naked body, books that offered "a false picture of life," books that emphasized a "defective social arrangement" rather than a character's personal "responsibilities."

Book selection inevitably required some kind of discrimination. But in their efforts to protect the morals of their patrons, librarians aggressively took on the role of censor. "Some [librarians] have greatness thrust upon them," proclaimed Arthur E. Bostwick, the president of the ALA, in a 1908 speech approvingly titled "The Librarian as Censor." Books should be judged, he said, on the basis of three categories—the Good, the True, and the Beautiful. Using these and similar standards, all sorts of books were banned from libraries or placed on restricted shelves, including Shakespeare's *Richard III,* Robert Louis Stevenson's *Treasure Island,* Edgar Allan Poe's *The Murders in the Rue Morgue,* and Arthur Conan Doyle's *The Adventures of Sherlock Holmes.* Theodore Dreiser was a particular target of library censors, as was Edith Wharton in the western Massachusetts communities that she wrote about. Other works, such as Boccaccio's *The Decameron* and Henry Fielding's *Tom Jones,* were purchased only in expurgated editions.

THE IMPACT OF ECONOMICS, SEGREGATION, AND CENSORSHIP

During the prosperous 1920s, library building continued. The United States was a global power with a renewed fascination with urban grandeur. As major civic construction projects were undertaken, inadequate libraries were replaced with new central facilities. Branches, too, sprang up here and there, accounting most likely for the impressive growth in book circulation at public libraries. Carnegie grants for the construction of libraries all but ended two years before his death in 1919. But now there was sufficient support among urban voters to float bond issues for new construction projects. Detroit built a new main library in 1921. Philadelphia followed with one of the largest library buildings in the United States in 1927.

Though Carnegie funds had gone into the building of six branches in Los Angeles, the city lacked an adequate central library. In 1908 the main library was moved to Hamburger's department store, where elevator operators announced the library's floor after carpets and furniture. From there the library moved once again, in 1914, to the three top floors of the newly constructed Metropolitan Building at the corner of Fifth and Broadway. Finally, after the usual internecine political conflict and two bond issue campaigns—featuring in one instance a negative comparison to San Francisco's new main library—a new central Los Angeles library opened its doors to the public on July 6, 1926.

In 1929 the bubble of prosperity burst, and libraries, like other civic institutions, suffered from the resulting economic deflation. The sickening downward slide of the economy did not start to impact many cities and their libraries until 1931, when cities began to cut their budgets. The downturn in library budgets came with an uncanny sense of bad timing. As unemployment increased, more and more adults went to the library. And those who did were reading more nonfiction than ever. This pattern *suggests*—there are no definitive studies—that adult readers were seeking explanations for the Great Depression and information that could lead to reemployment. Faced with a rapid decline in their budgets between

Rural America, particularly in the South, lacked libraries until federal funding for libraries began in the 1950s. Dorothea Lange photographed this library in the Piney Woods of southwestern Mississippi in 1937 for the Farm Security Administration.

"THE MOST CURSORY REFLECTION WILL MAKE IT CLEAR BEYOND DOUBT THAT BOOKS ARE A PRIMARY NECESSITY OF LIFE IN ANY CIVILIZED COMMUNITY."

✿

Douglas McMurtrie
The Book, 1943

With the 1950s craze for drive-ins that provided food, movies, and even church services, library service was bound to follow. This book drop was located in Cedar Rapids, Iowa.

1931 and 1933, librarians were forced to cut all categories of expenditures. They chose, however, to cut book-buying budgets more than salaries. Total circulation and the number of book borrowers began to decline, partly because of the lack of new books and partly because of a decline in unemployment. By 1935 the worst of the depression was over, and library budgets began to inch upward again.

The depression, despite the severity of its impact on libraries, produced some new departures. For one thing, it marked the federal government's first involvement with public libraries through the Agriculture Extension Service, the Emergency Education Program, the National Youth Administration, and the Works Progress Administration. The WPA, the principal funder of library work, contributed $18 million a year between 1934 and 1943 in an effort that employed some 27,000 people. Packhorse librarians and bookmobiles carried books into some of the most remote parts of rural America. In the WPA's Minnesota Demonstration Project, library stations were set up in out-of-the-way places such as barber shops, lunch counters, and general stores. In other states, libraries were established in prisons, mental hospitals, and military bases. These federal efforts marked the first systematic attempt to build up libraries in rural areas. They also led to greater degrees of cooperation between resource-starved libraries on the state and county levels.

There was a certain irony here. As the Examining Committee of the Boston Public Library put it, "the rediscovery of the Public Library is a by-product of the depression." It would take a while, however, for public libraries to recover. Boston, for example, had spent lavishly on books throughout the 1920s, and expenditures did not return to the highest level of that period until the budget for 1947 to 1949.

By these postwar years, every major city had a central library and branches. The picture was less rosy in rural America, but the issue of rural libraries was deferred until the federal government reentered the library funding business in 1956. Library development had reached a kind of plateau. In fact, during the immediate postwar era, libraries were very much on the defensive.

In 1947 the Carnegie Foundation funded the first major study of public libraries. The results shocked and dismayed the library community. Two of the books that reported the results of this study, Bernard Berelson's *The Library's Public* and Robert D. Leigh's *The Public Library in the United States,* situated reading habits and use of public libraries in the context of all mass media at a time when radio was a popular medium and television was just beginning its dangerously seductive pas de deux with the American mind. The communication revolution had produced an abundance of media. The problem was that books were not the medium of first choice. Only about one-fourth of the adult population was reading on a regular basis. Of the books that were read, only one-fourth of them came from public libraries. And of those who actually used the library, 10 percent of the borrowers took out 30 percent of the books. In short, the library audience, despite almost one hundred years of efforts to reach out to the public, was a rather small one.

Looking ahead, Berelson and Leigh argued that the picture was an alarming one. Library use was likely to *decline,* although the public needed libraries as much as ever. Polls, Leigh explained, indicated that even with an abundance of media Americans showed less knowledge and understanding of vital social issues. Berelson's and Leigh's conclusions were disheartening: libraries should focus on their natural audience—the better educated, the opinion leaders, the "widely distributed group leadership" that was "an inevitable part of the social structure of American communities in our day." Essentially, Berelson and Leigh were arguing that librarians should give up any broader social mission and return to their elitist roots. In the debate over the library inquiry, no one seems to have pointed out that the early years of the depression showed just the opposite: that the number of library patrons could expand dramatically in a time of need, even with declining book-buying budgets. The inquiry also failed to note that by the end of the war adequate library service was available to less than half of all Americans, and that in most rural areas library service was nonexistent.

The Harlem branch of the Tampa Public Library in Florida, 1923. Until the Supreme Court's 1954 desegregation decision in Brown v. Board of Education, *most public libraries in the South, like public schools, were segregated.*

Another issue that the library inquiry did not address was the availability of public libraries to minority communities, particularly African-Americans. A study of library facilities for blacks conducted in the South in 1938 showed that 6 million blacks were without library service and that 2 million lived in communities where whites alone had access to libraries. Blacks had been close to universally deprived of library service in the South until the beginning of the twentieth century. Then, during the first two decades of the century, a few public libraries extended restricted privileges to blacks. In other communities, beginning with Galveston, Texas, in 1904, separate branches for blacks were opened, while in a small number of communities, such as Charlotte, North Carolina, wholly independent black libraries were established. The WPA brought library service to thousands of blacks in the rural South, but by the end of the New Deal many blacks remained cut off from library service.

Library integration came quietly and slowly to the South beginning well before *Brown* v. *Board of Education,* the 1954 Supreme Court decision that banned separate but equal facilities in education. Integration proceeded with little fanfare

The Public Library and the Black Experience

◆

"When I reached the age of sixteen, I can remember a county library being erected. Before that time I had no knowledge of any public library. It was a lovely building, and this small town [Fayette, Alabama] took great pride in it. One afternoon after school, while working at my uncle's cab company, having read everything worth reading in our school library, I thought I would call the new county library and ask if I could come and check out books. I called because I was too afraid to go in person. I explained that I was a 'Negro' and wanted to know if I could use the library. This difficult and unusual question was immediately referred to the librarian. I remember, as if it were yesterday, her reply, in a very soft and mild voice, 'I am sorry, we cannot allow Negroes to come here.'"

James R. Wright
What Black Librarians Are Saying, 1972

▦

during the civil rights era; its leaders, for the most part, picked more important and visible targets than public libraries. In 1963 the ALA reported, however, that library segregation was "still widespread and severe" in the five states of the Deep South. Although 1960s civil rights legislation put an end to segregation, the ALA was correct in noting that library services available to both blacks and whites were "far inferior to those found in other major regions of the United States."

During the postwar malaise in the library world, public libraries came under attack on another front. As hysteria about the threat of godless communism spread, self-appointed guardians of the moral order became increasingly aggressive in their efforts to tamper with the book selection process at public libraries. The leadership of the American Legion in Illinois, for example, called for a general purge of "subversive books" in libraries, schools, and bookstores in 1948.

The ALA had long given up its glorification of censorship and had passed the Library Bill of Rights in 1939. Starting during World War II, the ALA championed the fight against book censorship through its Intellectual Freedom Committee. Studies conducted in the 1960s on the availability of controversial books, such as Karl Marx's *Das Kapital,* James Baldwin's *Nobody Knows My Name,* J. Edgar Hoover's *Masters of Deceit,* and D. H. Lawrence's *Lady Chatterley's Lover,* indicated that these types of books were fairly widely available. But a careful examination of the results shows that books written from a right-wing perspective were more commonly available than those written from the left. Describing one such survey in the *Library Journal* in 1962, the author tried to reassure readers that "extremes are rejected with equality, neither the right nor left coming off ahead." Indeed strong evidence was developed by Marjorie Fiske in a 1958 study of California libraries that librarians were continuing to act as censors simply by avoiding the purchase of controversial books. A new generation of librarians who joined the profession or grew up in the activist era of the 1960s were more willing to confront the censors. The problem of censorship did not fade, however; it simply shifted to new terrain. In the post–Cold War years, issues such as those associated with the Christian right's campaign for "family values" became the focus of censorship battles. Children's books, including Michael Wilhoit's *Daddy's Roommate* and Leslea Newman's *Heather Has Two Mommies,* which described gay relationships, were the new targets of opportunity.

A New Generation of Library Activism

The predictions about declining use of public libraries that came out of the 1947 Carnegie inquiry proved to be wrong. The Cold War years saw an enormous increase in the impact of higher education on the number of people who used libraries. Central city populations continued to grow, while new suburbs outpaced them, expanding almost five times as fast. Book use at public libraries expanded accordingly—dramatically in some major cities—with children's books leading the way by a wide margin.

Beginning in 1956, the federal government returned to the field of library funding with passage of the Library Services Act. Initially funding was directed at the problem of rural libraries. The U.S. Office of Education estimated in 1956 that 26 million rural Americans lacked library service and that 300 counties had no library. The LSA triggered more funding at the state levels, and in the act's first years new libraries were built, millions of books were purchased, and new bookmobiles provided service in many rural areas. When the LSA was amended to become the Library Services and Construction Act in 1963, additional funding was provided for library construction in urban as well as rural areas. Soon the federal mandate

Jacob Lawrence's painting
The Library *(1960) celebrates*
an American public institution.

The Los Angeles Public Library's bookmobile, "Little Toot," shown in the 1950s, when libraries were undergoing the greatest wave of expansion since the age of Andrew Carnegie. Community outreach efforts such as bookmobiles were negatively impacted by budget cutbacks that began in the early 1970s and accelerated after the passage of numerous antitax referenda inspired by California's Proposition 13 in 1978.

grew again, with funds provided for library service in disadvantaged neighborhoods and for the handicapped. Beginning in the 1970s, additional federal funds were provided through job training programs, literacy programs, public works programs, and the National Endowment for the Humanities. Federal funding leveraged more state dollars for library development, but the overwhelming share of funds for public libraries still came from local sources.

While library service spread steadily through the new suburbs and into rural areas, the big city library became a victim of the urban social crisis that was thrown into relief by ghetto rioting in several major cities in the 1960s. With white flight to the suburbs and the emergence of a large, poor, mostly nonwhite underclass, cities were increasingly hard-pressed to meet the needs of their residents. Whole new skylines arose in central business districts, but libraries sank slowly toward the bottom of the list of political priorities.

Fiscal constraints began to hit a number of major libraries like New York's in the late 1960s. By 1975 the ALA could report that public libraries had experienced their worst budgetary problems since the depression. Librarians were "moaning and groaning," according to the ALA; some "wept openly in the streets." Cutbacks were the answer. Hours were shortened; staff hiring was deferred; book budgets were cut. Not all the news was gloomy. Here and there a city like Dallas and later Chicago announced plans for the construction of a new library. Budgets increased for urban libraries in some western Sun Belt cities, and suburban libraries fared much better as construction continued in these areas. With the passage in California in 1978 of Proposition 13, a radical tax-cutting measure, librarians in other states held their breath for similar budget parings. Dramatic cuts did not materialize until recession hit in the late 1980s. Instead, big city library budgets tended to remain flat or to increase only gradually.

In the midst of the double crisis of urban life and library budget cuts, librarians attempted once more to redefine their mission. The social activism of the 1960s brought a new emphasis on outreach work to disadvantaged neighborhoods. When attention was drawn to the decline in adult literacy, libraries stepped up to provide a home for new literacy programs. Simultaneously the emergence of the facsimile machine and computer led librarians to view the library as an information center that could share resources, often out of economic necessity, over ever-expanding networks.

As public institutions such as libraries and schools continued to deteriorate, major urban centers witnessed an alarming shift in their cultural infrastructure.

Libraries might be forced to close branches and shorten hours, but private funds could be readily raised for large cultural complexes, such as New York's Lincoln Center, that served the city's elite. The polarization of income that became so glaringly apparent in America's inner cities during the Reagan years not surprisingly produced a similar polarization in the world of books. Those who could afford them could buy their own books—and they did, despite higher prices—or they could join a private library. Those who could not were jammed together in overcrowded facilities, which they frequently shared with homeless people. Library patrons all too often looked for books that had long ago disappeared or simply had not been purchased.

These conditions produced a new kind of library activism. Support organizations, such as the numerous Friends of the Library, had existed for decades. But with the stagnation and decline in library budgets, they took on a whole new role. If the business community and the politicians assigned a low priority to public libraries, various library support organizations turned for assistance to the community, for it was generally acknowledged in poll after poll that libraries were valued as an important civic institution by a large majority of the public. Campaigns were launched to prevent the closure of branches, to maintain hours, to stop staff cuts. Many of these failed; others succeeded. In the press of events, librarians discovered that a large world of readers supported them and their institutions. In the most successful instances, library support groups emulated the backers of private cultural institutions, such as the symphony and opera, by launching major fund-raising campaigns to supplement public funds for the construction of new libraries or to endow existing ones.

Although something approaching universal library service had been achieved by the 1990s, the 8,500 public libraries in the United States faced their most severe crisis since the 1930s. Big cities, often forced to choose between basic services such as fire and police protection and education and other institutions such as the public library, cut library budgets substantially. Hours were shortened, staffs reduced, and book-buying budgets trimmed. In California, beginning in

Artist William Wegman and his dog Fay promote reading and libraries in an American Library Association poster. Starting in the 1970s, libraries began to play a major role in the campaign against illiteracy.

WILLIAM WEGMAN and FAY FOR AMERICA'S LIBRARIES

THE NARROW TEMPLE

❖

I'VE HAD A LOVE AFFAIR with the printed word since the first time I finished reading a cereal box at the kitchen table. My great-grandmother, Grace, who raised me, was quite accommodating even though buying books was considered a luxury by the city of Boston's welfare administration. Her only requirement in reading material was that it not cost more than fifty cents at the Goodwill store. But her free-ranging curiosity and economic parameters combined to give me the most eclectic early education of just about any kid on my block.

Each book I opened was a door to a new world. The doors, unlike many others then and now, never said whites only. That I was wearing secondhand clothes or reading by the light of an oil space heater in a cold-water flat did not bar me from walking through those doors.

I finally got a library card but there was no library in my neighborhood. Eventually there arrived what I thought of as the magic carpet—the bookmobile. I always tried to be the first in line because they would let only a few kids at a time into that narrow temple. I can still hear the whoosh of the air lock on the door just before it opened and feel the excited pounding of my heart.

I decided simply to pick a shelf within reach and start reading. My hope was to read every book in the bookmobile. I worked my way through my grade level, then slipped into the adult section. Sometimes I focused on topics I wanted to investigate, like homosexuality. Even as a young girl I knew I was a lesbian and hoped to find a book to tell me more about it. No such luck. Not much in black fiction then, either. What I didn't know was that the supply of books was periodically changed. When I first realized it I was upset. Eventually I was incurably excited by the idea that somewhere there was a repository of more books, an endless store of words and stories that I would always have to look forward to.

Thirty years later I still get that rush of excitement when I walk into my little Glen Park branch of the San Francisco library. An extensive collection of work by writers of all ethnicities and a lesbian/gay collection are all at my fingertips. There is room for books by and about any type of person we can imagine.

Writer Audre Lorde (who held her degree in library science) declared in one of her essays, "Poetry is not a luxury. It is a vital necessity of our existence. It forms the quality of light within which we predicate our hopes and dreams toward survival and change." This really was what that little girl was standing in line for outside the bookmobile—not just magic but survival and change.

Jewelle Gomez

1993–94, the impact of these cuts was particularly severe. Hours were reduced by 14 percent. Children's services, hit the hardest, dropped by 25 percent; eight libraries eliminated children's services completely. Book-buying budgets, cut by 25 percent, resulted in the purchase of 1 million fewer books. At the end of 1993, Merced County in central California closed all nineteen of its branches and laid off the staff. Some branches were reopened selectively by volunteers.

Residents of Ozone Park, New York, demonstrate against the closure of their local branch of the Brooklyn Public Library in 1991. Budget cuts in the early 1990s led to reduced staffing, restricted hours, and branch closings at many public library systems.

A 1991 survey, however, showed that public library use throughout the country had grown dramatically since the 1947 public library inquiry. It continued to grow in the 1990s. Interestingly, the biggest users were those in the eighteen- to twenty-four-year-old age group. The typical library patron was still "white, well educated, and reasonably well off," according to *Library Journal*'s report on the survey. Conversely, library use among blacks and Hispanics lagged noticeably behind that of whites and other ethnic groups. This situation left public librarians with a number of formidable challenges: maintaining political, hence budgetary support; providing better service and more books for established library patrons; reaching out for new readers, particularly among nonwhite low-income people; serving new immigrants with multiple linguistic demands; and dealing with the new complex of problems arising from the use of information technology. Ultimately the challenge was this: to protect and build a vital civic institution in a world that was increasingly hostile to the public patrimony.

The American free public library was the outgrowth of more than two centuries of experiments in librarianship. Libraries were formed as part of book club cum debating societies, for religious and general educational purposes, for meeting the specific informational needs of different professions, for entertainment, and for a sense of connectedness with the world beyond the isolation of new urban and rural frontiers. All of these experiments eventually flowed into the movement for free public libraries. And although the earliest and most pronounced emphasis of the first free public libraries in the United States was education, public libraries, as they broadened their services, returned in a sense to the more diverse efforts of their numerous progenitors.

The American library experiment had proved wildly successful. No other society could claim the near universality of the public library system in the United States. But the age of true political support for public libraries was in years gone by, and it would take the determination and imagination of the first founders of American libraries to maintain this truly great heritage.

Chapter Five

GRAND PLANS, SOMBER REALITIES

❖

The First San Francisco Public Library

Like a tawdry Aphrodite born fully from the sea, San Francisco, begotten of greed and wanderlust, sprang to life after gold was discovered in 1848 and became the leading western metropolis almost overnight. The city sprawled along the strand by the bay, a confusion of old adobes, new brick-and-timber buildings, and abandoned ships

Preceding pages: An oil painting by an unknown artist depicts San Francisco's City Hall burning during the fire that followed the 1906 earthquake. The city's public library was on the third floor of one wing of City Hall.

This 1868 aerial view of San Francisco from the west shows the young city that in twenty years overwhelmed the bayside village of Yerba Buena. The Golden Gate is at the left, and the sand dunes in the foreground would later become Golden Gate Park.

tied together by rickety boardwalks and turned into raucous gambling saloons, hotels, and warehouses. Swarmed by young men from all quarters of the compass, Sierra gold flowed through the city's veins while its youthful inhabitants lived with an abandon and lawlessness that would, some later said, put Gomorrah to shame. Leveled by fire six times in the 1850s, the city was rejuvenated by a mighty transfusion of silver and gold that poured from the Comstock Lode after its discovery in 1859.

Once the impermanent home of the freebooting sourdoughs who roamed the Sierra Nevada pick and shovel in hand, San Francisco by 1860 had reached a population of 57,000 and settled into a more substantial life as the center of a mining frontier that stretched as far as the Fraser River in British Columbia. No longer an individual affair, mining was big business, a corporate endeavor financed as much by the wildly speculative investments wagered at the San Francisco Mining Exchange as by silver and gold. Mining meant machinery, pumps, hoists, steam drills, engines, and rails, plus thousands of men, who, no longer their own masters, slaved away for daily wages in the bowels of the earth. So San Francisco became an industrial city, a mercantile exchange, a bankers', stockbrokers', and lawyers' town, the trading center for the grain trade that sent thousands of bushels of California wheat east and west. It was a city of elaborate

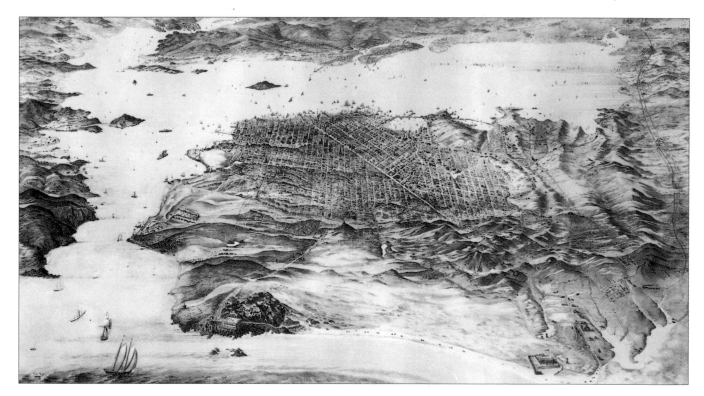

mansions, of poor and respectable working-class neighbor-hoods, a city with a Chinatown, a city that began to cover its growing tensions and challenging complexities with a patina of respectability.

And it was a literary town, a place, as the historian Franklin Walker wrote, that "had grown articulate enough in the days of its youth to speak while frontier conditions existed." After all, San Franciscans were both literate and cosmopolitan. There were more college graduates in early San Francisco, some said, than in any other American city. By the middle 1850s, the city could boast that it had a well-developed book trade and more newspapers (in more languages) than London, and that it published more books than all other cities west of the Mississippi. In an improbable mixture that foreshadowed modern California, its residents came from Asia, Latin America, and Europe as well as back east. The greatest number, of course, were those who came for gold. But others came to record, or by happenstance found themselves recording, one of the most extravagant episodes in human history.

Men from Asia, Europe, and Latin America gather in an ornate saloon during the height of the gold rush days. San Francisco could also brag about its bookstores, an early and abundant fixture in the city.

MINING THE LITERARY VEIN

At first San Francisco's literary life was a direct result of its remarkable outpouring of newsprint. By the mid-1850s there were twelve newspapers in the city and many more magazines, all of which employed some 1,000 people. Born of political strife, the city's newspapers and journals soon attracted a crowd of young editors and writers who turned to the local scene—the life in the Sierra diggings; the hustle and bustle of Virginia City in present-day Nevada, where the Comstock Lode gave birth to another instant metropolis; and the peculiarities of San Francisco itself.

The writers of the fifties were the first of a colorful lot. Dame Shirley (Louisa Amelia Knapp Smith), in her *Shirley Letters,* penned one of the most detailed accounts of life in the diggings. With wit and self-deprecation, Old Block (Alonzo Delano) wrote a series of articles that appeared in the leading news-papers and the *Golden Era,* the first of a long line of excellent journals that com-bined news with literature. Block's writings covered his westward journey by wagon and the grimmer realities of life in the mining camps. His first book, *Chips from the Old Block,* published in 1853, sold over 15,000 copies in the state. There were others: John Phoenix (George Horatio Derby), the humorist, gam-boled through town writing, drawing, and staging elaborate hoaxes, while Yellow Bird (John Rollin Ridge), the son of a Cherokee chief and a white woman, wrote poetry and *The Life and Adventures of Joaquin Murieta, the Celebrated Bandit,* a book that described the terrible iniquities practiced upon Hispanics.

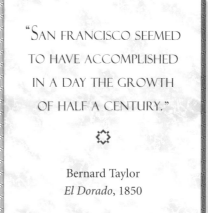

"SAN FRANCISCO SEEMED TO HAVE ACCOMPLISHED IN A DAY THE GROWTH OF HALF A CENTURY."

✧

Bernard Taylor
El Dorado, 1850

Robert B. Woodward included a library in his hotel for men who did not drink, the What Cheer House, when he opened it in 1852. Mark Twain is said to have visited, but undoubtedly did not stay.

These newcomers prepared the ground for the next wave of writers, whose popularity and names became synonymous with western literature, writers like Ambrose Bierce, Ina Coolbrith, Bret Harte, Joaquin Miller, and Mark Twain. Flush with the flow of silver and gold from the Comstock, San Francisco in the early 1860s witnessed another wave of immigration, and the city, with its fancy hotels, fashionable watering holes, theaters, and clubby editorial offices, took on a new sophistication leavened by bohemianism. The outpouring of words was as extravagant as the speculation on the Mining Exchange.

An embittered Civil War veteran, Bierce wrote over the next four decades fiercely satirical pieces for the *News Letter,* the *Californian,* the *Argonaut,* and the *Examiner* while penning poems and macabre short stories. Coolbrith's specialty was a kind of romantic, even sensuous poetry popular at the time. Harte, through his short stories, did more than any other of his contemporaries to promote the notion of the West as the land of hardened men and whores with hearts of gold. Miller also wrote poetry and drew on his adventures, including living for a time with the Modoc Indians, for a number of semifictional works. Twain, on a lark and on the run from Civil War, worked as a reporter and prose contributor for the *Golden Era,* San Francisco's *Dramatic Chronicle* and *Daily Morning Call,* the *Sacramento Union,* and Virginia City's *Territorial Enterprise.* Twain's great works lay ahead of him.

Early San Francisco Writers

Ambrose Bierce

Yellow Bird (John Rollin Ridge)

Joaquin Miller

Mark Twain (right) with actor John T. Raymond

In the end the city's writers, like all westerners, were a transient lot, and the best of the them, like Harte and Twain, having made their reputation in San Francisco, hearkened to the siren call of the East, where they would be closer to the centers of publishing power. Of course, there were plenty of writers left, and some good ones too. Ina Coolbrith stayed and went on to be Oakland's librarian. But San Francisco never again saw a literary era quite like the 1860s.

Libraries, like writers, came early to San Francisco. The first one was opened to guests and the public in 1852 by Robert B. Woodward in a large room in the What Cheer House, a men's temperance hotel that he built at the corner of Sacramento and Leidesdorff streets. Woodward was a wealthy real estate speculator and operator of the Mission Toll Road, the city's principal thoroughfare when Market Street was still a high-backed sand dune. Adjacent to this plank road, near the present-day corner of Mission and Duboce, Woodward built a mansion, which he later turned into an art gallery filled with copies of the works of the great European painters. The mansion was surrounded by gardens that

Woodward opened an amusement park in 1866 at what is now the corner of Mission and Duboce streets. Woodward's Gardens offered camel and ostrich rides, concerts, an eight-foot-tall Chinese man, and a pen where toddlers could play with baby alligators.

Bret Harte

Ina Coolbrith

Old Block (Alonzo Delano)

John Phoenix (George Horatio Derby)

The Montgomery Block was one of San Francisco's most enduring literary landmarks. From 1856 to 1906, it was home to the city's law library, where Adolph Sutro worked on his huge book collection, which later became the state's Sutro Library. The block's restaurants and saloons catered to artists and writers who lived upstairs. The block eventually was replaced by the Transamerica Pyramid.

became Woodward's Gardens, San Francisco's first amusement park. The Library Room at the What Cheer House held 2,000 to 3,000 volumes, including numerous works on agriculture and a large collection of biographies, classics, and books by many contemporary writers, such as Washington Irving, Charles Dickens, and Nathaniel Hawthorne. There was also a newspaper collection with papers from California, the eastern United States, and Europe.

In 1853 the Mercantile Association formed the city's first subscription library by raising funds through the sale of shares for $25 apiece. In a city where most anyone could call himself a businessman and booms were followed by the inevitable bust, the association's effort to place membership "within the means and power of almost every resident of San Francisco" was appropriate. For non-shareholders, dues were $1 a month after payment of a $5 initiation fee. The initial subscribers, according to the local press, were mostly clerks and mechanics. The library, its founders proclaimed, would offer hundreds of young men "an opportunity for moral and intellectual improvement . . . instead of wasting their time and substance in the follies and vices which hold out such tempting allures to the idle." According to the *Pioneer,* the library opened in three rooms on the second floor of the Montgomery Block (between Montgomery, Sansome, Washington, and Clay) "among the gambling saloons and other brilliant dens of iniquity with which our city teems in undue proportion to our population." Open on a daily basis, the library welcomed women from 12:00 to 2:00 P.M. Among the honorary members were Edward Everett, who was simultaneously playing a central role in founding the Boston Public Library.

Not satisfied with one private library, a second group met at the end of 1854 to form the Mechanics' Institute library. Five years into the gold rush, the bloom was already off the rose. The Sierra placers were running out, and the city was thronged with unemployed men who faced the problem of developing their skills in an inhospitable environment; none of the city's schools offered technical education. The first Mechanics' Institute library was located in a room in the Express Building on the northeast corner of California and Montgomery streets. The first four books, including a Bible and a copy of the Constitution of the United States, were donated. The Bible and the Constitution were soon stolen, leading Flora Haines Aponyi, a chronicler of early California libraries, to write in 1880 that this "would seem to indicate that the desire for religion and constitutional law was much greater at that day than it is at this." After moving several times, the library was finally lodged in 1866 in the Mechanics' Institute's own building at 31 Post where, rebuilt after the earthquake of 1906, it remains today at 57 Post.

Other libraries were opened by the International Order of Odd Fellows, the Society of California Pioneers, the Young Men's Christian Association, and La

Ligue Nationale Française. A group of lawyers put together a professional library in an old billiard room in the Montgomery Block. It was reorganized into the official San Francisco Law Library in 1870 by a board of trustees headed by the mayor and several district court judges. There were also a number of very fine personal libraries, such as Leland Stanford's 3,000-volume collection, which was kept in an ornate room finished with mahogany and rosewood on the ground floor of his Nob Hill mansion, and Robert Woodward's private collection at his estate in the Napa Valley, north of the city.

San Francisco's most famous book collection began as the private obsession of Hubert Howe Bancroft, who started work as a miner but then opened a bookstore and became a publisher in San Francisco. In 1869 he moved his business to a new five-story building erected in a cow pasture on Market Street. This became the Bancroft "history factory." In the Department of Literary Industries on the fifth floor, twenty men worked under the eye of Bancroft himself on the thirty-nine-volume *History of the Pacific States* and numerous other works. Starting with books on California, Bancroft ranged far and wide, buying anything that pertained to the history of the western United States. Ultimately he put together a collection that contained 20,000 volumes and included whole libraries as well as priceless documents bought in England, France, Germany, and Spain. In 1905 Bancroft sold his collection to the University of California at Berkeley, where it formed the cornerstone of the Bancroft Library.

San Francisco's early libraries were commensurate with its literary atmosphere and its increasing cultural self-consciousness. Culture was one thing; public amenities were another. Despite the city's enormous wealth, it was still an

Hubert Howe Bancroft (above), publisher of the thirty-nine-volume History of the Pacific States, *actually hired others to do the writing and put his name on the title page. At his "history factory" on Market Street (below), Bancroft published his works, sold books, and compiled an extensive collection of early books and documents pertaining to the history of the West.*

William C. Ralston, industrialist, rancher, and major downtown landowner. Ralston and his associates, known as the Ralston ring, tried to corner the silver supply on the Comstock Lode, the rich ore deposits in the Nevada Territory which fueled San Francisco's booms—and busts—for three decades.

"EARLY SAN FRANCISCO HISTORY IS NOT FOR BABES NOR FOR SENTIMENTALISTS."

✿

Josiah Royce
California, 1886

era across the nation when private enterprise prevailed, and little attention beyond the funding of public schools was given to investment in public institutions. Hence, it took three decades before San Francisco's civic leaders turned their attention to that relatively new phenomenon known as a public library.

ASPIRATIONS AMID THE TURMOIL

Ironically, the call for a public library came during one of the most troubled times in the city's short and troubled history. Once again boom followed bust, but this time it started with an event, the completion of the transcontinental railroad in 1869. Most businessmen thought that the railroad would assure permanent prosperity for the state. Instead, cheap goods flowed in from the East, swelling unemployment to an estimated 30 percent across California. In 1873 depression struck the East, and thousands fled to the West looking for work. They were met by an estimated 80,000 Chinese who arrived in the state between 1870 and 1875. Recurring drought drove farmworkers off the land and into the city, where they gathered with men idled by the end of construction on the railroad.

Then came the final catastrophe in San Francisco, the collapse of the so-called Ralston ring. William C. Ralston had arrived in the city in 1851, the captain of a steamer calling from Panama. From the steamship business, he moved into banking, founding and managing the Bank of California, and then into real estate, farming, manufacturing, and hotels including the Palace. His ultimate scheme was breathtaking in its ambition. Through ownership of a mining and milling company in Virginia City, control of bank loans, and construction of a railroad that supplied the mines, Ralston and his associates, who were among the leading businessmen in San Francisco, tried to bring all of the Comstock Lode within their grasp. There was only one problem. Despite their efforts to monopolize the mines, Ralston and his associates had missed the next and ultimately the biggest Comstock bonanza, which was found in 1873.

Ralston plunged ahead for two more years, sinking millions into efforts to protect the rapidly declining value of his numerous investments. Word got out, however, and on August 26, 1875, there was a run on the Bank of California. At 2:30 P.M., with over $1 million withdrawn in four hours, Ralston closed the bank's doors. The next morning he handed in his resignation as manager of the bank, signed over all his property to his closest associate, and walked down Sansome Street for his regular afternoon swim. He was never seen again.

The "terrible seventies" begat bankruptcy and turmoil in San Francisco. Over the past two decades, San Franciscans had witnessed an aggressive and brazen accumulation of economic power. Ralston and his associates had tried to monopolize the Comstock Lode and even attempted to control the city's water supply. Charles Crocker, Mark Hopkins, Collis P. Huntington, and Leland Stanford, while controlling rail access to California, had been granted an enormous landed empire by the federal government. The day of the solitary miner was long gone. Farm laborers were more common than the small farmer, and now this mythic American figure was threatened by ruthless land barons.

Resentment of these economic overlords and the empty dreams of easy prosperity triggered labor unrest in San Francisco. Demagogues from the Democratic party and the labor movement, egged on by many well-known San Franciscans and part of the press, directed their resentments against the hapless Chinese, who had been drawn into the city's workforce as a source of cheap and willing labor. On the night of July 23, 1877, after a year of anti-Chinese agitation, thousands of workers attended a rally at the sandlots south of City Hall, a favorite gathering place for political meetings, ostensibly in solidarity with striking railroad workers in the East. Shots were fired into the crowd, and a group of several hundred broke off and headed off to burn the Pacific Mail Steamship docks, attacking Chinese laundries and any Chinese on the streets along the way. Eventually the police quelled the riots, while the Committee of Public Safety, a new vigilante committee harking back to the vigilantes of 1851, was formed to assist the police.

Within a month, Denis Kearney, a fiery orator, former sailor, owner of a small drayage company, and recently member of the vigilantes' pickax brigade, assumed leadership of a new Workingmen's Party of California. The rich were using the Chinese to undermine the rights of workers, he proclaimed. Monopoly must end, and the Chinese must go.

During this turmoil a varied group of San Franciscans met on August 3, 1877, at Dashaway Hall on Post Street—men on the floor of the hall, a few women in the gallery—to form a committee to draw up a state law that would allow the city to fund a free public library through taxation. This effort was indicative of the fact that under the existing city charter, control of much of city affairs and the entire waterfront still resided in Sacramento, the state capital. The movement for a public library was initiated by Andrew S. Hallidie, the inventor of the cable car

On the afternoon of August 26, 1875, the doors of William Ralston's Bank of California were closed after panicked depositors rushed to withdraw their funds. They gathered outside the bank, frustrated and on the verge of a riot.

With the partially constructed City Hall in the background, labor agitator Denis Kearney harangues a crowd in 1877 at what was known as the sandlots.

and former president of the Mechanics' Institute, and State Senator George H. Rogers, who represented San Francisco and San Mateo counties. As president of the Mechanics' Institute, Hallidie had been frustrated in his attempts to turn its library into a privately endowed public institution with branches located on the Barbary Coast and in Happy Valley in order to draw the city's restless young men away from the bars and fleshpots of these two notorious neighborhoods.

While the newspapers asked why no one in a city of such rich men had offered to fund a public library, Rogers had sent letters to almost every American city with a population over 8,000 and several European cities seeking advice. He turned the results over to writer Henry George, who was already making a name for himself as a critic of the excesses of California "monopolists."

Rogers chaired the August 3 meeting. A number of people who spoke offered either books or cash. Dr. George Hewston, who volunteered to donate one hundred reference books, noted that a public library "would do more to overcome hoodlumism than the extremest rigors of the law." Referring to the Boston Public Library, Henry George spoke of a library that "would be open to all classes, but principally frequented by the poor; that the man in corduroy is treated with the same courtesy as the rich man in broadcloth; that the conduct of all is decorous; and that the charm of the place is its perfect freedom."

Not to be outdone, Denis Kearney, the Janus-faced agitator, proclaimed that "one hour in a public library was worth a whole day spent at San Bruno shooting bullets at a painted board and hitting nothing but the fields beyond it, or some unfortunate wandering cow. One educated man is worth a whole Committee of Safety and not nearly as liable to shoot his neighbor. One educated boy will come nearer rectifying the Chinese problem than a legion of rioters." He concluded, "I am a working man but will give my five dollars toward our free library."

On March 18, 1878, the governor signed the Rogers Act, which authorized any incorporated city or town to levy a tax not exceeding one mill (one-tenth of one cent) on the dollar of assessed property. San Francisco's supporters of a free public library had been approached by library advocates from other California cities and asked to make the legislation applicable to all municipalities. The act also called for the library to be governed by a self-perpetuating board of trustees. This was meant to keep the library free from the general corruption of city politics.

June 7, 1879—A Hard-won Opening Day

The library's first board of trustees was made up of George H. Rogers, Andrew S. Hallidie, Henry George, Irving M. Scott, Robert S. Tobin, E. D. Sawyer, John H. Wise, Andrew J. Moulder, Louis Sloss, and C. C. Terrill. It was clearly dominated by the self-made men who led the city's business community, among the most influential of whom were Scott, Tobin, and Sloss. Scott was the general manager of the Union Iron Works, the city's largest employer. Tobin was secretary of the Hibernia Savings and Loan Society, an Irish-American institution that was well on its way to becoming the city's leading savings bank. Sloss was an original partner and twice president of the Alaska Commercial Company, which for a time monopolized the sealskin trade in Alaska and was thought by many to be managing all the affairs of the Alaskan territory with the help of its Washington, D.C., lobbyist.

Under this portrait of Denis Kearney are the slogan "The Chinese Must Go" and the title "President Workingmen's Party." Kearney formed the party to push for workers' rights as well as the exclusion of the Chinese. He was also a participant in the first meeting to found a public library, held in August 1877.

Henry George was the odd man out, a radical among bankers, lawyers, industrialists, contractors, and insurance brokers. He was a wanderer who had tried the high seas, ranging from Australia to the Fraser River goldfields and the Sierra mining camps before settling in San Francisco. He had even enlisted in a filibustering expedition bound for Mexico in support of Benito Juárez in his fight against the French-imposed emperor Maximilian. This adventure ended at the Golden Gate when a revenue cutter intercepted George's ship with 10,000 rifles in its hold.

When he first came to San Francisco in 1858, George spent some time at the What Cheer House making use of its library to read Adam Smith's *Wealth of Nations*. Unable to earn a decent living as a miner and a printer, George turned to writing to supplement his income, starting with a series on the ever-popular subject of spiritualism. Eventually he turned his restless mind to economic questions, predicting that the concentrated ownership of land in California would re-create the same polarized class situation that persisted in the eastern United States and Europe. Basing his argument on the large size of the land grants awarded to the builders of the transcontinental railroad, George advocated in an 1871 pamphlet a single tax on land as a means to return land to the people. While participating in the founding of the public library, George was also researching his best-known work, *Progress and Poverty*. Published in 1879, it propelled him as a prophet into leadership of the single tax movement and on to New York.

The idea of a new library caused a minor stir in the press. There was talk of raising $250,000 to build "a very large edifice," of building one of the great libraries of the world, of merging the city's existing libraries into the new public

What Makes a Library

THE ONLY LIBRARY THAT, as a girl in Hong Kong, I had access to was the one at school: a single shelf in the classroom cupboard that held a sad collection of dog-eared discards with broken spines and missing pages. The children who brought in these books told me of libraries at private clubs to which their families belonged. These libraries, they said, were rooms as large as the school's assembly hall, rooms filled with books from floor to ceiling. And since these clubs—and therefore the books I coveted—were denied me, I grew up believing libraries were made by people of privilege for people of privilege.

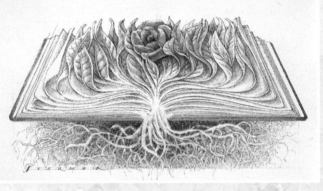

That there could be free libraries for the general public was inconceivable to me, so I was in the United States for almost five years before I discovered the public library. When I applied for a library card at San Francisco's Main, however, I was turned down. Disappointed and embarrassed, I might have thought the clerk's reason—I had no identification—concocted to keep me out. But the diversity of the patrons streaming through the doors told me otherwise, and when I returned with bills that proved my residency, the clerk gave me a card.

Had anyone asked me then what makes a library, I would have said, "Books." Books were all I saw, all I wanted. Checking out the limit of eight at every visit, I was fully satisfied.

Then I began researching the experience of Chinese in America. Suddenly, books were not enough. I needed photographs, newspapers, personal and public documents, and oral histories, materials that turned out to be scattered in libraries all across the United States yet librarians said were available to me through interlibrary loan or by writing to the libraries directly.

I carried out the first transactions with trepidation, sure the treasures I desired could not be so easily obtained. Twenty years later, I am still awed by the accessibility of the information I continue to seek, thrilled at its arrival. And working with libraries nationwide, I have come to see that what makes a library is a complicated interweaving of personnel, material, patrons, the larger public, and funding sources—with librarians responsible for building collections broad enough to satisfy myriad needs; librarians, clerks, and pages for making the collections accessible; patrons for making the best possible use of what is there and pressing for more; the larger public for ensuring the kind of funding that will increase collections and continue to provide access for all.

Ruthanne Lum McCunn

library. The new trustees were more realistic. They knew that there was one problem: they might exercise firm control over the affairs of the library, but funding for the library had to be approved by the board of supervisors, who were not in a financially expansive mood. In May 1878 the library's advocates took their case to the supervisors, requesting the modest sum of $75,000 for 1879. This amounted to a tax of three-tenths of a mill on the dollar, a little less than one-third the amount authorized in the Rogers Act. There was sentiment, one supervisor said, to oppose any new tax levy on the grounds that "wealthy men would contribute sufficient books to start the institution." In the end, the board voted nine to three to appropriate $24,000.

With regard to space for the new library, the supervisors were even less forthcoming. One plan was to locate the library temporarily in the old City Hall on Portsmouth Plaza in rooms that were soon to be vacated by the supervisors. The supervisors were about to move to the new City Hall near Market and Larkin streets, which had been under construction since 1871. They were unwilling, however, to provide the library with space in any public building.

The *Wasp*, the satirical weekly, could not resist commenting: "The Trustees have experienced the greatest difficulty in persuading our Honorable (?) Board of Supervisors to make anything like a reasonable appropriation for the support of the Public Library. If the Trustees of the Public Library would only get up a dog fight, a man fight, a cock fight, or something equally brutal and disgusting, the WASP has no doubt that the City Hall would rally to their support right royally." The politicians, the *Wasp* suggested, were more interested in collecting funds "for the purpose of paying fraudulent claims—large proportions of which go into the pockets of collusive city officials."

It was one thing to get the supervisors to agree to fund a new library; it was another actually to get the money out of City Hall. A year went by. A librarian, Albert Hart, former assistant to the state librarian, was hired. (The California State Library was founded in 1850.) He and his assistant went to work without pay. A large room was rented on the second floor of Pacific Hall on Bush Street between Kearny and Dupont. The California Theatre was in the same building. A stage was removed. Fresh oilcloth was laid on the floor. The room's frescoes were touched up, and an office was constructed in the corner of what was to be the reading room. A newspaper reading area was set up in the gallery. Shelves were built, and some 5,000 books were bought on credit or donated. Many of the latter turned out to be old and worthless. There were so few books that the trustees, even before opening the doors, announced that books would not circulate. They feared the prospect of a library where the collection went out the door in the hands of the first borrowers. Finally, a wire screen was installed in front of

Henry George, printer, gold miner, and adventurer turned social critic, served as secretary for the committee that founded the San Francisco Free Public Library in 1878. As author of Progress and Poverty, *he became a national figure advocating a single tax on land as a way to combat the concentration of wealth that he witnessed in California.*

The first San Francisco public library opened in 1879 in a large auditorium on the second floor of Pacific Hall on Bush Street, just west of Kearny Street. The California Theatre was next door in the same building. Women sat in their own section (foreground right).

the bookshelves to assure that only those employees sent to retrieve books for the library's patrons would have access to them.

All was ready, but there were still no funds. Mayor Andrew Bryant argued that because the Library Fund authorized by the Rogers Act had not been created, money could not be paid out of the General Fund for a new library. A Library Fund was created, but Bryant vetoed the supervisors' effort to transfer funds into it, and when Hart applied for his salary, the city and county attorney ordered the city not to pay him.

Still without funds, the trustees decided to open the library in a ceremony held on the evening of June 7, 1879. A goodly crowd of men and women filled the new reading room. Senator Rogers, in his introductory remarks, pointed out that the city had not turned over the library's funds yet. The city was insisting that all other forms of indebtedness be paid out of the General Fund before any money went to the library. With credit and borrowed funds, Rogers told the celebrants, the trustees had spent $10,000 on books and another $2,400 on furnishings. Hallidie and George addressed the crowd, and Judge E. D. Sawyer urged them to put pressure on their supervisors to release the library's funds. With that, the library was declared open with hours from 9:00 A.M. to 9:00 P.M. every day except Sunday, when it would open at 1:00 P.M. and close at 9:00 P.M.

GROWING PAINS

Though it opened under a cloud, the library was an instant success. Within days the tables in the reading room were so full that patrons had difficulty finding seats. New tables had to be bought, and often a line of would-be patrons was seen stretching along Bush Street. Within a few years, the single reading room was jammed with patrons, and employees were forced to receive and catalogue books on the tables and floor of the same room. Despite the impasse over funding, relations with the board of supervisors and the mayor remained outwardly cordial. The trustees invited the mayor and supervisors to the library soon after its opening for an informal discussion of how to bring about the release of the library's funds from the General Fund. They would need at least $50,000 more to buy enough books to make the library a circulating one, the trustees patiently explained. The matter was finally resolved when Judge John W. Dwinelle, one of the library's original supporters, ordered the city to release the funds. The struggle between the supervisors and the trustees was a fundamental one. The supervisors wanted control of the library because it was a potential source of patronage jobs. The Rogers Act denied them. Ultimately the issue of the autonomy of the self-perpetuating board of trustees was decided in the California Supreme Court in favor of the trustees.

The stress of opening the library without funds took a heavy toll on Albert Hart, the new librarian, who resigned before the end of the library's first year. He was replaced by Charles Robinson, who also claimed overwork and resigned after seven months. With $48,000 in the 1880–81 annual budget and enough books to form a circulating library, the trustees turned in 1880 to Frederic Beecher Perkins to head the library. Perkins was a member of the Beecher family. His uncle was Henry Ward Beecher, the eminent clergyman, and his daughter, Perkins's cousin, was Harriet Beecher Stowe, the author of *Uncle Tom's Cabin*. Perkins had worked with the two leading figures in the public library movement, Justin Winsor, head of the Boston Public Library, and Melvil Dewey, inventor of the Dewey decimal system and a founder, along with Perkins, of the American Library Association. Perkins brought to San Francisco the experience of *the* American library after which San Francisco wished to model itself.

As it turned out, Perkins's tenure in San Francisco was not a happy one. The board of supervisors had come under the control of Christopher Buckley, the so-called Blind Boss. In addition to handing out lucrative franchises in exchange for bribes, the supervisors were committed to rolling back taxes on behalf of their small-business clientele. Starting in 1885, the supervisors began to cut the library's appropriation, reducing it to $18,000 a year, and in one year wiping out the book-buying budget and preventing the printing of a new catalogue to describe books recently acquired. Perkins went on the attack in the annual ALA conference issue of the *Library Journal*. Comparing the new San Francisco library negatively to its counterparts in other large

THE WAY IT WAS

❖

Joy Lichtenstein went to work at the San Francisco Public Library in 1886 at the age of thirteen and worked there until the library was destroyed in 1906. Here is his description of the first library.

"When I entered the employment of the library it was on Bush Street, on the north side above Kearny. . . . The library was up one flight of stairs. As you entered a long hall there was seated at the entrance an old man, in fact there were two of them—combined janitors and doorkeepers. The one in attendance would hand you a brass tag, fairly large, which you carried in with you and which you absolutely had to deliver before you could leave. The library itself was in back of a tall wire screen and there were no books which the public could touch except by making out applications. The wooden bookstacks rose to the ceiling, and the boys scrambled around by means of sliding ladders which resembled those used in shoe stores. The books had class and shelf numbers but the Decimal System was still far in the future. The catalogs were printed and very much out of date. The public secured books either by reference to the catalogs or by asking the attendants; and used therefore, when consulting the catalogs, either a pink or a white oblong slip. . . . These were handed through openings in the fenced off portion and three ladies were always in attendance. They were ladies who had secured their positions by means of influence not political. They were not bookish and of course the boys were not; so it was a sort of hit or miss proposition for a member of the public to procure a desired book."

California Library Bulletin, June 1950

With his peremptory manner and emphasis on strict rules, Frederic Beecher Perkins, the city's third librarian, drew the attention of a cartoonist from the Wasp *in 1886. A Boston librarian, Perkins resigned after being fined for manhandling an unruly child.*

cities, he suggested that "on pretence of economy" the library's opponents, if they could not control the library, were bent on destroying it altogether.

Despite his efforts on behalf of the library, the tall, bearded, and combative Perkins brought a measure of rigidity to his job that was typical of his day, but was his undoing when added to his political contentiousness. Upon his arrival he scanned the collection and removed numerous "dirty books," such as the novels of Émile Zola. Then he got into a verbal brawl with a local reporter, who insisted on his right to borrow Henry Fielding's *Jonathan Wild,* which Perkins described as a "brutally gross story."

Eyeing the library's motley downtown crowd, Perkins wrote in the *Library Journal* that "a library is not for a nursery; a lunch-room; a bed-room; a place for meeting a girl in a corner and talking to her; a conversation-room of any kind; a free dispensary of stationery, envelopes and letter-writing; a free range for loiterers; a campaigning field for mendicants, or for displaying advertisements; a haunt for loafers and criminals." Insisting on quiet and orderliness, Perkins equipped the library's pages with slippers so there would be less noise as they moved up and down the ladders used to retrieve books from the shelves. With his idiosyncrasies, Perkins became a perfect foil for the press. The *Wasp* honored him with a full-page cartoon.

Perkins's downfall came when he was the object of a citizen's arrest by Captain Eagan of the U.S. Army, who accused him of giving his nine-year-old son a severe beating. Perkins acknowledged that he had ejected the boy from the library, but denied that he had handled him roughly. He was fined $20 and roundly criticized by members of the press and the board of supervisors. Attacking the trustees and the supervisors for lack of financial support for the library, Perkins resigned in 1887.

Perkins was replaced by another Bostonian, the poet John Vance Cheney. Cheney began his working life in Boston as a lawyer, but gave that up for poetry and California, where he was working as a cashier in the post office when he was called to replace Perkins. A handsome and personable man, he is said to have had political connections that landed him a job for which he showed no apparent qualifications. Cheney turned out to be an excellent librarian, successfully accomplishing two of Perkins's principal objectives—to move the library out of the theater district into safer, more respectable, and sizable quarters and to establish branch libraries. Perkins disliked the library's location in the midst of one of the city's entertainment districts with its theaters, saloons, and other attractions.

It was a problem of "the professional immorality of notorious localities," he said. Perkins also objected to the $200 monthly rent paid for Pacific Hall and the $50,000 insurance policy the library had to carry because of its proximity to a theater, which he thought would inevitably burn down.

In 1888 the library relocated to the Larkin Street wing of City Hall while discussions were initiated about building a separate structure for the library. In 1893 the library moved again into more commodious and elegant quarters on the third floor of the McAllister Street wing of the building. A work in progress, City Hall was a true monument to the venality of San Francisco politics. Construction had commenced in 1871 and was finally completed in 1898. With its curious towers and disproportionately narrow dome, City Hall was a strange agglomeration of various additions that were built from time to time as the city, in its parsimonious fashion, released funds on an annual basis. Some were used for construction, the rest to line the pockets of both the supervisors and the contractors. In fiscal year 1888–89, the public library opened its first three branches: in the Mission, in North Beach, and on Potrero Hill.

An engraving from the San Francisco Call, June 13, 1897, shows the Juvenile Department at the library, which opened in 1895.

The library's second move within City Hall proved to be an expensive undertaking. In the late 1880s the library's appropriation began to inch up again, leveling off at $35,000 in the early 1890s. But the cost of the 1893 move, plus the impact of the depression that struck in the early 1890s, led the trustees in their 1894 annual report to note that they had not been able to buy any new books for six months while they contemplated closing the Potrero Hill branch for a time. The library also reported that its thirty-eight employees were paid less ($48.95 per month) than other city employees even though they worked longer hours. The library's budget recovered quickly, as did the city's economy. Under the aegis of a new librarian, George T. Clark, appointed in 1895, the library began a period of expansion during which circulation doubled in five years. A new periodical room was added and then a Juvenile Department with its own 3,000-volume collection. The Juvenile Department replaced the ladies' reading room on the second floor, which was moved to the ground floor where, according to the *San Francisco Call*, the tables where patrons sat would be provided with travel books and other literature that would "take from them the desire for trashy literature." In 1897 an elevator was added, and the next year 10,000 books, about one-tenth of the collection, were placed in open stacks. The North Beach branch was moved from Stockton to Powell Street. New branches were opened in the Richmond near Golden Gate Park (1892), on Harrison Street (1896), and on Fillmore Street (1899).

Despite the improvements made at City Hall, the library was still jammed into cramped quarters, and the trustees were still eager to move into a separate building. They thought they had found the solution when in 1895 a trustee of the Mercantile Library suggested a merger that would require the public library to absorb the Mercantile Library's $75,000 debt while inheriting its collection of 70,000 volumes and moving into its building. Such an arrangement, according to the *Call,* "will render [the San Francisco Public Library] a not unworthy rival to the great Public Library in Boston." In the end, the trustees of the Mercantile Library voted against consolidation, arguing that the patrons of their library were of a different class than the public library's.

REFORMS LIFT THE LIBRARY'S FORTUNES

As the city emerged from the depression of the 1890s and the next century dawned, San Francisco was shaking off its frontier garb. A new generation of political and business leaders was looking beyond the era of primitive accumulation and political bossism to a time when a more cultured, well-governed, better designed city with an improved infrastructure would take its place among the great metropolises of the world. Despite the enormous wealth of its business leaders, its gigantic hotels, and its impressive office buildings, the city as a whole retained much of the ramshackle shabbiness of its earliest days. Streets were poorly graded and full of potholes. New neighborhoods in the western part of

In 1877 Eadweard J. Muybridge photographed a panorama of the city from the top of Mark Hopkins's Nob Hill mansion. These two plates show Russian Hill rising to the north. Advocates of a planned city pointed out that the grid system of streets laid out at right angles, established as early as 1839, made no sense in a city of hills.

the city were still not served by paved streets. The public hospital was a wooden firetrap. The debts of the hospital, almshouse, and jail were so high that merchants refused to deliver food for patients and inmates or hay for the horses that drew the wagons and ambulances. The sewage system poured human waste into the bay from 125 different outlets. There was widespread concern that the firefighting system could not deal with major fires like those that had repeatedly gutted the city in the 1850s.

With the exception of Golden Gate Park, public amenities, such as they were, were the gifts of private benefactors. For example, Adolph Sutro—the mining engineer who built the Sutro Tunnel under the Comstock Lode, owned block after block of city real estate, and served as mayor from 1895 to 1897—rebuilt the Cliff House and built the Sutro Baths on the Pacific Ocean beachfront for public use. But beyond the schools, jails, almshouse, hospital, and necessary city offices, there was little public investment. For one thing, the city lacked the legal ability to issue bonds, which were central to funding an improved public infrastructure.

Foremost among the men who sought to change this situation was James Duval Phelan, who would serve his city as mayor and the state as a United States Senator. Phelan's father, James, was typical of the forty-niners who had seized the

William C. Ralston's Palace Hotel, completed in 1875, was the largest hotel west of Chicago and the largest of several luxury hotels lining Market Street. Not far away were the dives and shabby wooden houses of Happy Valley.

My Librarian

Of course there are others, young ones, old ones, even, yes, male ones, but the librarian I am thinking of is the classic one, the one with the black bun and black shoes who never approves of the books I select. I have tried everything: history, romance, travel—no use. She drops her eyes, lips pursed, silent as she checks me out. Her breath smells like cold coffee and her wrists smell like Jean Naté. She keeps a vase of pussy willow on her desk in the spring, a jar of ditch licorice by the clock in the summer, and a huge spray of poison oak by her computer in the fall. She has not missed a day of work in her life; her health is supernatural; so are her powers. With the lift of an eyebrow she can cast spells: children behave like adults in her presence and adults behave like angels. She moves briskly through the aisles, straightening shelves, slipping stray volumes back into place, bending to pick up dropped pencils and scraps of paper which she reads, with no interest, before pocketing inside her cardigan. She holds out her hand, palm up, to receive the knife the teenage boy is gouging the walls of his carrel with; she collects, in the same pale hand, decorated only with her dead mother's diamond, an unlit cigarette from the drunk behind the *New York Times*, and a water gun from two little boys which she later uses on her philodendron, pleased at the way it gets water under the leaves without spilling onto the oak table. She has spent a lot of time

rubbing water stains out of that old oak table. She has also spent a lot of time fixing the microfiche, loading the Xerox, unplugging the toilet in the men's room, pulling the staples out of the bulletin board with her fingernails and flicking them without a single miss into the waste-paper basket. Her glasses, hanging from the requisite chain of amber beads around her neck, bounce lightly as she steps down from the footstool and returns to her desk. It is piled high with books. She herself does not read books and has not for years; she doesn't have time. Her one passion is ice-hockey games and her voice the day after a victory is harsh from shouting. She is especially patient on such days as she tallies overdue fines, gives directions, grants small grace periods, listens to lies, explains the new file system, and announces the closing hour. "No sir," I hear her say to the grateful old man swaying before her on bandy legs, his arms full of books on the Civil War, Japanese joinery, and Marilyn Monroe, "I do not know everything. But I know where to find everything. And that is almost as good, if not better." From my hidden place on this page, I clap. She raises her eyebrow, finger to her lips. "You," she says. "Shhh."

Molly Giles

main chance. When the first reports of the gold rush reached New York where this native-born Irishman was living, he sent three shiploads of goods around Cape Horn and hustled to San Francisco to meet them. Two of the ships made it, and Phelan was in the chips. By the time his son was born in 1861, Phelan had moved into banking and real estate. His son would grow up in an entirely different atmosphere from that of his father. He attended the best Catholic schools and then went to Europe, where he spent two years studying the workings of European cities from sewage systems to architectural design and city planning.

With his inherited wealth, young Phelan intended to play a role in reshaping his beloved city. Thus he joined the civic reform efforts of the 1890s that curtailed, only temporarily, some of the excesses of a city polity that was dominated by bossism and the needs of the Southern Pacific Railroad. Elected mayor in 1896, Phelan pushed for reform of the city charter and spoke of a city government conducted like a business. He extolled the benefits of fine public buildings and clean streets, and a city attractive to tourists, who were just beginning to draw the attention of San Francisco's business leaders.

Influenced by his study of Rome, the Athens of Pericles, and Paris as redesigned by Baron Georges-Eugène Haussmann, Phelan was particularly interested in questions of urban design and a civic aesthetic. "Cities are the repositories of everything that science and art and invention have done for mankind and they are a dear possession of every country. We must make them fit for a free and enlightened people," he wrote in the *Overland Monthly* the summer before his election. San Francisco, Phelan argued, must be the capital of an empire and the chief outlet into the Pacific for American trade.

After his travels in Europe, Phelan reconnected with the world of urban design as vice president of California's World Fair Commission and manager of California's exhibit at the 1893 Columbian Exposition in Chicago. There he was exposed to the work of Daniel Burnham, chief of construction, and the group of talented fellow architects that he had gathered around him. These architects, a number of whom were educated at the École des Beaux-Arts in Paris, became advocates of the City Beautiful movement, an effort to produce a planned and unified approach to the redesign of major cities and the construction of monumental public buildings to fit within that design.

When Phelan sought reelection in 1899, the platform of his party, the Democrats, called for the city to act with confidence and to plan for the city's future on broad and liberal lines. At the same time the San Francisco Art Association, a civic beautification group, which Phelan had served as president, asked him to draft a comprehensive plan for the beautification of the city. Having championed a new charter, which was approved by the voters in 1898, Phelan now had the power to

James Duval Phelan, reform mayor, philanthropist, and advocate of urban planning, was also a patron of the library and a trustee for more than three decades.

Phelan donated the funds to build this South of Market branch library in 1901, when he was mayor. In an expanding city, branches were essential to good library service. The building was destroyed in the 1906 earthquake.

raise funds for public structures through the sale of bonds. He immediately went to work, receiving voter approval in 1899 for the sale of bonds to pay for an improved sewer system, a new hospital, seventeen schools, and two new parks. Under Phelan the city's bonded indebtedness rose from $186,000 in 1897 to $11 million in 1901. Phelan had launched the first part of a program to rebuild San Francisco, and the stage seemed to be set for a massive remaking of the city.

Out of office at the end of 1902, but with continuing support from important civic leaders and parts of the press, Phelan and the San Francisco Art Association formed the Association for the Improvement of San Francisco, which turned to Burnham to draft a plan for the city. After visiting a number of Mediterranean hill towns to prepare himself for his work, Burnham built a shack on the eastern side of Twin Peaks, which afforded him a panoramic view of the city, and went to work, with the help of Edward Bennett and Willis Polk, redesigning the city.

Meanwhile the fortunes of the public library improved somewhat because of the new reform atmosphere. In 1896, to further insulate the library's staff from the political purveyors of patronage jobs, examinations were required for a library job. This innovation foreshadowed civil service reform that would come with the passage of the new city charter in 1898. The new charter increased the tax assessment for the Library Fund, setting a minimum appropriation of $75,000. It took five years, however, before the library actually began to receive that amount.

City Beautiful, Library Beautiful

From the start, the library's trustees had pressed for a new, separate building, noting repeatedly that other major American cities had better libraries in appropriate buildings. When James Phelan was elected mayor in 1896, he joined their effort. An enthusiastic supporter, Phelan was also a patron of libraries. He gave libraries to the city's almshouse and to two high schools, and in 1901 he donated $16,000 to build a new branch for the South of Market area, at the corner of Fourth and Clara streets (replacing the Harrison branch). Soon after it was built, a library and a reading room for the blind were moved into the structure. With the construction of the Eureka Valley library (absorbing the Potrero branch) with a $45,000 gift from Andrew J. McCreery in 1902, there were now six branches. In 1901 Phelan also proposed that the city build a new main library. From the Carnegie Foundation, Phelan secured a commitment to spend $750,000 for a new main library and several branches.

This proposal was quickly opposed by the San Francisco Labor Council. Carnegie's gift, its members argued, was a "presumptuous claim of a wealthy nonresident to dictate our municipal policy in the assumed name of philanthropy." Moreover, Carnegie's money was not wanted because it was acquired "by notoriously questionable means" through his sale of armor plate for warships at extortionate prices to the United States government. And not to be forgotten was Carnegie's "cruel, heartless and degrading policy toward his employees" during the 1892 strike at his steel mill in Homestead, Pennsylvania. A library constructed with Carnegie money, the Labor Council concluded, would "stand as a perpetual charge against the morals of the community."

Despite the opposition of labor, the supervisors voted to accept the Carnegie gift. Because the Carnegie funds were insufficient for the construction of a new main library, the supervisors put a $1.647 million bond measure on the ballot in 1903. The measure passed, but the bond issue was undersubscribed.

Phelan, who had been followed into the mayoral office in 1902 by Eugene Schmitz of the Union Labor Party, stepped in to arrange for the sale of some of the bonds to local bankers, specifically for the library. But not without a price: the law was changed so that the board of supervisors, which was still controlled

B.J.S. CAHILL: "FATHER OF THE CIVIC CENTER"

English-born architect B.J.S. Cahill developed the first plan for a San Francisco Civic Center, which included a library, in 1899. His proposal called for a commercial island with a hotel and a theater with roof garden in the middle of Market Street between Seventh and Ninth streets. Cahill urged the city to condemn property and then sell it at a higher price for the commercial venture in order to raise funds for a new library that would be located on McAllister Street adjacent to the Hibernia Bank. (The library is to the left of the B in "Bird's Eye." Hibernia Bank is to the left of the library.)

Without the proper connections, Cahill never saw either this or a later plan submitted to Daniel Burnham in 1904 for a Civic Center west of City Hall realized. In 1912, his 1904 plan became the basis for plans for the present Civic Center, and he was named "father of the Civic Center" by the press.

The Hibernia Bank was gutted by fire after the 1906 earthquake and then rebuilt. It became the headquarters of the chief of police in 1994.

Right: Daniel Burnham, Chicago architect and leader of the City Beautiful movement, worked closely with James Phelan and other reformers to produce a comprehensive plan for San Francisco.

by Phelan's Democratic allies, not the mayor, would control site selection for the library. Plans for the $1 million granite-and-marble structure were completed by the city engineer. But with $647,000 available for the site, in 1904 all parties involved commenced fighting over the location. The supervisors had instructed the library's trustees to select Block 67, which was bounded by Van Ness, Fulton, Polk, and Grove (the south side of the present City Hall). Immediately nearby property owners and architects began to pressure the supervisors to change the location. Central to the discussion was whether the site of the new library was consistent with the master plan that Burnham was developing for the city.

Some years later, architect B.J.S. Cahill insisted that Burnham had been coerced into changing the site of the library by Phelan, who demanded an extension of the Golden Gate Panhandle that would link up with the Civic Center at Market and Van Ness. Phelan wanted the library facing the extension in Block 73, which was bounded by Fell, Franklin, Hayes, and Van Ness. Cahill, who claimed to be working with Burnham, said that he went to the board of supervisors early in 1904 and asked them to postpone their decision about a library site until Burnham, who was not in San Francisco at the time, would return. The supervisors agreed. Upon his return in September, Burnham assured Cahill that the library would be located in Block 66 in a large complex of civic buildings due west of City Hall. (Cahill preferred Block 67.) Both blocks were consistent with a plan that Cahill drew up and submitted to Burnham in the same year for a Civic Center located west of the old City Hall, with a boulevard that would run west along Fulton Street to Alamo Square and from there southwesterly to the Panhandle.

A drawing from the Burnham plan of 1904 shows a new Civic Center at the intersection of Market and Van Ness. (View is from the south side of Market looking north along Van Ness.) A new library was to be located along the Panhandle extension, which radiates from the Civic Center in a north-westerly direction. An opera house (top) is shown in the middle of Van Ness.

According to Cahill, when Phelan found out that Burnham supported plans that were not consistent with Phelan's Panhandle extension and library plans, he got Burnham to change his mind. When Burnham finally appeared before the supervisors, he was carrying new drawings that showed Phelan's Panhandle extension with the library located in Block 73. *Town Talk,* a chatty newsweekly for the better classes, claimed that Phelan was not exactly a disinterested participant in the debate. Phelan, the paper also charged, had persuaded Burnham to change the plans for the Civic Center so that Block 73 could be selected for a library site. Part of Block 73, the reporter went on, was owned by a friend of Phelan's, who had bought the lot through the agency of some of Phelan's business associates. Whatever the case, when the dust settled, the board of supervisors settled on Block 73 in March 1905.

In September 1904, Burnham and his associate, Edward Bennett, who did most of the work, completed their plan for the Civic Center and presented it to the board of supervisors. Bennett and Burnham, who insisted that civic reformers should "make no little plans [because] they have no magic to stir men's blood," conjured up a spectacular vision for a new San Francisco. Taking advantage of the city's hilly terrain, they mixed new streets that followed the hills' contours with boulevards that radiated out from the new Civic Center and a number of other circular plazas spread throughout the city. The new Civic Center would contain "structures, public or private, of monumental character and of great civic interest, relating to matters literary, musical, esthetic, expositional, professional or

This two-page spread in the September 24, 1899, San Francisco Examiner *accompanied an article by Mayor Phelan calling for an extension of the Golden Gate Park Panhandle from the park to the corner of Market and Van Ness as visualized by the* Examiner's *artists (upper right). The* Examiner's *correspondent reported from Paris, which Phelan regarded as a model for a series of planned public improvements for San Francisco.*

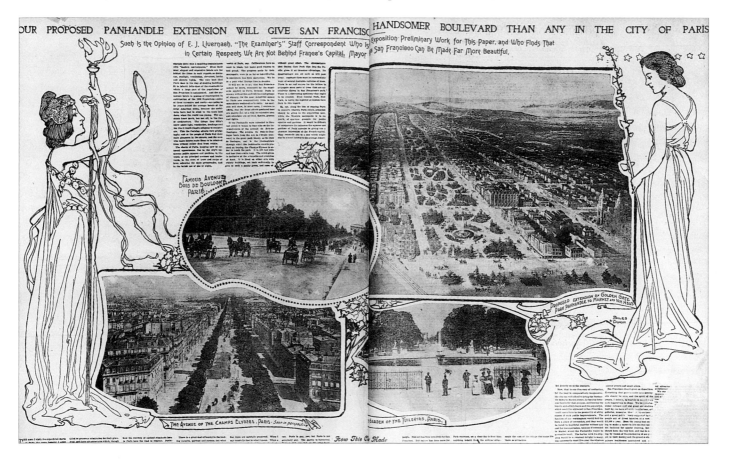

CATHEDRAL

❊

WHAT DOES A LIBRARY mean to me as a writer? Everything. I became a writer because I read an older brother's Renaissance library at home and because I got my third job after high school at age seventeen in the Oakland Public Library. It was a grand old Victorian slate gray granite building, with huge walls and high ceilings and windows that could have been in a cathedral and Roman columns and glass floors that you could see through in the stacks. Like looking up through the bottom of a Coke bottle. Thick and beautiful as frozen ice. Beautiful the upper stacks where only the employees went, where pages like myself were called to get reference material by a buzzer.

Beautiful the sense in my teenager's head of the quiet and seriousness that hung like a light mist over the readers' bent brows, as if they were bending to prayer. Beautiful to sit down on a stool when I stacked the books on the public shelves and read passages out of book after book after book. Beautiful to take book after book after book home when I really got interested. I'd work hard and get my work done. Then make myself scarce in the public stacks and read by the hour, everything from *Black Boy* and *Native Son* to *This Is My Beloved* by Walter Benton to *The La Guardia Reports on Marijuana* to *Mother India* to books on black magic and the psychology of dreams and the life of Soapy Smith, con man extraordinaire in Alaska, and Joaquin Murieta, the California bandit. Life was rich. My head was full of words and stories and great ideas on how my mind worked and made visions at night. I'd dream of the bookshelves at night. Wandering among them. Lost and happy and a little bewildered by the magnitude of the journey of the mind that stretched ahead of me. The idea even came into my mind then that I could maybe do a little writing myself. I did become a writer and won a few awards and got good critical reception and thanked God I got to work in a public library where education was free.

For that reason a public library is the first bastion against tyranny. The first thing the reactionaries do is cut off education so people won't be smart enough to see through them. The battle over government support for the arts came out of right-wing Republican think tanks, whose members know that the control of consciousness is the key to control of the country and command of profit.

The library is the most socially important structure that can be built. Without libraries we will become ignorant and enslaved. President Kennedy quoting Lincoln said, "Whoever wants an uneducated society to be free, wants something that never was and never will be." Fight for freedom. Support the library.

Floyd Salas

religious." It would be connected to Golden Gate Park by an extension of the Panhandle, which would run on to the Pacific Mail Steamship docks on the Embarcadero along the bay. On Ashbury Heights, an amphitheater and sports fields would offer a grand view of the Golden Gate. On the west side of Twin Peaks, there would be an Athenaeum modeled after Hadrian's Villa, with a colossal statue of Athena facing the sea. Bennett and Burnham continued this Mediterranean theme with a proposal to reserve certain pieces of real estate for villas that would obviously be for the very well-to-do. New parks were scattered all over the new city, including one along Islais Creek in the vicinity of present-day Cesar Chavez Street designed to resemble the Bois de Boulogne in Paris.

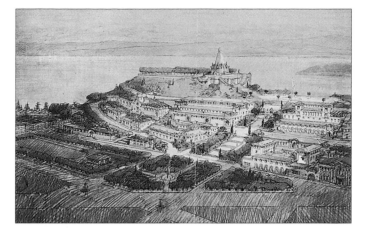

Burnham emphasized a street plan that would follow the contours of the city's famous hills. In his vision for Telegraph Hill, curving streets pass large commercial and civic structures and Roman villas as they sweep up to a park and a monument on the crest of the hill.

The new Civic Center was to be clustered around a semicircular *place* at the intersection of Market and Van Ness and was designed as a constellation of subcenters, each with a major public complex. The existing City Hall was to be one of these. In addition there would be a new railroad station, a new auditorium for conventions, a new opera house, and the new library, which both Phelan and Burnham considered to be an integral part of any civic center. This immense plan would cost $50 million in the first phase alone, but being realistic, Burnham described it as a fifty-year undertaking and urged the city to start with the Panhandle extension, which would cost $6 million.

DREAMS BURIED IN ASHES AND RUBBLE

The Burnham plan was received with great fanfare in certain circles such as the Merchants' Association. The city had enjoyed almost a decade of prosperity. Bolstered by the expansion of American trade in the Pacific after the United States seized the Philippines in 1898, San Francisco remained the preeminent port on the Pacific littoral. Along Market Street, the city's main business axis, automobiles could be seen maneuvering around horse-drawn wagons and electric and horse-drawn streetcars. The street was lined by modern office buildings, including the Call Building, which at eighteen stories was the tallest, and the Chronicle Building, designed by Burnham and an associate. All of the buildings were served by electric lights and telephones. The Burnham plan seemed consistent with the modern city's rollicking optimism.

In April 1906, the plan was printed and bound, ready to be distributed to the board of supervisors, when an unprecedented catastrophe struck the sleeping city. At 5:13 A.M., April 18, as the gray dawn light broke over the East Bay hills, an enormous earthquake raced at 7,000 miles per hour in a southeasterly direction

down the San Andreas Fault. It hit the city with an impact that made the streets rise and fall in great waves, and the office buildings on Market whiplash back and forth over the street. Brick facades tore loose, falling into the streets with a sickening roar amid great clouds of dust. Numerous wooden structures danced and skittered on their foundations before collapsing or falling against each other. At City Hall thousands of tons of stone facade pulled loose from the rotunda while walls fell and pillars toppled, including one that tore the front off an apartment building across the street. City Hall had finally become what the wags had called it—a ruin, with the steel frame of its rotunda towering over the broken walls like an empty birdcage. In the midst of the rubble lay the remains of the public library.

With its block after block of ornate, often poorly built wooden structures, many of them constructed on landfill, San Francisco was destined to fare poorly in a disaster. These houses on Golden Gate Avenue near Hyde Street collapsed during the 1906 earthquake.

In about a minute and a half the quake was over, but the destruction had just begun. Fed by kitchen fires and broken gas mains, flames rushed through the city, consuming block after block. Fires started in numerous places, were checked here and there by water and dynamite, and then flowed together into new and larger fires.

The "Ham and Eggs Fire," said to have been started some time before 11:00 A.M. by a woman cooking breakfast in a house with a damaged chimney at 395 Hayes Street, was driven eastward across Van Ness by a strong westerly breeze. Sparks flew onto the roof of the immense wooden Mechanics' Pavilion, which stood at the site of the present Civic Auditorium. Here many of the injured were being treated, and the bodies of the dead were stacked unceremoniously out of sight. With the pavilion soon in flames, it took little time for the fire to jump across Larkin Street to City Hall, where jumbled furniture, wooden cabinets and shelves, tons of records, and tens of thousands of books, newspapers, and magazines fed the flames.

Some 3,000 people died as the result of the earthquake and fire, and 250,000 lost their homes. The fire leveled over four and one-half square miles of the city, leaving a scene of appalling desolation. Little was left but the burned-out remains of an occasional building standing like a lonely cenotaph. In the fire area, only 303 structures were still standing, and some 28,000 buildings were razed. As for the public library, the heart of its collection was decimated. At the main library in City Hall, 138,000 books plus newspapers and periodicals were consumed by the Ham and Eggs Fire. The South of Market branch donated by Phelan was destroyed, as was the North Beach branch. The new Eureka Valley branch was heavily damaged. At the time of the earthquake, 15,000 books were out on loan. Only 1,500 of them eventually came back, the last one in 1981. A new library would have to be built around the 25,000 books left at the four remaining branches.

Opposite page: San Franciscans gather on Russian Hill to watch fire consume the city after the earthquake. The earthquake and fire, the greatest urban disaster since the Chicago fire of 1871, killed at least 3,000 people, destroyed 28,000 buildings, and led to the evacuation of 250,000 people.

Eureka Valley was severely damaged, leavir
mond branches operating.

Despite the devastation, the library's
There was $40,000 in the Library Fund, an
library carried a small insurance policy. With
library's trustees were faced with the problem
functioning once again. Headquarters were
branch, then to the McCreery, while the trus
fire fighting to retain ownership of Block
Franklin, and Fell, this was the site bought
library. In August 1906, the board of supervi
in this block and were only dissuaded when th
tion in October barring the board of public v

Efforts to rebuild the library system g
earthquake, Andrew J. McCreery offered to
branch, which he had originally funded. In e
temporary main library at the corner of Hayes
brick structure with two reading rooms feature
entrance to the stacks. Additionally, the supervi
branch that was to be built somewhere a
Panhandle. For fiscal year 1907–08, the library
history that exceeded the legal minimum. Wit
trustees began to make plans for a bond issue th

George Clark, like Lichtenstein, who
one of those who did not stay to see the library
become head librarian at Stanford University. Cl
and taciturn—"not a man of very attractive per
For twelve years he had presided over an expans
it grew to be the eighth largest in the Unite
appointed the new city librarian. A graduate of
in Albany, New York, Watson had been supe
Pittsburgh and then first assistant librarian at th

Scandal Impedes Rec

"Come at once!" library trustee and former may
Daniel Burnham in Chicago immediately after
cent opportunity for beautifying San Francisc
owners will gladly cooperate, now that their
swept away. I am sure the city will rise from its

Chapter Six

THIS MAGNIFICENT
TEMPLE OF LEARNING

❖

The Rebuilding
of San Francisco

On April 20, 1906, two days after the earthquake, city librarian George Clark and assistant librarian Joy Lichtenstein trekked through the rubble that surrounded the still smoldering City Hall on their way to inspect the remains of the library. City Hall was a scorched ruin, most of it heavily damaged, though much of the McAllister

Preceding pages: The San Francisco Public Library during a visit by the combined Atlantic and Pacific naval fleets in April 1925. The column and statue at the right were installed as a World War I memorial and were later removed.

City Hall was devastated by the 1906 earthquake. Several hours after the earthquake, the "Ham and Eggs Fire" began in a chimney on Hayes Street and spread to City Hall, where it reduced the main library, housed in the McAllister wing, to ashes. Only a handful of books survived.

Eugene Schmitz, the handsome head of the musicians' union and conductor of the orchestra at the fashionable Columbia Theatre, was picked by his longtime friend and lawyer Abe Ruef to run for mayor and served from 1902 to 1907.

The city revived, but the Burnham plan, copies of which had been saved from City Hall even as it burned, would linger on its deathbed while Phelan and his supporters, now known as the dreamers, struggled on. Their ambitions for a planned metropolis with a new Civic Center and library were blocked by the city's major property owners led by Michael De Young, owner of the *San Francisco Chronicle.* "The crying need of San Francisco today is not more parks and boulevards," the *Chronicle* editorialized, "it is business." The city had to be rebuilt quickly, and any plan that might raise the issue of property rights, especially the property rights of the powerful downtown business community, through redesigning the street plan would only hold back the rush toward reconstruction.

But first the city had to wallow through the corruption scandals that originated before the earthquake with the activities of Republican political boss Abraham Ruef; Eugene Schmitz, Ruef's handsome but feckless mayoral creation; and a board of supervisors described by historians T. H. Watkins and R. R. Olmsted as "an ambitious gaggle of boodlers." With Ruef's backing, Schmitz had been elected on the Union Labor Party ticket in 1901 and then reelected in 1903 and 1905, sweeping a Union Labor board of supervisors into office with him. In 1905, *Bulletin* editor Fremont Older—with financial and moral support from Phelan and Rudolph Spreckels, Phelan's close friend and a member of the Spreckels sugar family—began to attack Ruef and Schmitz in a series of exposés.

Following an investigation not known for its respect for legal niceties, Ruef and Schmitz were indicted in November 1906 for accepting $10,000 in protection money from owners of the city's so-called French restaurants, which were really fancy houses of prostitution. Special prosecutor Francis J. Heney and district attorney William H. Langdon slowly traced the trail of corruption as it snaked through the board of supervisors into the private clubs and corporate suites where the city's elite congregated.

In June 1907, Schmitz was convicted of extortion and sent briefly to jail, which meant he had to vacate the mayor's office and the supervisors were empowered to elect his successor. In July, Heney, Langdon, and Spreckels settled on Dr. Edward Robeson Taylor as a suitable reform candidate for mayoral office. He was elected by the supervisors in July and reelected in citywide elections in November.

Printer, newspaperman, poet, doctor, and lawyer, Edward Taylor was a remarkably well-rounded individual. His long ties to the San Francisco literary community included friendships with Henry George—Taylor had proofread the manuscript for George's 1879 *Progress and Poverty*—and Gelett Burgess, whimsical poet-editor of the experimental magazine *The Lark* and one of the free spirits of the 1890s. Taylor had served as head of a medical college and was the dean of Hastings College of Law. Most importantly, he had a long history of reform

Recognizing the pressures that [...] finances, the trustees at first spoke of a [...] considerably less than the $1 million s[...] The Carnegie Foundation continued to [...] library, which required the city to provi[...] the Carnegie gift. In addition, the city'[...] bonds in 1903 for the construction of a m[...] to be divided between a main library an[...] raise additional funds. Some of the 1903 [...] was that they bore a 3.5 percent interest [...] closer to 4.5 percent. This problem was r[...]

NEW HOPES FOR A [...]

Although the Burnham plan in all its glo[...] Hall and its Civic Center (with library [...] Burnham plan called for a Civic Center a[...] the north side of an extension of the Pa[...] Now a new element added a sense of urg[...] the Civic Center. In December 1908, a [...] formed a company to submit a proposal [...] city as the site of the celebration that wou[...] Canal in 1915. To host this ambitious ev[...] Hall and a new convention center to repla[...]

In the spring of 1909, the superv[...] Civic Center. Burnham came to town to ba[...] Ness plan, which was drawn up by Willis[...] Newton Tharp. The second proposal, pres[...] 1904 plan, which Burnham had rejected. It [...] City Hall, to be rebuilt on its pre-1906 sit[...] extending westward along Fulton Street [...] southwesterly direction to the Panhandle.

In April 1909, the supervisors reje[...] an $8.48 million bond measure for a Civic [...] November ballot. Mayor Taylor, who was a [...] sure. The measure won a majority, but with[...] down to defeat. The election spelled the en[...] which the library still owned, became just a [...]

In 1911 San Francisco was selecte[...] Panama-Pacific International Exposition. In [...]

---

activity and was in no way associated with the city's political shenanigans.

Inevitably, the library was caught in the political cross fire. Taylor had been a library trustee since 1886, Phelan since 1896. It was Taylor, in fact, who suggested the lines from Seneca, *Vita sine Literis, Mors Est* (Life without letters is death) for the library's bookplate. So for a time after Taylor's first election, two of the library's strongest backers were at the center of city politics. As mayor, Taylor immediately increased the library's appropriation. Additional funds were set aside for a new Park branch near the Panhandle, which opened in 1909, and to rebuild the book collection. Rental space was located for the North Beach and Mission branches, and discussions began on building a new main library. At the same time, the finance committee of the board of supervisors exacted revenge for the fight over the location of City Hall by refusing to appropriate $1,850 for a sidewalk adjacent to the new Park branch. Taylor served only one term, refusing to run again, and the library suffered accordingly.

By 1908 a curious alliance of Republicans and Union Labor Party supporters had had enough of the corruption prosecutions. Despite their differences, too many important figures from both camps were threatened with jail sentences. These two would-be antagonists successfully backed Patrick H. "Pinhead" McCarthy, the Union Labor head of the Building Trades Council, for mayor in the 1909 election, and ultimately only Ruef went to jail for any length of time.

McCarthy's ascendancy rekindled the feud between the supervisors and the library's trustees. In 1910 the supervisors, calling the present arrangement "un-American and unconstitutional," proposed an amendment to the city charter that would change the board of trustees from a self-perpetuating to an elected board. The *Chronicle* and the *Examiner* leapt to the trustees' defense. The *Examiner* claimed that the amendment was designed "to make the San Francisco Public Library a part of Mayor McCarthy's machine." The *Chronicle* noted that the library was well managed, "with an air of decency and courtesy about it" and never so much as a suspicion of scandal. In November 1910, the charter amendment was defeated. Unsuccessful at trimming the trustees' sails, the supervisors cut the library budget to the minimum allowed by law and refused to fund the construction of additional branches.

With the new San Francisco going up at the rate of a building every 104 minutes, the trustees began to push for the construction of a main library. The temporary main library had reached capacity. During its busiest hours, patrons were forced to sit on the window ledges in the reading rooms. On March 1, 1912, city librarian William Watson retired for health reasons and was replaced by Robert Rea. Rea had no professional experience outside the library, where he had taken a job as a page at the age of thirteen.

Abe Ruef, the most notorious of San Francisco's political bosses, rose to power with the Union Labor Party and its mayoral candidate, Eugene Schmitz. In the years after the earthquake, Ruef and Schmitz became the principal targets of an anticorruption crusade, whose twists and turns delayed plans to rebuild the library.

Workers grade Fulton Street in 1915 between the site of the main library built two years later on the right and Marshall Square on the left. The new City Hall, almost complete, stands in the background.

district businessman with no previous political experience, defeated Pinhead McCarthy at the polls. "Sunny Jim" entered office committed to key elements of the reform agenda that had been backed by Phelan and his associates since the 1890s. By sheer force of personality and an astute handling of his connections with business and labor leaders, Rolph would transcend the bitter conflicts that divided the city and begin the greatest era in the development of the city's infrastructure.

Rolph had run on the promise to build a new Civic Center. He immediately set up an advisory committee headed by University of California architecture professor John Galen Howard, Willis Polk, and Edward Bennett, the shadowy hand behind the Burnham plan. Could it be that the Burnham plan for a new Civic Center still had not succumbed? Polk and Bennett argued for the Market and Van Ness site, but Howard, using notes prepared by Cahill, ultimately prevailed. The city already owned the site of the old City Hall, and it was cheaper to purchase land to the west of this site for a new Civic Center. Cahill may have been repeatedly rebuffed and ultimately excluded from its design, but he was annointed "father of the civic center" by the newspapers.

With planning for the Panama-Pacific International Exposition under way, the pieces of a new Civic Center rapidly fell in place. Rolph secured broad support from business and labor for another bond measure, which would pay for City Hall and for land for other Civic Center buildings. The exposition company agreed to pay $1 million for the construction on the south side of the new Civic Center of what would become the Nourse (later the Bill Graham) Civic Auditorium, while the state committed $500,000 for a new office building on the north side. Money was being raised for a new opera house. Also to go on the November 1912 ballot was a charter amendment that permitted the city to sell the 3.5 percent library bonds at 4.5 percent.

Then came another impasse. Library trustee and former mayor Taylor decided to raise the issue of Carnegie money once again. He had always been against the Carnegie gift, Taylor told the *San Francisco Call.* "Nothing could be more humiliating than the spectacle of this great city holding out its hat to Carnegie." The Labor Council backed Taylor, as did Catherine Hittell, who said

The Place to Be

FROM THE START in 1977 the Dashiell Hammett Tour has met on the steps of the main library. I incline to symbolic value and liked the fact that Hammett was a frequent user of the Old Main in the early 1920s, walking the three blocks down Larkin from his rooms in 620 Eddy Street. And if you go for symbolism, what better place to start a literary tour than the library?

I saw the library as a locus for that kind of activity, courtesy of my friend Donald Sidney-Fryer. In the early 1970s, as The Last of the Courtly Poets, Don, in Elizabethan garb, was

staging the set piece "St. George and the Dragon," from Edmund Spenser's *Faerie Queene*, in libraries all over town. He was not alone. I went with Don to a library performance by a fellow who portrayed James Boswell, acting out brilliantly the text of Bozzy's *London Journal*, even scribbling in a diary at an antique desk. Somehow I got the idea that you should dress up and go down to the library and do something. Tights and sword. Periwig and quill. Trenchcoat and hat. Contribute to the culture.

The Hammett Tour has never been sponsored by the main library. I just sit on the front steps and the library does not object. I have never been a City Guide, which seems odd now—how did I bypass becoming one of the library's City Guides? I have no idea, but I regard them as Fellow Cicerones of the Mean Streets, of the Historied Past.

I have worked on projects with and in the library over the years. The reading of poetry from the California Romantics in the Lurie Room of the Main, November 17, 1982, was one of the best. We had Donald Sidney-Fryer recite verse by the inimitable Clark Ashton Smith and for a *tour de force* finale lined up the fantasist Fritz Leiber with George Sterling's epic "A Wine of Wizardry," a favorite of Ambrose Bierce, but not the sort of poem the average person can get into today. Son of the Shakespearean actor of the same name, Fritz knew all of *The Scottish Play* by heart from listening to rehearsals as a child, and his tonal range was as rich as rolling thunder. Immediately after, Lawrence Ferlinghetti came over to me and said that Fritz's rendering was the best reading of a poem he had heard in San Francisco since Dylan Thomas came through in the 1950s. That night I felt the Lurie Room was *the* place to be.

With the opening of the New Main, I suppose I'll move my starting point to a fresh set of steps. The Old Main remains the authentic Hammett site, but after all these years I'm partial to sitting in front of *The* Library, waiting to see who will show and what fun will ensue.

Don Herron

Library leaders look over the winning plans for a new main library in May 1914. George W. Kelham, winner of the competition to design the library, was picked by a jury made up of James Duval Phelan (standing second from left), Paul Philippe Cret (seated center), and Cass Gilbert (seated right). Also shown are library trustees Joseph O'Connor, John H. Wise, Judge Ralph G. Harrison, Edward Robeson Taylor, and Eustace Cullinan.

that the ladies of the California Club would grow vines to cover Carnegie's name if it was put on a new library. Ten thousand names were gathered on a petition to reject the Carnegie gift, and the issue was debated before the supervisors. Meanwhile the library's trustees voted eight to one, with Taylor voting against, to accept the money, and the supervisors did the same by a vote of thirteen to three.

The measure against tainted money, however, qualified for the November ballot, where it appeared along with the Civic Center bond issue and the charter amendment permitting a higher interest rate on library bonds. San Franciscans voted two to one to accept the Carnegie money. The bond measure and charter amendment, which were virtually unopposed, passed by a margin of ten to one. Phelan, acting as a library trustee, had remained in touch with Carnegie, and in early January 1913 he visited Carnegie's office in New York and spoke with the retired steel magnate. Carnegie was gracious, saying that the money would be forthcoming.

AMBITIOUS PLANS FOR A CIVIC CENTER

With the sale of bonds, the library's financial problems seemed to be solved. That left the question of a site. The library still owned Block 73 on Van Ness, but the new Civic Center was to be located in the blocks bound by Hyde, Grove, McAllister, and Van Ness. The plans showed an opera house located in the block bound by Grove, Larkin, Fulton, and Hyde. Money had been raised through the sale of boxes and seats, which in fact were oversubscribed, and plans were drawn up for an elaborate structure modeled after the Paris Opera House. Suddenly, the new mayor turned against the opera, declaring it undemocratic and calculated to promote aristocratic pretensions. For a time, the library was slated for the opera house site, but then John Galen Howard, working with the supervisors, arranged to trade Block 73 for the block bound by Larkin, McAllister, Hyde, and Fulton.

In June 1913, the trustees announced a competition to select the architect for the main library, and six local architects were chosen to enter. The three-man jury was made up of Phelan, head of the trustees' building committee; Cass Gilbert, the well-known New York architect who had designed New York's Custom House and Woolworth Building, one of the first skyscrapers; and Paul Philippe Cret, professor of architecture at the University of Pennsylvania, a native of France, and a graduate of the École des Beaux-Arts in Lyons.

In May 1914, the trustees announced that George W. Kelham had won the contract. Kelham, who had come to San Francisco in the wake of the earthquake, had designed the new Palace Hotel and contributed to the design of the Bohemian Club. Later he was appointed chief of the office of architecture at the

Panama-Pacific International Exposition. Born in Massachusetts, Kelham was a Harvard graduate and had studied at the École des Beaux-Arts in Paris. The library's design, which was "in the spirit of the Italian Renaissance," according to Kelham, was very much in the tradition of the École and consistent with the new City Hall, which was going up across the Civic Center's new central plaza.

In the mind of one of the contestants, Edgar Mathews, Kelham's plan was a little too consistent—with Cass Gilbert's design for the Detroit Public Library. Mathews filed a complaint with the trustees, claiming that Kelham copied Gilbert's plans and even used one of his draftsmen. Kelham dismissed the charge as "childish talk." Two years later, Mathews sued for breach of contract, but the case was thrown out of court. His problem was that he misunderstood the historically derivative nature of neoclassical architecture. The *Chronicle* put it most succinctly, if a bit crudely, when it editorialized, "We must admit that the art of the architect is the art of plagiarism. There has been little new in architecture in the last hundred years—that is, monumental architecture."

There was, of course, much that was new in American architecture. But through a long and mostly fruitless struggle to break with the banality and inappropriateness of a grid system in a wonderfully hilly waterside terrain that cried out for something innovative, the city fathers had settled on another form of confining orthodoxy that emanated from the École des Beaux-Arts. The end result was a monumentally conservative complex of civic structures, albeit the most complete, unified civic center in the United States. In the spirit of deference to tradition common to much of American architecture, the Boston Public Library looked back to Paris's Bibliothèque Ste. Geneviève, Detroit to Boston and Paris, and San Francisco to all three.

With Kelham's drawings completed, groundbreaking was scheduled for early 1915. But the library was still facing financial difficulties. Not enough bonds, even at the 4.5 percent interest rate, had been sold to release the matching Carnegie funds. As the war in Europe pushed prices upward, the trustees used what funds they had to buy crucial materials before prices went higher. Finally, in February, the trustees had enough money to let the contracts for excavation and construction of the foundation. On April 15, 1915, ground was broken, but then work was suspended because of the poor sale of bonds. An arrangement was made with the San Francisco Municipal Railroad to use its surplus funds, which

A silver trowel was presented to the board of supervisors by the McGilvray and Raymond Granite Company to commemorate the laying of the library cornerstone (below) on April 16, 1916. Mayor James "Sunny Jim" Rolph kneels at the center of the picture.

A riveter works on the steel frame of the new main library in 1915. In the background are the new City Hall and civic auditorium.

were earning only 2 percent, to buy library bonds. The library's problems were only temporary, however, because in October the supervisors authorized the sale of $120,000 in additional bonds to pay for the construction of a facade in granite, rather than the planned brick, along McAllister Street.

On April 16, 1916, ten years almost to the day since the earthquake and fire, the cornerstone was laid in a ceremony that included speeches by Mayor Rolph, Edward Taylor, George Kelham, and Joseph O'Connor, a library trustee and president of the board of education. Rolph and Taylor used the occasion to defend the self-perpetuating status of the board of trustees. "All these years this Board has been free from politics. No political boss, no politician, has been able to influence in the slightest degree the management of this institution," Rolph said. Somehow, Rolph did not see Phelan and Taylor, both former mayors and both with a long history of political activism, as politicians. Perhaps regretting the populist excesses of his earlier attack on the opera, Rolph gestured across Fulton Street toward Marshall Square and predicted the beginning of work on the opera house, which did not happen, and not at that site, until the end of his mayoral career in 1932. Kelham, in his remarks, noted that only New York's and Boston's main public library buildings could compare with San Francisco's.

Returning to work, the contractors rushed ahead as prices continued to rise. Seemingly everywhere but at the library, the number of strikes and violent confrontations between pickets and strikebreakers grew as employers tried to weaken the city's unions. The strife culminated in June 1916 in an attempt by the chamber of commerce to "end class warfare" by imposing the open shop and

· WEST ELEVATION · COMPETITION FOR SAN FRANCISCO PVBLIC LIBRARY · · SO V

creating a Law and Order Committee. War hysteria was also spreading as the United States was being drawn into the European conflict. All of this was brought home with a vengeance on July 22, when unknown assailants bombed the Preparedness Day Parade on Market Street, killing ten people.

The Temple Opens

In this increasingly ugly atmosphere, the library was completed without incident and dedicated on February 15, 1917, a warm, overcast day. Five hundred participants jammed together under the painted beam ceiling in the main delivery room to hear speeches by the mayor, the library trustees, and George Kelham. Referring to "this magnificent, chaste temple of learning," trustee O'Connor said, "Perhaps they will say 'those Trustees built for a village.' They should have known that this city was bound to become the New York or the London of the Pacific." Business leader Reuben B. Hale, another trustee, pointed out that in only one year since the destruction of the library in 1906, the board of supervisors had provided the library with more than the minimum amount of funds required by law.

Architect George W. Kelham presented the city with a truly grand building, which evoked an appropriately somber atmosphere. The steel-framed granite structure, which cost $1.153 million, was designed to hold 500,000 books and to have the ability to expand to 1 million volumes. The exterior featured Roman arched windows set off in front by Ionic columns. Later added in the alcoves above the front door were five statues by Leo Lentelli. Patrons entered from Larkin Street through three heavy, brass-framed doors into a colonnaded vestibule that led up a broad staircase to the distribution room. The vestibule, stairway, and delivery room were finished in pockmarked travertine marble from Italy intermixed with

Front and south elevations of George W. Kelham's 1914 design for the main library. The south elevation in particular bears a striking resemblance to Paris's Bibliothèque Ste. Geneviève, the Beaux Arts masterpiece that also influenced the design of the Boston and Detroit public libraries.

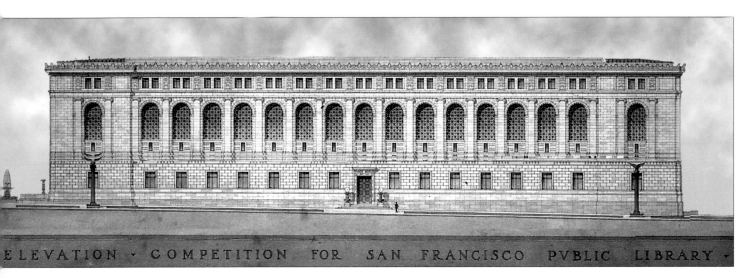

ELEVATION · COMPETITION · FOR · SAN · FRANCISCO · PVBLIC · LIBRARY ·

The Public Library, Civic Center, San Francisco, Cal.

Above: Hand-tinted postcard of the San Francisco Public Library. Below: Library card issued to its holder on April 4, 1906, two weeks before the earthquake.

(Form No. 88—8-23-05—10M)

Olney, Emma A.
1965 Pacific

NO. 24225 ISSUED APR 4 - 1906
EXPIRES APR 30 1908

SPECIAL CARD
Books classified as fiction will not be issued hereon. This card must not be used by any one not of your own household.

a locally concocted ersatz marble that was indistinguishable from the pure stone. The delivery room, reference room, and main reading room had painted beam ceilings, and the bookcases, ornamental doorways, and other wooden fixtures were covered with an antique oak finish—all of which were meant to evoke the interior of an Italian Renaissance palazzo.

Kelham had been saddled with a difficult problem. The design competition called for a building of a certain volume to be constructed within a block of fixed dimensions. The building also had to harmonize with City Hall and the civic auditorium, which were completed in 1915. Kelham chose a fully finished curtain facade with a cornice the same height as those of City Hall and the civic auditorium. This facade stretched along Larkin and Fulton streets, the sides that faced the Civic Center's central plaza and the supposed site of the new opera house. The extra bonds authorized by the supervisors allowed for the use of granite on the McAllister Street side of the building where the stacks were built. But the McAllister facade remained plain and unadorned. Kelham's plans show space in the empty corner of the block at McAllister and Hyde for a later addition. Both Cahill and Edgar Mathews, the architect who sued when he lost to Kelham, pointed out that when the library was approached along Fulton Street from Market (later the United Nations Plaza), one was presented with the unfinished rear of the building, facing Hyde Street. The problem of finishing the building bedeviled the library for years after it reached maximum capacity during World War II. Nevertheless, the library had finally found an appropriate home in the new Civic Center.

Beginning in 1914, $375,000 from the Carnegie funds were being used to construct new branches in the Richmond, the Mission, Noe Valley, the Sunset, and Golden Gate Valley. George A. Mullin, secretary to the board of trustees, was regarded as the expert on branch libraries. In some ways his work, such as his travels in the east with Kelham to visit various libraries for ideas about the main library, overshadowed that of chief librarian Robert Rea. All of the branches repeated the monumentality of the main library, only on a smaller scale. The Mission branch, in particular, with its Spanish revival architecture—green tile roof, glazed terra-cotta tile around the windows, and timbered ceilings—was hailed as "one of the finest in the United States."

The size of the library's book collection had returned to pre-earthquake levels. But the library was operating a vastly more demanding system, which now included a large main library and eight branches. The library's budget had increased

THIS QUIET HALL

※

THE MISSION BRANCH of the San Francisco Public Library stands prominently in the setting of two of my novels. In one of them a child reads the mysterious but awesome names TOLSTOY, HUGO, DUMAS, HAWTHORNE, BALZAC, and GEORGE ELIOT carved on the outer walls of the building. In the other novel a child climbs what seems to her a long, grand staircase to the adult section, a crucial initiation proving "that I am worthy to enter this quiet hall with its sacred smell of bookbindings and glue."

I was that child.

I was born in San Francisco's Mission District at the beginning of the Great Depression. My parents were immigrants from a poor village near Turin, Italy. Both had worked from the age of ten, but attended as much school as they could. My mother had even—against great odds—succeeded in completing high school in America. My parents worked and saved to provide a home, food, clothing, and medical care and—someday, they said—a college education for me.

But for all my parents' respect for learning, there were no books in our house, nor in the homes of friends. These were the days before cheap paperbacks began to appear in drugstores and supermarkets. No such thing as a bookstore (either new or secondhand) existed in the Mission. Books were expensive luxuries owned by schools and libraries.

I can't remember who introduced me to the public library. Probably my older sister walked me there the first time. I do remember—vividly—being issued a card that would grant me the privilege of taking books home. Books I could choose for myself, from rows and rows of shelves. I remember my excitement at the choices now open to me.

From then on I walked at least twice a week from our home on York Street, up Twenty-fourth Street to the library on Bartlett. The library became both a second home and a wider world to me. I always carried home the limit—four books—returning them on time, of course. The very thought of an overdue fine was not only a financial disaster but a disgrace.

One day—I must have been about ten or eleven—I summoned the courage to ask for an adult card. The children's librarian hesitated—there were so many rules in those days—then decided to give me one, and I made my proud ascent up the stairs to the adult section, where the choices were wild, incredible.

I recently visited the Mission branch and saw that the children's section had been moved upstairs. There were other changes. But one thing has not changed—the excitement on the face of a child I see pushing a pile of books—the limit—up onto the desk to be checked out.

Dorothy Bryant

Dorothy Bryant

A *Kelmscott Press edition of* The Works of Geoffrey Chaucer *printed by William Morris in 1896. This gem is from the Max J. Kuhl Collection, the cornerstone of the San Francisco Public Library's excellent collection of rare books by fine printers and binders.*

at roughly 10 percent a year since the earthquake. Until 1920, however, San Francisco was spending appreciably less than other West Coast cities, including Oakland, on its library and was employing one-third fewer staff members than libraries of a comparable size. Although the library still had $160,000 in Carnegie funds to build another branch, it was not receiving sufficient funding from the city to operate it. So the branch remained unbuilt.

Civic improvement clubs, the equivalent of contemporary neighborhood organizations, continued to petition for new branches, particularly in Bayview and Visitacion Valley. By 1921 the library's budget was large enough to permit the construction of the last Carnegie branch, in the Presidio on Sacramento Street, and to rent new space for the North Beach branch. The year before, voters approved a charter amendment that raised the maximum assessment to .0375 cents per dollar's worth of assessed property. The library immediately received a $40,000 increase in its budget, its largest ever. For fiscal year 1907–08, the library had received $64,445 from the board of supervisors. By fiscal year 1921–22, the amount had reached $185,282. Librarians worked forty-two hours a week and were paid $85 to $95 a month, a lower wage than other city employees.

Later, when the library's budget grew at a faster pace, six more branches were added to the system between 1925 and 1928: Excelsior, Ingleside, Ocean View, Glen Park, Bayview, and Portola. In 1929 a special business branch was opened in rooms rented in the Russ Building on Montgomery Street in the heart of the downtown financial district.

THE COLLECTION GROWS

There were notable changes in the book collection, starting even before the main library was built. In 1911 Julius Rehn Weber, a pianist and music teacher, arranged for the purchase of the 10,000-item music library from the Boston Music Company, a branch of G. Schirmer's Music House of New York. Over the next decade and more, Weber personally supervised the development of this collection, which was ranked among the best in the country. In 1918 the library offered a lecture series on music in conjunction with the University of California Extension. The library also began to attract donations from wealthy patrons. In 1908 the Lilienthals, a prominent local banking family, donated Philip N. Lilienthal's book collection to the library. Somewhat later John Cebrian began a series of donations of Spanish language books, some from the fifteenth and sixteenth centuries.

In 1920, at the instigation of library trustee William Young, the library began systematically to collect rare books and the works of San Francisco's fine printers. In 1927 a memorial collection was set up in memory of Max J. Kuhl. Kuhl, who died at the age of forty-six, had served as the attorney for the Panama-

Pacific International Exposition and had worked with Phelan, Taylor, Young, and Albert Bender to build the library's collection of rare books. The Kuhl collection contained rare works printed by famous printers such as Aldus Manutius, Italian Renaissance inventor of italic type and master of the Aldine Press, and William Morris, the nineteenth-century English writer, designer, and master of the Kelmscott Press. It also marked the beginning of a collection of the works of San Francisco fine printers and binders, who since the earthquake had gained national and even international stature. Foremost among these printers were Edward Robeson Taylor's sons, Edward DeWitt and Henry Huntly Taylor; John Henry Nash; and Edward and Robert Grabhorn. Besides corporate work, many of San Francisco's printers derived part of their support and renown from jobs commissioned by the Book Club of California, which the elder Taylor had helped organize in 1911 and served as its first president.

With the budget increases triggered by the 1920 charter amendment, the library began a three-year period of book buying. As early as 1916, Rea arranged for regular purchases of art books through dealers in Paris, Vienna, and other European cities. Fiction, of course, was a mainstay of the collection. But Rea felt that the library was successful in using fiction as an entrée to more serious reading in nonfiction. The library's policy—according to Rea, who exercised tight, some would later say dictatorial, control over book buying—was to buy ephemeral fiction with roughly 15 percent of the book-buying budget. These books represented 55 percent of the circulation. At the same time Rea prided himself that San Francisco bought more books in other areas, such as drama, costume design, interior decorating, science, and business, than other libraries of its size. For example, in 1925 San Francisco had the largest collection of chemistry books in the West. In 1927 the library's two most popular books were Will Durant's *The Story of Philosophy* and Theodore Dreiser's *An American Tragedy*.

WARNINGS OF TROUBLED TIMES AHEAD

Despite its growing book collection and new programs, the library was not without its problems. In 1926 the San Francisco Center produced a survey of the library. The study has since disappeared, but from the response of head librarian Robert Rea, it appears that the center found that the board of trustees was undemocratic, that funding was insufficient, and that the library lacked adequate children's services. According to the center's report, the library was "the one large public library in the country which does not appreciate the value of assistants who are graduates of library schools."

Rea responded in a bitterly dismissive tone. The charge that the board of trustees was undemocratic was "academic theorizing," and the criticism of staff

GOINGS-ON AT THE LIBRARY

❖

"Mysterious hands that grab girls' ankles have caused consternation among some of the feminine attaches of the public library. Women members of the library staff whose duties call them among the stacks have experienced the startling grasp of the hands. Strange men have been disappearing in the corridors, simultaneously with the molestations, which led John [sic] Rea, the librarian, to appeal for police protection."

San Francisco Examiner,
December 5, 1920

"It is about time the librarians in charge of the study and reading rooms of the San Francisco Public Library curb the chatter and patter of love-enmeshed swains in their teens who come to use these places of mental reflection."

Letter to the Examiner
from a student, December 11, 1920

A librarian in 1930 wearing a pedometer, which indicated that she walked ten to fifteen miles a day.

The public library's nine branches in 1925. Clockwise from upper left: Sunset, North Beach, Richmond, McCreery, Mission, Park (center), Golden Gate Valley, Noe Valley, and Presidio. All of these except the North Beach, McCreery, and Park branches were built with funds donated by library philanthropist Andrew Carnegie.

training was "quite unjustified" because "the greater part of the work done in any public library does not call for graduates of library schools." A suggestion that the library publicize its activities was derided as savoring "too much of the age of jazz and sham."

The next year, while James Phelan was serving a term as president of the trustees, the trustees asked Sydney B. Mitchell, director of the library school at the University of California, and Judson T. Jennings, Seattle's librarian, to conduct a survey of the library. In their 1928 report, Mitchell and Jennings pointed out that the board as a self-perpetuating institution was undemocratic and inconsistent with the majority of public libraries, whose trustees were elected, and that "the present double-headed administration with a secretary [of the board of trustees—George A. Mullin] and a librarian" led to divided loyalties and divided opinions.

Mitchell and Jennings next turned to Rea, the untutored librarian who had grown up with the system. Responding to "numerous criticisms both from his own staff and from those outside of the library," they found that, though Rea was good at selecting and buying books, he was "temperamentally unfitted for administrative leadership." The listing of Rea's faults was brutal and succinct: lack of an administrative mind, autocratic supervision, inability to delegate authority, and finally "a very noticeable lack of appreciation of the value of better educated, better trained, and experienced assistants, and even evidence of hostility towards the idea of engaging such employees." Mitchell and Jennings recommended that Rea be replaced at the earliest possible opportunity with a successful, trained librarian. To do this, the trustees would have to arrange to waive or change the requirement in the city charter that an appointee reside in the city for a year and would have to increase the librarian's salary.

With regard to the staff, Mitchell and Jennings found a staff that was almost entirely made up of women and that suffered from "intellectual inbreeding" and lack of initiative because of the absence of encouragement from the head librarian. There were also serious shortcomings caused by the librarians' lack of training, particularly for librarians working with children.

Despite the increase in library budgets since the earthquake, the survey found that San Francisco ranked last among thirteen major cities in library expenditures per capita. The American Library Association recommended $1 per capita library spending. San Francisco spent .497 cents.

The library had its strong points, according to the survey. The book collection was excellent, particularly given its almost total destruction in 1906. The buildings, because many of them were new, were in fine condition. The general

A Writers' Room

❉

WHEN WE HAD TOO MANY CHILDREN and too little quiet in our apartment in New York, I got a space in a writers' room at the New York Public Library. For me, it was like being admitted to Valhalla. These were eminent Writers bent with research, fortified by file cards, pecking incisively at their typewriter keys. I meekly took my seat and assembled my miserable few notes and books.

At the time, I was writing paperbacks about a spy who killed for the Pope. It's a long story. Even longer if you make a series out of it, which I did. Anyway, I was not "sharing" with the writer next to me who was preparing the definitive tome on constitutional law. He looked like Ben Franklin without the twinkle. At best, I hoped to go unnoticed.

Wasn't to be. On the first morning, I caught certain alarmed glances in my direction. By the afternoon, whole tables of writers stopped their labor to look at me with the shock of mourners watching a dear departed dance on the coffin. By the end of the day, I figured it out. I was the only fiction writer in the room. Fiction writers don't just write. They mutter. Their expression alters with each character. Unaware, they begin to act out dialogue. How else can they catch rhythm, pace, nuance?

"Put down that gun!"

"I won't put down that gun!"

"You better put down that gun! Because shoot me and you'll fry. I shoot you, I'll only have to say the 'Hail Mary' a hundred times."

Twenty nonfiction writers and twenty serious books came to a halt while I honed that scene. Then I packed up my machine and erasable bond (That's how young I was. Erasable bond? Hah!) and left. Now I work at home.

I still do research at my local library. Couldn't work without it and am astonished by the speed of the new retrieval system. And if they put in a padded cell, I might go down and write.

Martin Cruz Smith

The Panama-Pacific International Exposition of 1915 commemorated the completion of the Panama Canal. It announced to the world that San Francisco had been successfully rebuilt after the 1906 earthquake and provided momentum for the construction of a new City Hall, civic auditorium, and main library.

reference service was deemed of excellent quality and highly appreciated in the community. To improve its services, Mitchell and Jennings concluded, the library needed a new librarian, staff training, better pay for all librarians, more library assistants, more branches, and above all more money.

The League of Women Voters, after its own survey, responded by defending Rea. The Mitchell-Jennings report, the league argued, was designed to discredit Rea and to increase the demand for librarians that would be trained at the University of California. Nothing was said about the report in the press, which did print letters complaining about the library on a regular basis. The trustees noted in their annual report that many suggestions included in the Mitchell-Jennings

report would be discussed at length in the future. Nothing happened to Rea, who finally retired in 1945. Some minor changes were made in library operations. Patrons were allowed to borrow four books at a time rather than two. Fines were reduced from five cents to two cents per day. More emphasis was put on encouraging the staff to take library courses at the University of California Extension, and librarians were granted a pay increase. And in one of the more peculiar innovations, the police department in 1931 was given space in the basement of the main library for a shooting range.

In the end, the trustees had squandered an important opportunity to put well-paid, trained librarians in command of what was then a good book collection housed in what were for the time very fine buildings. Mitchell and Jennings's report could not have been more accurate or more prophetic. Rea, after all, had prided himself on running a major city library system with a small, underpaid staff. Unfortunately the library had peaked and was at the beginning of a slow descent that would accelerate over the next thirty years until the library came under attack in the press in 1957 as a national disgrace—for all the reasons and more that had been pointed out in 1928.

THE EXPANSIVE AND EXCESSIVE TWENTIES

One can speculate about why the library came only so far on the road to recovery after the earthquake. Sunny Jim Rolph's first term was a period of remarkable expansiveness. The Panama-Pacific International Exposition was a great success, and major parts of the civic infrastructure—such as City Hall, the civic auditorium, the library, the Hetch Hetchy water delivery project, and an improved, municipally owned transportation system—were either built or initiated during those years. Despite fear of competition from Los Angeles, San Francisco remained the premier city on the West Coast, the headquarters for larger and ever more complex corporate empires. The city's transportation, banking, agribusiness, oil, and utility companies, with names like Bank of America, Standard Oil of California, Pacific Gas and Electric, Natomas Company, DiGiorgio Fruit Corporation, Southern Pacific Railroad, and California Delta Farms, dominated the western economic landscape.

The library benefited to a limited degree from this wealth and expansiveness and continued to do so through the 1920s. But the city, led by its hedonistic mayor, subsided into excess. Rolph, one of the great characters in the history of a city known for its characters, set the tone. Despite the wealth that he earned early in shipbuilding, insurance, and banking and later squandered, Rolph was a true man of the people, a mayor who would instruct his driver to stop at a corner to give a stranger a ride to work. Rolph was happiest at the head of a parade or off in the

As a builder and a reformer, Mayor James "Sunny Jim" Rolph oversaw the construction of the Civic Center and brought about municipal ownership of the city's water and streetcar systems while turning a blind eye on a thoroughly corrupt police department. Rolph had an early Hollywood sensibility and favored a wide range of campaign outfits from cowboy to Indian chief. And he loved the ladies, particularly shapely young movie stars, whom he entertained at what his friend San Francisco madam Sally Stanford described as a "Caucasian geisha house" at 699 Sanchez Street.

THE CHURCH & CLUBHOUSE OF SAINT LIBRIS

FOR A LONELY CHILD in an American suburb, the public library was a place of worship, a place to find others afflicted with the love of books, a refuge from small-town conformities, even an alternate family. I went to the library in order both to breathe easy and to have adventures. It was a fortress against the world outside, but it also celebrated the world. At the long tables I fell in love with words, their power and seduction. I was enclosed between walls and stacks which accepted this passion. There, in the public library, I found others like myself.

At open stacks, attracted by a title, a binding, sometimes an author's name, even the smell of the book, I learned a benevolent promiscuity. It was exhilarating to be able to explore a subject about which I needed to know (beehives, the history of oil exploration, sex). Perhaps it was even better to wander and pluck books almost at random, just because I was hungry for the adventure of wordplay.

I came upon Hart Crane's poetry because he was displayed among "Cleveland Poets." I too was a Cleveland poet, but at fifteen years not yet displayed. I murmured lines from his work, "like pearls that through some doge's hands," as incantations to speed me on my way toward righteous genius.

I persuaded a teacher at Emerson Junior High School to write a letter authorizing me to read *Gone With the Wind*, which was on the restricted adult shelf, on the grounds that I was mature enough to deal with whatever filth might be contained therein. The librarian studied the letter, studied me, and slid the book across the counter. On the strength of that precedent, later she allowed me to read the work of James Branch Cabell, George Sylvester Viereck, Catullus, Rabelais, and the collected tales of Boccaccio—an endless banquet of some great, some deservedly forgotten writers. The confrontation of book and myself challenged essential metabolic processes of growing up.

In middle years I escaped to libraries to write. I could mutter over my papers, lip-reading the words I had magicked out of my soul. I was soothed and coddled by the evidence of creative study, of the history of books, their dignity and implied judgment. On the shelves all around me stood living models of curiosity, passion, talent, occasional genius. And also, in this place of mental commerce, communal immersion in the worlds of imagination, there is the record of the joys and griefs of the ages, an essential version of the great civic marketplaces in the plazas in front of cathedrals. At our best, we're all still lonely questing children and the library is a home for dreaming.

Herbert Gold

hills, holed up in a shack, hunting and drinking with his buddies. He was the patron saint of a wide-open city, where many citizens worshiped willingly. San Francisco became known for its wealth and beauty, but also for its illegal booze (served openly by "refined and well-dressed ladies" at the Democratic National Convention in 1920), for its gambling, and for some of the finest houses of prostitution in the country, all of which were protected with civic zeal by Rolph's police department.

The 1920s was not a particularly impressive era in the city's literary history. Dashiell Hammett, William Saroyan, and John Steinbeck worked and visited here but were just beginning their writing careers. Long gone was the heady atmosphere of the nineteenth and early twentieth centuries when the city was a writers' town. Publishing was becoming centralized in Boston and New York. Only fine printing and book binding graced the San Francisco literary landscape.

In contrast, the 1920s were formative years for the opera and the symphony. Opera was one of San Francisco's first love affairs. Early opera, beginning with Bellini's *La Sonnambula* in 1851, was a crude endeavor produced under dripping candelabra for a crowd mostly of men, who talked, drank, and spat tobacco juice throughout the performances. After the city's first opera house burned in 1906, San Franciscans saw only touring companies until Gaetano Merola organized the San Francisco Opera Company in 1923. Symphonic music and ballet were relative latecomers to the city's cultural scene. The first known symphonic performance was in 1881. The San Francisco Symphony Orchestra was organized in 1911, and the San Francisco Ballet not until 1933.

The library was the oldest of the city's four most important cultural institutions, which came to share the growing Civic Center. As the darlings of the city's elite, the ballet, opera, and symphony had ample funds to draw on and would achieve national and international stature in the years after World War II. The library, in contrast, was dependent on the foibles of politics; with a constituency of needy everyday people and only a small, but dedicated handful of wealthy patrons, it lacked both political and financial muscle. Libraries in other cities, such as Baltimore and New York, attracted wealthy patrons who gave substantial amounts to help build major libraries. San Francisco, despite its enormous wealth, did not.

Sunny Jim Rolph, unlike Phelan and Taylor, who were serious patrons of the arts, showed no particular interest in literature or the library, but then, with the exception of Phelan, very few San Francisco mayors ever did. Eustace Cullinan, one of Rolph's oldest friends and closest advisors, sat on the library's board during Rolph's mayoralty, and the library fared better when budget time came around. Ultimately, the library was left alone with an aging board of self-selected trustees and a poorly trained and underpaid staff. Rea had done a good job building the book collection, and the library certainly looked impressive. What more was needed?

Robert Rea, with his high, starched collars, was the last of the old-school bachelor librarians, unmarried until he retired. Lacking professional training, he grew up in the library knowing no other work. He built up the book collection, presided over the construction of seventeen branches, and successfully held off one brief attempt in the 1920s to reform the library.

CHAPTER SEVEN

THE ORPHAN CHILD OF CITY GOVERNMENT

❖

Troubled Years for the Library

With the advent of the Great Depression, dark days loomed over the library. After an increase in 1928–29, the library's appropriation flattened out in fiscal year 1929–30 and then after an increase for 1930–31 began to drop. As the depression closed down on the city, unemployment rose, the lines at soup kitchens in the

A depression-era soup kitchen at the corner of Ritch and Clara streets. The unemployed also flocked to the library for warmth and entertainment and to fathom the reasons for the collapse of the economy.

Preceding pages: The grand stairway at the main library. Stately Beaux Arts elements in the 1917 building proved to be a problem when the library reached capacity in 1943. It was estimated that approximately half of the floor space was unusable.

Tenderloin and South of Market grew longer, and the number of people using the library skyrocketed. The library had become a refuge, a free source of entertainment, a place to probe the underlying causes of the depression and to rethink one's employment possibilities if there were any.

In 1931 Sunny Jim Rolph went to Sacramento as governor, and Angelo Rossi, another successful businessman turned politician, was elected mayor by the board of supervisors. Rossi would govern the city under a new charter passed by the voters in March 1931. Under the charter, the library's self-perpetuating board of trustees was replaced by an eleven-person commission appointed by the mayor. The door was finally opened to a different kind of politicization of the library, and Rossi would soon take advantage of the patronage potential created by vacancies on the commission. The commission would come to resemble a revolving door, with commissioners coming and going, some to more prestigious and powerful city posts. Many of the appointees had little knowledge of or connection with libraries, but there often remained a small core of commissioners who were truly appreciative of the library's needs.

With the depression deepening, Rossi convened a Citizens' Advisory Committee on Unemployment Relief in January 1933 to look for ways to cut the city budget to pay for relief. Rossi emerged from one of his first meetings with the committee to announce that he was willing "to close down some of these municipal projects" to get the funds he needed—specifically, the library, the de Young Museum, the Palace of the Legion of Honor, parks, and playgrounds. At first Rossi fixed on a 50 percent budget cut for the library. "Curtailment of library activities," librarian Robert Rea pointed out, "will hamper one of the greatest safety valves of the depression."

The library was already suffering, particularly in the book-buying area, where the budget began to lag in the late 1920s. For fiscal year 1931–32, the supervisors cut the budget by $40,000, and the trustees pointed out that with the book-buying budget going to replace books, the library's collection was shrinking.

For a city hard-hit by the depression, in certain ways the library fared remarkably well after 1934. Funding seesawed and then flattened out until the war years, although with the gradual growth in employment and at first the lack of new books, book circulation began to decline. Money was found for new branches on Anza Street (1932) and in Visitacion Valley (1934). The library benefited particularly from the influx of dollars from both state and federal employment programs. In 1934 the California Works Administration funded twenty-one new typists and employees for the library's book bindery. The same year thirty women, supported by the State Emergency Relief Administration, began working on the California newspaper collection.

For fiscal year 1935–36, Rossi backed the library commission's plea for additional funds for branches. Receiving only $40,000, the commission proposed putting new branches in rented storefronts. Rossi instead turned to the federal government and asked for $150,000 in Works Progress Administration funding for permanent buildings. It was an adroit move since Rossi was able to garner major headlines the month before his reelection in November 1935. Early the next year he asked the commission to trim its next request for funding, now getting headlines as a careful fiscal manager. Ninety thousand dollars in federal funds were forthcoming and were used in 1936 for new branches in West Portal, opened in 1939, and Bernal Heights, opened in 1940.

With the return of economic optimism in the late 1930s, Rossi and the library commission developed ambitious plans to expand the branch system. In 1940 the commission completed a survey calling for five more branches—in North Beach, the Marina, the Outer Sunset, Potrero Hill, and Ingleside. The next year Rossi and Rea announced a plan to establish a branch in every public school to eliminate double purchasing of books by the schools and the library. These plans looked good on paper—and in the newspapers—but when North Beach residents launched a campaign for a new library in their neighborhood, Rossi merely said that he would consider their request.

The library lacked the funds to expand the system, and at first neither Rossi, nor Roger Lapham, who was elected to succeed Rossi as mayor in November 1943, nor the supervisors were interested in increasing the library's budget enough to carry out the branch-building plans. The city, anticipating the continuation of New Deal programs after the war, applied in 1943 for $437,000 in WPA funding for the construction of ten branches. The next year Lapham, looking to the peacetime needs of San Francisco, announced a six-year plan to spend $131.8 million on 277 public works projects, including $584,000 on new and existing branches. Federal funding for libraries, however, was a thing of the past and would not be revived until 1956. Instead Rea and the commission, looking to increase spending on the library starting in 1944, began to squirrel away funds for the branches.

This cartoon from a 1933 San Francisco News *reveals the level of public anxiety over Mayor Angelo Rossi's threatened major cuts in the library budget. When the budget was finally cut, the library was aided by federal and state relief projects.*

In 1934 thirty women were hired through the State Emergency Relief Administration to mend bound volumes of San Francisco newspapers.

Building branch libraries accomplished two things: it brought much-needed library service to the city's far-reaching neighborhoods, *and* it was good politics. Branch building, because of its political returns, may well have been the only way that the library commission could get the mayor and the supervisors to respond to the library's funding needs. The branches, particularly beginning with the construction of the Bernal Heights branch, served as more than libraries; they were community centers or, later, as in the Marina and the Outer Sunset, parts of a larger complex of community buildings. There was a definite limit, however, to the amount of money that the supervisors were willing to appropriate for the library. When Rea asked Mayor Lapham's charter revision committee in 1944 to raise the minimum tax rate for the library, the proposal was voted down. In a poignant letter, one of the librarians, Frances K. Langpaap, wrote to the *Chronicle* after the charter revision committee vote asking if the library was "to be treated forever as the orphan child of the city government."

Sadly, because of budget constraints, the building of branches was promoted at the expense of the main library, the veritable heart of the system. As early as 1938, Rea had noted that the main library was close to capacity and that the addition George Kelham had provided when he designed the library during World War I would soon have to be built. The library, in fact, reached capacity in 1943. Once again the city turned to the federal government and asked for $700,000 in its 1943 request from the WPA for an addition to the main library. When it became apparent that the federal well had run dry, the library commission with the support of the planning commission began plans for a bond measure to fund construction of an addition.

The postwar malaise that would lead to serious concerns about the viability of the country's public library system (see Chapter Four) had already set in at the library. In the immediate postwar era, city fathers faced the dismaying fact that the city's population had failed to grow at all since the beginning of the depression. It looked for a while as if San Francisco would continue to atrophy as new suburbs sprouted up around the Bay Area. But then the city's population began to grow and would increase dramatically; yet cardholding and circulation were declining. In this context the library was not an attractive funding opportunity for the city's politicians.

A Gadfly Emerges

In 1944 Nat Schmulowitz, who had been appointed a library commissioner in 1941, was elected president of the commission. He was well known in legal circles for his 1921 defense of Roscoe "Fatty" Arbuckle for the alleged rape of a "film starlet" during a wild party at the St. Francis Hotel. After two hung juries, the silent-movie comic was acquitted, although his movie career was doomed in the growing attack on Hollywood's hedonistic values.

Before he reappointed Schmulowitz to the library commission in 1944, Mayor Lapham asked for a list of suggestions about the library. Schmulowitz responded the next year with a scathing report that cast some revealing light on the inner workings of the library commission. Borrowing his metaphors from Jonathan Swift's *Battle of the Books,* he argued there was a group on the commission that treated books as sarcophagi for knowledge, the library as a cemetery, the librarian as an undertaker, and the commission and staff as honorary and active pallbearers. At the same time, another group took a more positive attitude that the library should cooperate with other community agencies to improve existing service and make excursions into new fields of service. Most progressive librarians and commissions were finding "new means and ways by which books will chase the readers instead of waiting for the readers to chase the books."

Further, Schmulowitz disclosed that he had found that a number of the commission's members were not even attending committee meetings. Their reports were prepared by the commission's secretary, Laurence J. Clarke, so that they could be read by the committee chairs at commission meetings. Commission members avoided contact with the staff and were not fully informed about the function of departments. Election of officers was a mechanical affair, jobs rotated according to seniority, and women declined to run for president of the commission. Schmulowitz found that, rather than develop a carefully thought-out way to get support from the mayor and the supervisors, commissioners generally accepted the attitude that they would be denied funds whatever they did.

Schmulowitz recommended that the commission undertake an outside survey of the library, something that did not happen for more than a decade. The only public response to Schmulowitz's blistering report was a defensive statement by commissioner George Kemper in the *San Francisco News:* "This report is full of inferences that things are wrong here at the library."

Schmulowitz continued to be a major supporter of the library even after his retirement from the commission. Afflicted with what he described as "a wonderful, wonderful disease," he started collecting humor books and magazines in the 1920s. On April Fool's Day, 1947, with a $500 check, he began to transfer to, and expand his collection as part of, the public library. The collection would eventually reach 17,000 books in thirty-five languages spanning four hundred years and become one of the greatest in the world.

Nine months after Schmulowitz's report, Robert Rea, who Schmulowitz made abundantly clear was not at fault for the library situation, resigned as city

Attorney Nat Schmulowitz served the library as a commissioner and was a founder of the first Friends of the Library. He caught the collector's disease and began assembling the Schmulowitz Collection of Wit and Humor, which he donated to the library in 1947. International selections from the 17,000-volume collection are shown below.

What Horton Hatched

My earliest memory is of sitting on my mother's lap listening to *Horton Hatches the Egg:*

I meant what I said
and I said what I meant,
an elephant's faithful
one hundred percent. . . .

(How good is my memory after fifty-seven years?) As the only child of a working-class family during the Great Depression, I was read to constantly, and sung to constantly, and talked to constantly.

Language and imagination were my companions.

Books in particular came to be magical instruments to me. My folks didn't have enough money to own many volumes, but my mother visited the Oildale branch of the Kern County Library weekly, frequently taking me with her. There I gazed at illustrated editions while she made her choices—both children's and adults' books each visit. As nearly as I can recall, she always allowed me one choice of my own.

Those books were revered in our house, often read aloud, frequently discussed by the adults, and I was taught to read before beginning classes at Standard School. As soon as I acquired my own library card—a rite of passage in my family rivaled only when I received my driver's license ten years later—I became a regular at our neighborhood library.

There I, like my pals, was encouraged and directed by generous ladies who seemed to believe that all we barefooted, we burnished, we generally disheveled kids were worthy of their hope. What we couldn't recognize (but those librarians certainly did), as we dug through dinosaur books and pirate yarns, was that we had begun the process of sharing the accumulated wisdom of our culture . . . indeed, of our species. That idea was far too remote and elevated to have crossed our minds at the time.

But that is exactly what we—Okies, Bloods, Chokers, whatever we were called then—were doing: building the foundation that has allowed us to participate in our shared culture. And in doing so, we have changed and shaped it. In our cultural hearts, we are all part African, all part Asian, all part European, all part of everything that filled those books that stirred our minds.

For me everything started with a faithful elephant sitting on a lazy bird's egg, and with my mother's voice. Sadly, Mom is no longer with us, but that egg continues hatching, a library's enduring legacy: mother to son, son to granddaughter, granddaughter to . . . the world, *faithful, one hundred percent.*

What Horton hatched for me was my life.

Gerald W. Haslam

librarian after fifty-six years with the library. Rea epitomized the provincialism of the public library in its middle years, a time when library policy forbid looking outside San Francisco for librarians. Without professional training, Rea worked his way up through the ranks and, having known no other library except San Francisco's, was suspicious, even hostile, when it came to the professional world of librarianship. Ultimately, he was a survivor, probably most of all because the library, with its problems and its accomplishments, was largely ignored.

THE MAIN DECLINES, THE BRANCHES SURVIVE

Upon Rea's resignation, Laurence J. Clarke, the secretary to the library commission, was appointed city librarian. Born in England, Clarke was a graduate of the University of San Francisco and the Library School at the University of California. He worked as a librarian from 1933 to 1937, when he took the job as commission secretary. As the 1928 survey of the library pointed out, the commission secretary was a kind of shadow city librarian. Consistent with the recommendation of the 1928 survey, there was a faction on the library commission that preferred to look for a new librarian outside of San Francisco. Ultimately the decision to appoint Clarke was made at a stormy meeting of the commission in Mayor Lapham's office after Lapham hurriedly reappointed commissioner George Kemper. In December 1945, Clarke became city librarian after a five-to-four vote by the commission.

A tall, debonair gentleman who favored a flower in his lapel, Clarke immediately called for more funds, more staff, a resurvey of the branch expansion plan, and improvements in the main library. Seemingly energized, Clarke asked for a $200,000 increase in his first budget, and he and the commission began planning to place a bond issue on the May 1946 ballot to raise funds for an addition to the main library. The bond issue, designated Proposition E, which soon became a more ambitious plan to raise $2.5 million for eighteen branches and an addition to the main library, did not reach the ballot until November 1948.

Meanwhile Clarke warned the supervisors that the library faced curtailment of its services due to a serious shortage of librarians because librarians had to be recruited in San Francisco. Clarke tried to reorganize the main library into departments, which had long been typical of most public libraries, but the supervisors cut the funding for his plans. In frustration the commission warned that the lack of funding was becoming a deterrent to wealthy patrons who wanted to donate books to the library. In addition the federal government threatened to stop providing government documents free of charge after it discovered that the library was not making the documents available to the public. Clarke and the commission hoped that their funding problems were only temporary and would

Laurence J. Clarke, city librarian from 1945 to 1960, served the library during its darkest hours. He is looking over bound volumes of the Alta California *newspaper.*

LIBRARIANS ORGANIZE

Left to right: Librarians Lorraine Fahs, Marian McCarthy, and Vivian Goodwin, who were active in the 1940 campaign to win civil service status for librarians.

One of the earliest signs of activism by the library's staff was the 1940 campaign by the San Francisco Public Library Staff Association to secure civil service status through a ballot measure. The city's librarians were notoriously underpaid, most of them making less than the telephone operators at City Hall. They chose, however, to seek job security as a way to secure higher wages and shorter hours at a later date. The campaign was headed by Ella Paine, who was supported by Stuart Boland, Harriet Collopy, Dick Fazackerley, Guspava Millinovich, Marian McCarthy (daughter of former Mayor P. H. McCarthy), Peter McCormick, Barbara Stevens (retired president of the staff association), Vivian Goodwin, and others. Employees leafleted and gave speeches at civic organizations. Support for the campaign was widespread, ranging from the Labor Council to the chamber of commerce. It ended with a motorcade on the night before the November 1940 election. The measure won by a margin of two to one.

be solved by the bond issue. They must have been encouraged by the widespread support coming from the Citizens Committee for Proposition E, the Central Council of Civic Clubs, and numerous other organizations. But in the end the measure failed by the infinitesimal margin of 12,000 votes. As a consolation prize, the library received a temporary office building at 45 Hyde Street, which the Navy had constructed during the war and intended to tear down. (The library was still using the building in 1995.)

After the failure of the bond measure, the library commission carefully assessed the library's strengths and weaknesses. The collection was strong in general reference, California and western Americana, and rare books. The music collection was rated third in the nation, the art collection fifth. But the main library was "crowded to the point of inefficiency," and there was insufficient room to house these collections. Moreover, the book-buying budget had been flat for ten years.

Demands on the library had grown to the point where "complaints from the public and petitions for service from districts of the city have long since become a chronic condition." Reference work was hindered by civil service regulations that kept reference librarians at the lowest pay grade and then forced them to leave the department to find better-paying jobs. Government documents were stored in the basement still in their original cartons. On the brighter side, funds were already allocated for the construction of four new branches, which were built over the next decade: Parkside (1951), Potrero Hill (1951), Marina (1954), and North Beach (1959). Without funding to do much else, Clarke was deeply involved in the construction and design of new branches.

"The history of the library," the commission concluded, "clearly shows the lack of interest by the City Administration in the building up of library service. . . . Unless a realization of the Library's important function to the community, particularly by the Board of Supervisors, is forthcoming, the type of service will continue to deteriorate."

The commission's desperate wake-up call to city hall went unanswered. However, it is important to note that the library was only one of many city institutions that were in poor condition. During the Great Depression and World War II, the city's infrastructure—schools, hospitals, municipal railway—was sorely neglected. Only after the election of Mayor George Christopher in 1955 did city hall begin to attack maintenance that had been deferred for too long.

A number of citizens did respond to the library commission's plea for support. At the instigation of Mrs. Lucille Mohr, who was appointed to the library commission by Lapham in 1944, a meeting was called in December 1949 to form the Friends of the Library. Clarke and the commission were heartened by the appearance of 160 people, a larger number than expected. Nat Schmulowitz chaired the meeting, and Dr. Albert Shumate, who was to give up his medical practice to become a historian, was elected president of the new organization. In his remarks Schmulowitz touted the organization as one without a

constitution, dues, and bylaws. This informality may well have been the organization's undoing. According to Shumate, the organization accomplished little, and its members' interest soon faded.

A banner above a dentist's office reads, "Vote Yes on E, 18 new branches for our city. E is for everyone." Despite widespread support, Proposition E lost by a very narrow margin in November 1948. It took forty years to get another library bond measure on the ballot.

The consequences of the library's continued decline were soon felt. Just before the 1948 bond vote, Moore S. Achenbach, a local advertising executive, announced that he and his wife were giving their collection of 100,000 prints covering five hundred years—a collection that included works by Dürer, Van Dyck, Rembrandt, Hogarth, Goya, Whistler, and Picasso—to the public library. Achenbach stipulated in his agreement with the library that the library would provide a separate room, a curator, and funds to increase the size of the collection. The Achenbach gift was a coup for the library, giving it a world-class print collection to enhance its already strong art book collection. A curator was hired in 1950—at the same time that the supervisors eliminated the commission's request for eight new librarians—but by 1951 the Achenbachs, who were supporters of the Friends, decided that the library was not the appropriate place for their collection. It was moved to the art museum at the Palace of the Legion of Honor.

Gradually library service was curtailed. First came the closing of certain branches on Saturday nights starting in 1949. By 1952 the main library and all branches were closed on Saturday nights and then on Sundays for want of $12,000 in a year when Mayor Elmer Robinson made almost all of his cuts in the city's budget from the library's. Library buildings deteriorated as the library's carpenter and painter were cut from the budget. Conditions at the library did draw the attention of the press. Unflattering, but sympathetic articles describing the decline of the library began to appear regularly in the city's newspapers.

FALSE HOPES FOR A NEW LIBRARY

Clarke and the library commissioners still dreamed of doing something about the main library. They were heartened by discussions about expansion of the Civic Center. Since the end of the war numerous proposals had been floated by the city,

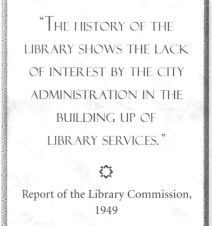

"THE HISTORY OF THE LIBRARY SHOWS THE LACK OF INTEREST BY THE CITY ADMINISTRATION IN THE BUILDING UP OF LIBRARY SERVICES."

✣

Report of the Library Commission, 1949

During World War II the library joined the war effort. The American Women's Voluntary Service operated a bookmobile, containing six hundred public library books, that visited schools and community centers at the huge housing complex for war workers at Hunters Point.

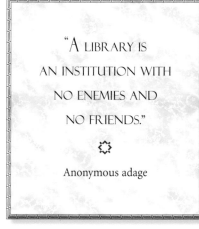

"A library is an institution with no enemies and no friends."

Anonymous adage

state, and federal governments calling for office buildings, fire and police department headquarters, new courtrooms, and a cultural center for the visual arts, music, and drama. They all boiled down to the fact that a growing city needed more space for its administrative and cultural activities.

In 1953, after holding hearings, the Department of City Planning published *An Introductory Plan for the Civic Center.* The city's planners were no longer enamored with the grand architectural gestures of the École des Beaux-Arts. The construction of the Civic Center marked an era when "the search for a native architectural style had hardly begun . . . when the greatest achievement in civic reconstruction, the opening of the boulevards of Paris by Haussmann, was still fresh and accepted uncritically as a model for all civic building endeavors."

Calling for "new buildings of simple and straightforward design," city planning proposed a major expansion of the Civic Center which would double its acreage by surrounding the present buildings with modern ones in order to accommodate all the demands made by different government agencies. Included in the proposal was a new courtroom building in Marshall Square just to the south of the main library.

Knowing that the Hall of Justice, then located on Kearny Street downtown, would eventually have to be moved, Clarke proposed turning the main library into the Hall of Justice and building a new, more functional library in Marshall Square, which was bounded by Fulton, Hyde, Grove, and Larkin. "I learned long ago," Clarke said to a *Chronicle* reporter about the main library, "that what was grandeur in 1917 is just so much waste space today."

Rebuffed again, Clarke and the commission scaled back their assessment of the library's needs. All that was required in a new bond measure, they argued, were funds for an internal reorganization of the main library. The library failed, however, to achieve even this limited goal, for a new bond measure placed before the voters in 1953 was turned down, again by a slight margin. After this, Clarke and the commissioners essentially gave up on the main library. With San Francisco librarians required to do four times the work of librarians in comparable systems in other cities and patrons at the main library enduring outrageously long waits (often six months to a year) for books, like best-sellers, that had to be reserved, the commission predicted that the main library would become "a warehouse research center and servicing department for the branch library system." They anticipated that the Children's Department would eventually be moved out of the main library, and that any increases in circulation would come through the branches.

Clarke's gloomy state of mind was clearly reflected in a series on the library that appeared in the *Chronicle* in August 1952. Citing the old saying "a library is an institution with no enemies and no friends," he noted, "We know what

SIGNS OF LIFE

HERE IS WHY we must join together to do everything in our power to keep our libraries open and thriving: because when a country's libraries close, it means the barbarians are truly at the gate. Open libraries are signs of life and hope; they are the cornerstone of democracy. They mean you can think and wander and discover and read and reread at will, and no one is telling you what to learn or think, and no one is looking over your shoulder. There is something holy about this. It is a communion of thought and experience and action. During the Dark Ages, the only glimmer of light came from the monasteries, where the monks painstakingly kept the great books alive, making copies one by one, word by word.

When I was a child, my family went to the Tiburon-Belvedere branch of the Marin County Free Library every single Thursday night, to stock up on books for the coming week. In books I found solace and direction and light, and dizzying enjoyment. Now I have a five-year-old boy, who got his first library card last month. When the librarian handed the card to him, he clutched it to his chest and closed his eyes, like he had just won something, which, of course, he had. The librarian and I looked at each other, and smiled.

That night in bed, when he said his prayers, he gave thanks for his library card; he really did, and I did, too.

Libraries won't necessarily make everyone believe in God, but faithfully attended, they do make people believe in infinite possibility, and intimacy, and wonder. If someday they are no longer open, all we will have left are five hundred cable stations: watching infomercials will be the order of the day. When libraries are no longer open, the light might not have gone off entirely in the world, but it will indeed have become dangerously dim.

Anne Lamott

San Francisco's Hyde Park

Men gather on the south side of the library in the 1950s.

In the 1930s, when the unemployed flocked to the main library in droves, Fulton Street, to the south of the library, became San Francisco's Hyde Park, a place where radical orators mounted their soapboxes and people gathered to debate the issues of the day. As the years went by and the area remained a gathering place for the unemployed, the library became concerned about the use by large numbers of "indigents" of the newspaper reading room and the men's lavatory, both of which in those days were located on the first floor near the Children's Department. Librarians Larry Clarke and William Holman tried unsuccessfully in the 1950s and 1960s to rid the library of these regulars. Beginning in the 1970s the number of homeless people using the library rose dramatically, and today the homeless are accepted, if reluctantly, as regular library patrons.

❖

the library needs, and we know how much it will cost. What we don't know is whether the people want it. If the handful of letters that come to the Mayor and the Board of Supervisors is any indication, people don't much care." Clarke compared the library with the city's other cultural institutions: "If the opera or the symphony, or the art gallery were in a bad way, the music and art lovers would stir up such a row, you could hear them from Twin Peaks to Telegraph Hill."

A Library in Disgrace

In 1957 the *Chronicle* ran another series under the headline "Public Library . . . Disgrace to S.F." More sustained editorial than reportage and biting at that, the articles by Hale Champion repeated most of the criticisms that were familiar to anyone who had read earlier newspaper stories or the commission's and librarian's reports for the past decade. Under the headline "Librarian, Others Share Blame," Clarke and to a limited extent unnamed mayors took the blame. The "others" remained anonymous. Champion brought up Clarke's appointment over "a storm of oral and written protest" from those commissioners who had wanted to conduct a nationwide search for a librarian. Champion characterized Clarke as an affable bumbler who "directed most of his attention to the building program for new branches." Champion either had not read or had chosen to ignore the candid critiques and detailed plans for dealing with the problems of the main library which Clarke and the library commission sent regularly to at least two mayors and the board of supervisors, who ignored them, and twice put before the voters, who turned them down.

Whatever the intentions of Champion's articles, they did cause enough of a stir that efforts were begun over the next two years which would finally lead to major changes in the library, including Clarke's departure. The library commission, meeting within the month after the series was published, voted to request funds from the supervisors to conduct a survey of the library. It took the clerk of the board of supervisors *four months* to write back to say that the finance committee did not have sufficient information about the need for the survey to provide the $7,500 sought by the commission. Finally, on May 15, 1958, the funds were released, enabling the library commission to hire Emerson Greenaway to conduct a survey. Greenaway was one of the most eminent of American public librarians. Having served as head librarian at the Enoch Pratt Free Library in Baltimore, he was chief librarian at the Philadelphia Public Library and president of the American Library Association.

The Greenaway report, delivered in October 1958, contained no surprises: the library lacked funds, books, trained professionals, and a functional main library. Greenaway's most significant recommendations were to create a committee of prominent citizens to study, support, and publicize the library; to reorganize the library by departments; to take immediate steps to buy more books; to hire an architect and library consultant to make recommendations for the rehabilitation of the main library; to hire more professional librarians; and to increase in-house training for the staff. According to Greenaway, the lack of trained staff was the library's greatest weakness. Over the next five years he recommended that the library hire 127 trained librarians while increasing its overall budget by $120,000 a year.

The library commission's immediate task was to prepare a budget for 1959–60 on the basis of the Greenaway report. Having received $1,607,754 for 1958–59, the library requested $1,953,311. The increase was more than double what Greenaway had recommended, but the commissioners hoped that the release of the Greenaway report would enhance their prospects with the board of supervisors. Included in the request were funds for sixteen new employees and $115,000 for new books. The supervisors approved a budget of $1,782,360, agreeing to fund four new positions and to put $65,000 in the book-buying fund. Although the supervisors approved far more than Greenaway had suggested as a target for annual increases, the additional funds went not to meet the library's needs but, as required by the city charter, to pay for salary increases for a staff that was sorely underpaid. The library commission tried valiantly to put the best face it could on what amounted to a rejection by the supervisors of Greenaway's most important recommendations.

Meanwhile Mayor George Christopher joined the fray. In early 1959 he announced that he would seek a $15 million bond issue for renovation of the Nourse Civic Auditorium and the main library, rebuilding the Palace of Fine Arts, and construction of Ferry Plaza (later Justin Hermann Plaza) at the foot of Market Street. Christopher's recommendation was in part an outgrowth of a plan for the Civic Center, published in August 1958, which added detail to the broad-brush proposal put together by the Department of City Planning in 1953. The Civic Center plan called for a first phase, the most important elements of which were the construction of a new civil courts building in Marshall Square, the remodeling of City Hall and the civic auditorium, and the completion and rehabilitation of the main library.

At the same time Christopher, in line with Greenaway's recommendation, appointed a Committee of Fifty to build support for the library and encouraged the

Headlines from the 1957 San Francisco Chronicle *series by Hale Champion that led to the first study of the library by an outside consultant since 1928 and the resignation of librarian Laurence Clarke. Many of those who fought for a new main library regard the series as the event that triggered the thirty-one-year struggle for a new main library.*

A TOY SHOP FOR THE MIND

❋

MY MOTHER FIRST TOOK ME to a library. I must have been very small, only four or five, because I remember the immensity of what was really just an ordinary building in an ordinary Long Island town. I remember the huge silence of the place, too, a sort of reverential calm like the one I knew from church, and I tried hard as I browsed not to make any noise. Books for young children are often quite thin, composed more of pictures than of sentences, and I could not believe how many of them I got to take home —dozens, it seemed, and all for free. That appealed to my greedy instincts. The library, I understood even then, was a toy shop for the mind.

In a way, my mother had created a monster. As I grew older, I demanded a trip to our library three or four times a week, devouring the Hardy Boys' mystery novels and any book about baseball or basketball, my favorite sports. I developed a habit of reading aloud in the kitchen every evening, entertaining my mother with, say, choice anecdotes from the life of Mickey Mantle while she slaved over our dinner. That she tolerated such performances stands as testimony to her belief in the power of the word. It was a belief I was beginning to share. Books, I saw, could transport a reader, could comfort him and fill him with dreams.

So the library became a kind of sanctuary for me. I visited it whenever I needed to know something, whenever I felt baffled or curious or in doubt about the relevance of a piece of information that I had gathered at random. Sometimes I went simply for the quiet, escaping from my family for a while to rest in a public space where, oddly, privacy was encouraged. On our high school basketball court, I had learned to be a team player, but at the library I searched out a sense of my own individuality. Like most teenagers, I was awkward, shy, and deeply protective of my many horrible secrets, so it did me a world of good to stumble on such writers as Jack Kerouac and William Burroughs, who were telling *their* horrible secrets in public. Maybe it's okay, I thought, to be a little weird.

Libraries convey to us, then, the beautiful richness and diversity that we share as human beings. We are all the same and yet all a little different, all a little weird. That is the great strength of our species—it is how we evolve. There have been times when a book has saved me, quite literally, when a voice rising from the pages has kept me from feeling entirely alone. I could survive without a library nearby, I suppose, but it would make for a lesser existence.

Bill Barich

library commission to ask for increased funding from the supervisors. The membership list for the Committee of Fifty read like a registry of the city's most prominent families and business, educational, and cultural leaders. There were Fleishhackers, Rosekranses, Slosses, Spreckelses, and Zellerbachs. There were people from the Bank of America, Pacific Gas and Electric, and the chamber of commerce. There were well-known bookstore owners like Warren Howell and David Magee; fine printers like Robert Grabhorn; opera director Kurt Herbert Adler; and even a publisher from the local office of the McGraw-Hill Book Company.

The committee met for the first time in April 1959 and drew up a list of proposals that focused on the main library. They found that patrons were deterred by the lack of parking in the Civic Center, which, they pointed out, was going to be solved by the completion of a new garage under the Civic Center plaza. Patrons were also fearful of the "casuals," elderly men, most of them unemployed, who lived in the area and could regularly be found sitting on the ledge on the south side of the library. The committee called for an elaborate reorganization of space in the main library and the formation of a subcommittee to solicit books from the public.

The Committee of Fifty formed another subcommittee to discuss the future of the main library. In May the subcommittee announced its recommendations. The main library was "a real white elephant" that was too antiquated to be used as a library. But the subcommittee opposed a bond issue for rehabilitation. In their list of priorities, decisions about the future of the main library should come last. "Why build a new building until we have books and a staff?" the subcommittee asked.

The library commission, however, decided to proceed with discussions about the rehabilitation of the main library. In October 1959, the city planning commission, at the request of the library commission, rewrote an earlier study calling for expansion of the main library and relocation or remodeling of a number of the older branches. The planning commission report was used as a basis to request funds for a study of the main library as recommended by Greenaway.

Chronicle cartoon that accompanied the Hale Champion series. Library patrons were burdened by an antiquated closed-stack system that required librarians and pages to bring books from the shelves. The wait for a popular book often stretched to six months.

A CITY AND ITS LIBRARY IN TRANSITION

In an attempt to start somewhere, the Committee of Fifty announced a drive to solicit books for the library. But in December 1959, the committee reported that

The Co-existence Bagel Shop in North Beach, beatnik gathering place in the 1950s. City Lights bookstore, founded in the same neighborhood in 1952 by Lawrence Ferlinghetti and Peter Martin, published many of the Beat writers, including, shown below on the cover of City Lights Journal, *Michael McClure, Allen Ginsberg, Richard Brautigan, and Ferlinghetti.*

it could not proceed with the drive because there was not enough staff at the library to catalogue the books that were being contributed. Understaffed and using antiquated methods, the catalogue department was months behind in its work. Ultimately it was found that 100,000 books were not catalogued, including all new books bought for the branches. This relatively minor conflict proved to be the beginning of the end for Laurence Clarke. Clarke was given an ultimatum in April 1960: report back in a month about how he planned to streamline the cataloguing process.

It quickly became clear that key members of the library commission had lost confidence in Clarke. According to the *Chronicle,* Clarke was scolded by the commission for failing to carry out the recommendations of the Greenaway report. Then on April 14, 1960, Christopher held an emergency meeting of the library commission in his office. Two hours later he and commissioner Rose Fannucchi emerged to tell reporters that "the library department has encountered administrative problems that have not been resolved" and that the commission expected to take definitive actions to correct the problem. Clarke was privately asked to resign or be fired.

Clarke did not go without making some final comments: "I had been making the same recommendations for ten years before Greenaway came here. Each time our budget requests were slashed." To emphasize his point, he referred to the library's latest budget request: the library asked for twenty-seven new employees (Greenaway suggested he request fifty-seven); Mayor Christopher had supported four. The supervisors had also cut funding for $25,000 in equipment needed to modernize the cataloguing process.

Memory Tomes (1958–1959)

I AM IN THE BIG READING ROOM where the reference books are kept. There are oversized volumes of art and architecture and science. I am at the large, polished wooden table near the center of the room and the gray San Francisco light of summer is coming through the windows. A volume of the lithographs of the turn-of-the-century French artist Odilon Redon is open in front of me. Redon's visionary heads and faces float in space on the pages; angels and roses mix together in shades of black and white and gray stippling. I turn the pages, absorbing the painter's ideas. I am troubled and I come here almost every day to give myself a task; to help keep my thoughts in order.

After looking at the Redon lithographs I go to a textbook of morphology. It helps me understand; I am interested in learning to grow, and how I may *literally* hold myself together. In the morphology book are illustrations of simple algae, and complicated patterns of flat colonial algaes evolving to make a single larger, coherent being. There are drawings of *volvox,* which are algae colonies that have become one organism and formed themselves into a sphere with other spheres of "child" volvoxes floating inside of them. The individual cells of the volvox are specialized and cooperative. The text is on soft paper. The words give me an idea of how I am one being and yet have many beings inside myself.

The library has a special still quietness. There is the calming smell of the oil and the sawdust used to clean the floors. Earlier, when I came in, I walked up the long flight of steps, taking several steps at a time to feel the strength in my legs. I enjoyed passing the tall murals of idealized California landscapes. These murals fit—even as old-fashioned as they are.

I hopped on a bus and rode down here. Now I'm out of money but I will walk back; my head is clearing. There are organizing thoughts in my mind. Before leaving, I go to the card catalogue to order books from the closed shelves. I ask for a spiritual text by Jacob Böhme and a book on alchemy. A self-contained, firm-spoken woman brings them. Holding the old, dark blue book in my hand, I look at Böhme's words again. I believe, as Böhme does, that our world is the rubbing together of a golden universe with a dark fire world. In the alchemical text there are explanations of the *negredo* and the *imago* and other transformations. This is a language to understand.

On other days I take down the dictionaries of argot, and archaic words, and especially the Old English dictionaries. There are many feelings that I do not have words for—I find the words for them here.

Michael McClure

Cartoon from the Chronicle, *April 13, 1960, depicting the library as a wallflower while other aspects of city life dance away. Two years after the Greenaway report, which called for dramatic increases in funds and staffing, little had been done to rebuild the library.*

Up until Clarke's last year, both the grand jury and the Committee of Fifty had made a point of praising Clarke's efforts in a very difficult situation. Mayor Christopher said in 1995, however, that he had lost confidence in Clarke before the Greenaway report. Whatever the case, the blame was focused on Clarke, and he was asked to fall on his sword. He had taken the job as librarian in the midst of controversy; he left in the same atmosphere.

Clarke had been librarian for a San Francisco that had been set in its ways for decades, but was on the cusp of fundamental changes. It was a city of working-class ethnic neighborhoods, more Irish and Catholic than anything else, a city whose sons and daughters often followed a well-worn path from parochial school to city government, whether it be city hall, the police and fire departments, or the library. It was a city with a small, firmly entrenched business elite, intermarried and intermingled, more Jewish, Irish, and Italian than WASP. San Francisco was a union town where Harry Bridges dominated the waterfront, a low-rise city of powerful corporations that had looked for the most part to California and the West, and were now looking outward in the expansionist fifties to the Pacific Basin. With its fine ballet, symphony, and opera, the city enjoyed a surfeit of cultural riches, although the opera and symphony were having their own financial problems.

Rapid transformations were on their way. The Giants had come to town, making San Francisco a major-league baseball city. New high-rises loomed downtown, and a new generation of writers, some of them called Beats, were making their way to this Paris on the Pacific, some to stay, some to pass through. Always a city of good bookstores, San Francisco was once again a city aspiring to be at the center of a young publishing industry. Whatever it was, it was not a library town.

Clarke served the library at a time when all of the staff had to be local, and much of it was, as he was, Catholic, when members of the church hierarchy were regular visitors to his office. Only 18 of the 110 employees were professionally trained librarians; many of the rest lacked even a college degree. Employees were often the relatives of city officials or other persons with connections to city hall. Employees from the Rea and Clarke eras describe the library as a congenial place to work—like a large family, said one—despite the poor pay, long hours, and atmosphere of neglect. People came to work out of high school or college, often found spouses there, and remained for their entire working career. Although Clarke publicly supported additional training for his staff, he told a staff meeting in the spring of 1959 that he had successfully resisted pressure from the city's general manager of personnel to require future librarians to have masters degrees in library science. This requirement, he argued, would undermine staff morale.

Clarke was a cautious administrator who was not averse to occasional acts of censorship. In 1946 he backed a drive against obscene books, stating that the library occasionally bought books based on an author's reputation only to find that they were degrading. These books were immediately withheld from circulation. In the same year it was revealed by *Chronicle* columnist Herb Caen that, when a city prosecutor went to the library requesting a copy of Edmund Wilson's *Memoirs of Hecate County* with its explicit sexuality, Clarke was keeping six copies in the safe. Six years later Clarke removed a book titled *USA-Confidential* from the shelves, saying that the portion about San Francisco was an example of poor writing. When the American Civil Liberties Union protested, Clarke argued that he was returning the book to its publisher because of lack of shelf space.

According to a number of his associates, Clarke's problem was that he was too close to city hall—too eager to grant favors, but not forceful enough to gain political support from three mayors and the board of supervisors. He was asked to command a ship whose rigging was gradually being stripped away by indifferent politicians. Clarke repeatedly offered the city plans to refit his vessel. Whether he could have done it if he had been given the funds early in his career remains an unanswered question. He was not to be given the chance.

The San Francisco skyline in the 1950s before the beginning of Manhattanization. The Top of the Mark in the Mark Hopkins Hotel (tallest structure to the left) was the fashionable spot from which to view the city while sipping cocktails.

CHAPTER EIGHT

BATTLES WON AND LOST

❖

Two Decades of Activism and Promise

The resignation of chief librarian Laurence J. Clarke in April 1960 added to the unsettled atmosphere in and around the library. Clarke had been popular with his staff. More than half of them, at the instigation of William Ramirez, who was head of the Library Staff Association, greeted his resignation with a telegram expressing

William R. Holman, city librarian from 1960 to 1967. Holman never forgot the comment made by library commission president Albert Schwabacher Jr. when Holman, then in his late thirties, acknowledged that he was "rather young" for the job. "Well, I think we need someone who's young and foolish and doesn't know what the hell he's getting into," Schwabacher replied.

Preceding pages: Front entrance of the old main library, which served as the flagship of the city's library system from 1917 to 1995.

confidence in his leadership. Part-time librarians were organizing in response to the job threat posed by Emerson Greenaway's recommendation in his 1958 report that part-time workers be replaced by full-time employees. With the librarians' qualifications and some of the library's more arcane practices the subject of repeated press criticism, many staff members were feeling demoralized.

In September 1960 the commission reported that it had hired William R. Holman, the director of the San Antonio Public Library. Holman, a young Oklahoman, had just turned thirty-six. Educated at the University of Oklahoma and holding a library science degree from the University of Illinois, Holman had worked at a small college library before serving as director of the Rosenberg Library in Galveston, Texas, which is known for its excellent collection of Southwestern historical materials. After that, Holman led the successful effort to transform the San Antonio Public Library into an award-winning institution with a reputation for public outreach.

A tall, lanky man with a decided drawl, Holman blew into town like a breath of fresh air. He held his first press conference even before being sworn in. Describing him among themselves as "Billy the Kid" and "the bookish Paladin," reporters were taken aback by what one described as his "rapid-fire straight-from-the-shoulder answers" and self-confidence "to the point of brashness."

Holman was deeply impressed by San Francisco, particularly its bookstores. "There are more good bookstores here than in the entire state of Texas," he told one reporter. "San Francisco is a bookish, unique city," he concluded, "and it certainly doesn't deserve a third-rate library."

Holman found a main library that, according to the grand jury, was gloomy, soiled, and odoriferous, a sort of skid-row hostel that provided public lavatories for the homeless, a building that was out-of-date from the standpoint of efficiency, a monument to wasted space. Additionally, only 1,500 books had been checked out from the main library in 1959, a dramatic decline from the 12,000 that had been checked out annually in previous years. The bulk of the collection at the main library remained in closed stacks, accessible only through a paging system or on those rare occasions when a librarian would escort a patron into the stacks. The library was organized not by subject but largely according to types of books (reference, fiction, nonfiction, government documents), an organization that, along with closed stacks, had long ago disappeared from public libraries.

Holman, in his first appearance before the library commission in December 1960, requested an emergency appropriation to deal with the backlog in the cataloguing department. On one of his first days in the library, Holman had asked for six well-known titles. The librarians could find only three of them; the other three were not checked out. After a closer look, Holman estimated that the catalogue department was three to five years behind in its work. Thousands of index cards were missing, and tens of thousands of books, including all the books acquired for branch libraries since 1957, had not been catalogued.

The emergency appropriation was not forthcoming; Holman would have to wait until the next year's budgeting process to receive additional funding. He nevertheless pushed ahead, laying out his plans for the library in a letter to the library commission president. First he had to inventory the collection, simply to find out what was in the library. The cataloguing operation had to be modernized. Librarians had to be shifted out of clerical work, and their work week shortened to five days and forty hours. The collection had to be reorganized and opened as much as possible to the public. Finally, funds were needed to survey the main library to assess whether it should be rebuilt or abandoned.

Holman's first encounter with the supervisors was an eye-opener. As the only city department head from out of town and a young man with an alien accent, he was at a decided disadvantage, recalled Vivian Goodwin, who would become one of his chief lieutenants. When Holman appeared before the supervisors' finance committee in April 1961, he asked for funding for nine new positions at the library. He was cut off in midsentence by a supervisor who snorted, "Welfare!" Ultimately, the supervisors approved a budget of $2,183,479, a small increase over the previous year. Without sufficient funds for new staff, Holman was forced in August 1961 to close the library on Sundays.

The Friends Reorganize

While Holman was fighting the perennial budget battle, the various citizen support groups were pulling themselves together into a single organization. George and Sally Williams had been inspired to start a library support organization in April 1960 after they decided to read the entire works of Ernest Hemingway and had found only a limited number of his novels at the main library and a general lack of accessibility to the fiction collection. Outraged by conditions at the library, Williams and his wife formed San Franciscans for a Better Library with Jack and Judith Pollatsek and William Mackey.

Simultaneously, the Committee of Fifty was shedding those who had lent their names on behalf of the library, but had little time for work, and was shaking down into a group of activists. During the spring of 1961, a large group from

This conveyor belt was part of the modern cataloguing process installed at the main library under city librarian William Holman in 1962. For want of $25,000 worth of equipment, the cataloguing process had broken down completely in the late 1950s, leading to the resignation of city librarian Laurence J. Clarke.

Margaret Mayer, Mary Louise Stong, and Marjorie Stern (left to right)—known as the "three Ms"—photographed in 1995, the thirty-fourth year of their fight for a new main library. Principal leaders of the struggle to build a new library, Stern and Stong were founders of the Friends of the Library. Mayer was its first director.

the committee and the original Friends of the Library, joined by other library supporters, met at the home of Mortimer and Janet Fleishhacker Jr. to discuss forming a new support organization. They included Holman, Marjorie Stern, Mary Louise Stong, John Bransten, Lucille Mohr, William Mackey, and Jack Pollatsek. With advice from the Blyth-Zellerbach Committee, the elite business group that was shaping San Francisco's redevelopment effort, and Walter Haas, the patriarch of the family that owned Levi Strauss, these library supporters put together a list of founding sponsors that read like a who's who of San Francisco: Mrs. Nion Tucker from the family that owns the *Chronicle;* Mrs. Dean Witter, whose husband founded the famous brokerage house; Mr. and Mrs. R. Gwin Follis (Follis was chairman of Standard Oil Company of California); Mr. and Mrs. John Bransten of the MJB coffee family; Mr. and Mrs. Albert Schwabacher Jr. (Schwabacher was another well-known broker); Mr. and Mrs. J. D. Zellerbach (of the Crown-Zellerbach Paper Company); Mrs. Walter Haas; and Dr. and Mrs. Frank Gerbode. Despite the list of powerful personalities, "funds were difficult to raise," recalled Alan K. Browne, the Bank of America vice president who served as the first president of the Friends of the Library, "and the [Friends'] objective had low priority in the city's budgetary process."

In April, after some contentious negotiations, San Franciscans for a Better Library—a younger, seemingly more confrontational support group—merged with the new support organization, which at first called itself the San Francisco Library League. In June, the league held its first public meeting at the Officers' Club in the Presidio and then in February 1962 reorganized with 177 sponsoring members and a treasury of $2,000 as the Friends of the San Francisco Public Library. Browne was elected president; General E. L. Johnson, first vice president; Marjorie Stern, second vice president; Jack Pollatsek, third vice president; William Mackey, treasurer; and Mary Louise Stong, secretary.

Over time, Marjorie Stern and Mary Louise Stong, later joined by the Friends' first full-time, paid director, Margaret Mayer—collectively known as the "three Ms"—would emerge as the core of the new organization's leadership. Stern's father, Morgan A. Gunst, was a well-known local book collector, who chose to give his collection to Stanford University because of the lack of enticements at San Francisco's public library. Stern got her first taste of activism when she led the campaign that brought the Avery Brundage collection of Asian art to the de Young Museum. Because of her close work with Mayor Christopher on this effort, Christopher appointed her to the Committee of Fifty, where she played a key role in organizing the Friends.

Mary Louise Stong was a member of a library family from the San Joaquin Valley: her grandfather founded the Porterville Public Library. Stong was working at the United States Steel Company when she met Lucille Mohr at a party. Mohr recruited her in 1957 as secretary-treasurer of the original Friends. Stern and Stong would serve the library for the next thirty-four years as officers of the Friends, library commissioners, lobbyists, and campaigners for a new main library.

Margaret Mayer started as a volunteer at the Friends' book sale and then joined the Friends as a part-time staff member in 1966. She was working with Stern raising funds for her college alumnae association when Stern got a look at Mayer's extensive list of contacts and immediately asked Mayer to work in the Friends' office. Mayer became the full-time director in 1967.

The Friends of the Library's annual book sale, shown here in 1976, became both a significant fund-raiser and a major West Coast book event.

The Friends' first efforts were varied. They helped furnish the new Rare Book Room, bought uniforms for the guards at the main library, continued the San Franciscans for a Better Library's program for shut-ins, and garnered contributions for a small scholarship fund for librarians. In 1962, with $10,000 from the Merrill Trust, their first large grant, the Friends launched a newsletter, *Among Friends,* and the next year established a modest acquisition fund. More significantly, by helping to organize and publicize a series of literary programs at the main library, the Friends attracted thousands of San Franciscans to a building that had been all but abandoned. Starting with a panel on censorship, the Friends brought Aldous Huxley, Christopher Isherwood, Mary McCarthy, Wallace Stegner, and numerous other writers to the library. For the first time in its existence, the library began to play a central role in the city's literary life.

The Friends was committed to publicizing the situation at the library while building up a membership organization that would provide grassroots support for the library. "After all," said Marjorie Stern, who was chairing the Friends' membership committee, "what is really needed to make our library system an excellent one is solid citizen support." She noted that cultural support groups in San Francisco turned repeatedly to the same small group of people. "We tried hard to get out in the community for support from every section of the population. We believe that every citizen has a responsibility to the library."

Additionally, the Friends was committed to raising funds for the library, but not, according to a Friends internal document, "to make up for the city government's indifference because the usual reward was to simply reduce the budget by the amount of the private support and to unload basic responsibility for public library services on private, rather than public, resources." Beside membership

"A LIBRARY
SHOULD HAVE
SOME PERSONALITY,
JUST LIKE AN
INDIVIDUAL."

✿

William R. Holman, 1994

FRONTLINE DEFENDERS

❈

I'VE BECOME INCREASINGLY AWARE of the role of librarians as frontline defenders of the First Amendment in an era when censorship of books and speech presents a growing threat.

A few years ago I was invited by the Ohoopee Public Library in Vidalia, Georgia, to speak as part of a symposium on death. These deathly meetings were scheduled to be held every Tuesday, addressed by experts in various fields. I was the leadoff speaker on the subject of the death industries.

Vidalia is a tiny community, so small that even people in Savannah, one hundred miles away, have hardly heard of it. But when my forthcoming lecture was announced, the American Legion attacked with full force. They sent out press releases denouncing the Ohoopee Public Library for giving a platform to a known radical, citing reports on me from the early 1950s by the House Committee on Un-American Activities. This made the front pages of the Savannah newspapers.

The Ohoopee librarians fought back: "Everybody can have his or her say at the Ohoopee Public Library!" was their battle cry, duly recorded in the Savannah press. To underline this point, they sent special invitations and free tickets for the lecture to all the funeral directors and allied industries in the area.

As a result of this unexpected barrage of publicity, the lecture was moved from a small meeting hall to the high school auditorium. The chairman led off, reiterating the library's free speech stand in the now familiar refrain:

"EVERYBODY can have his or her say at the Ohoopee Public Library." And were there any representatives of the funeral profession in the audience? he asked, upon which twelve black suits sitting together in a row got up in unison and sat down.

My talk was well received. Announcing the question period, I followed the lead of the chairman: "First, I should like to hear from any member of the funeral profession who may have a question." A black suit rose to his feet. "I am a vault man. I sell vaults. I've listened to Miss Mitford's speech and she never mentioned that when Jesus Christ our Lord was crucified, a rich man gave him his vault." And he sat down. I replied that I am well aware of the story of Joseph of Arimathea, who gave his vault to Jesus; but I added that if you read on, Jesus didn't stay there long; he was up and out in three days.

The outraged vault man shouted to his colleagues, "Let's go!" upon which the twelve black suits filed out of the hall. It was a tense moment: would the rest of the audience follow? After all, Vidalia is in the deepest Bible Belt. But not a soul stirred. They all wanted to stay around to discuss the depredations of the funeral salesmen. A most enjoyable evening, I reflected, made possible through the courage of the Ohoopee librarians.

Jessica Mitford

Jessica Mitford

fees, which were kept low to attract a wide range of supporters, the Friends found that their annual book sale, begun in 1964, was the most significant source of funds. The $4,000 raised that year were placed in a fund to purchase rare and unusual items in honor of Mayor Christopher. In time the sale grew into one of the most important book sales in the West, netting the library $58,000 in 1995.

While the Friends was organizing, Mayor Christopher made his own contribution to reforming the system by placing a measure on the November 1961 ballot that reduced the size of the library commission from eleven to seven members. This measure, decidedly unique because it involved a politician *relinquishing* some patronage positions, passed overwhelmingly.

A Library Transformed

By 1962 there were noticeable changes at the main library even without a dramatic increase in the budget. In April of that year, the new Literature, Philosophy, and Religion Department, with 100,000 books on shelves accessible to the public, opened on the second floor where the reference room had been located. The ceremony was attended by Lawrence Ferlinghetti, Tillie Olsen, Barnaby Conrad, Kenneth Rexroth, Oscar Lewis, Mark Schorer, and Eric Hofer, the longshoreman, autodidact, and author, who would eventually give his papers to the library. Two months later the commission approved a total reorganization of the library into departments, adding Art and Music; History, Travel, and Biography; and Special Collections to the Literature, Philosophy, and Religion Department. The next year the Business and Science Department was opened on the first floor.

With the reorganization came new assignments for key staff members and the hiring of new personnel. Holman appointed Harriet Collopy adult services coordinator and hired Effie Lee Morris, the children's specialist at the library for the blind at the New York Public Library, as children's services coordinator. Morris was a nationally recognized children's librarian who had won the E. P. Dutton–John McCrae Award, and was one of the leading African-Americans in the public library field. This was the first time that the library had staffed such positions. Vivian Goodwin became head of technical services, overseeing cataloguing, acquisitions, and the bindery, and soon regained control of the cataloguing process. Mary Moses became chief of branches. Avis Stopple, librarian at the College of Santa Rosa, became the chief of the main library, with Harold Martelle, director of the Dearborn, Michigan, public library, serving as assistant librarian.

Part-time employees were replaced by full-time clerical workers, and finally—more than thirty years after the first report urging that all librarians should have a library degree—Holman made a master's degree in library science a requirement for new librarians. Holman at first found the staff generally receptive

Effie Lee Morris, the first coordinator of children's services at the library, pioneered the effort to select children's books that were devoid of social stereotypes. Many of the innovations in children's services under Morris influenced other public libraries. In 1981 the library established the Effie Lee Morris Historical and Research Collection of Children's Literature to chronicle and preserve trends in children's book publishing.

A RARE GIFT

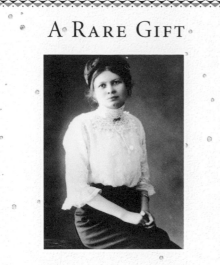

One of the most heartening developments in the history of the library was the construction of a new branch library in Bayview–Hunters Point. This was the result of a $186,000 bequest by Anna E. Waden, a city health department employee. Waden was a quiet and reclusive individual whose $285 monthly salary belied her gradual accumulation of funds over the forty years she worked for the city. She lived in a small cottage at 945 Fourteenth Street and was known to her few friends as a woman who was shy, but kindly, hardworking, and frugal to the point of lunching on a piece of fruit. When she died in 1957, she left $90,000 in securities, $9,000 in real estate, and the balance in cash deposited in twelve bank accounts. The Anna E. Waden branch opened on Third Street in 1969. George Alfred, described by a branch librarian as one of the saints of the library, was the first Waden branch librarian. While building a collection of books by and about African-Americans, he worked tirelessly to encourage young African-Americans to feel that this was their branch library. Alfred died of AIDS in the 1980s.

and supportive of his changes. He made a particular effort to work with older staff members, whom he described as very literate and well educated if not formally trained. A few were resistant. Some were disciplined; a smaller number were let go. There were other minor problems that had to be rectified, such as the sale of liquor and eggs by a staff member in the basement.

To put an end to the long waiting lists for best-sellers, the library turned to the McNaughton rental service, which also meant a significant reduction in the cost of book acquisition. At the same time Holman decentralized the book selection process and then worked closely with his staff and local rare book dealers Warren Howell, David Magee, and William Wreden to buy as many whole collections as possible.

In response to complaints about the unemployed who gathered on the south side of the library and were habitués in the newspaper reading room, the library commission authorized Holman to make certain changes at the library: guards were posted at the front door, the key to the men's room was kept at the circulation desk, and current issues of newspapers were removed to the library's business branch. These changes drew much attention and criticism in the press, but editorial support from the *Chronicle* and *Examiner*.

Holman himself was a fine printer, with an interest in rare books, calligraphy, and the history of the West. Part of what attracted Holman to San Francisco was the possibility of meeting other fine printers like Robert Grabhorn, Andrew Hoyem, and Adrian Wilson. To build this part of the collection, Holman appointed William Ramirez head of the Rare Book and Special Collections Department, which held the Phelan, Kuhl, Schmulowitz, and other collections. Ramirez in turn hired Gladys Hansen to build up the local history collection and run what would become the San Francisco History Room in 1964. Hansen later became the city archivist. Holman felt strongly that the public library could become a major research facility. "A library should have some personality, just like an individual," Holman said of his efforts to build collections that would reflect San Francisco's literary persona.

Starting in 1963, the library began to receive significant increases in its book-buying budget. "I had a budget that the fellow who was in charge of the rare books department at Stanford was jealous of," Ramirez recalled. He and Hansen scoured the city, including the damp basement of the de Young Museum, for historical materials. Meanwhile Holman had developed an astute way *not* to draw the supervisors' attention to what they might have thought were extravagant expenditures. Rather than send a large annual purchase order to City Hall, the library sent smaller orders on a regular basis.

By 1965 the library was showing marked signs of progress. This was a crucial year in the development of the Friends, its leaders recalled. The Friends had regularly mobilized its members to back the library's budget request. In 1965 these efforts paid off when the library's book-buying budget was raised from $381,000 to $500,000 with an additional $60,000 coming from a state grant. By 1967 the overall library budget was double what it had been in 1961.

The turbulent 1960s prompted the library's many experiments with community outreach, including using a car hood to display books on a street corner in the Fillmore District. Books were sent to community centers, and inexpensive paperbacks were given away on the street in poor neighborhoods.

Building the Last Branches and Seeking a New Main

The Holman era marked the final chapter in library branch building. Ironically, Holman himself thought that the city was "over-branched," with the exception of the need for a bigger downtown business branch. There were too many branches too close together even given the city's sprawl, Holman argued. However, planning for the last four branches, in the Excelsior, Eureka Valley, the Western Addition, and Bayview–Hunters Point, had begun soon after World War II. In 1962 the Eureka Valley branch was opened at 3555 Sixteenth Street, replacing the original McCreery branch, which had been damaged beyond repair in the 1957 earthquake.

Since the 1920s, branch building had generally followed the westward expansion of the city, the more prosperous white neighborhoods having been shown preference when branch sites were chosen. In multiracial working-class neighborhoods like the Excelsior and Bayview–Hunters Point, there were run-down rental facilities, and in the case of the Western Addition, no branch library at all. The board of supervisors added funds to the library budget for new branches in the Western Addition and Excelsior in 1961. Mayor Christopher made his own addition to the library budget for these two branches the next year. The Excelsior branch opened in 1967. The Western Addition branch, the twenty-sixth branch, opened in 1969 with an outpouring of enthusiasm from the mostly African-American community, which was experiencing massive dislocation because of urban redevelopment efforts.

Central to the plans of both Holman and the Friends of the Library was the construction of a new main library. For Holman, a strong main library was

Harrison Collection

In 1963 William Holman persuaded Richard Harrison, a local calligrapher and collector of calligraphy, to give his collection to the library on the condition that the library would enhance it with gifts and purchases. To announce the acquisition, the library commissioned Hermann Zapf, world-renowned calligrapher and type designer, to produce an original work (right). In his collection Harrison focused on English calligraphers such as Marie Angel. The Richard Harrison Collection of Calligraphy and Lettering has since been broadened to include young American calligraphers such as John Stevens and Thomas Ingmire, and has become one of the finest and largest collections of twentieth-century calligraphy in a public library.

Thomas Ingmire, *Saucy Jacks*, 1983

Theo Varlet

AN E
THROU
is a compar
can depress
no enemy a

* At home, a
introduction
and in socie

Without ba

Hermann Zapf, 1966

Marie Angel, *Exotic Birds*, 1968

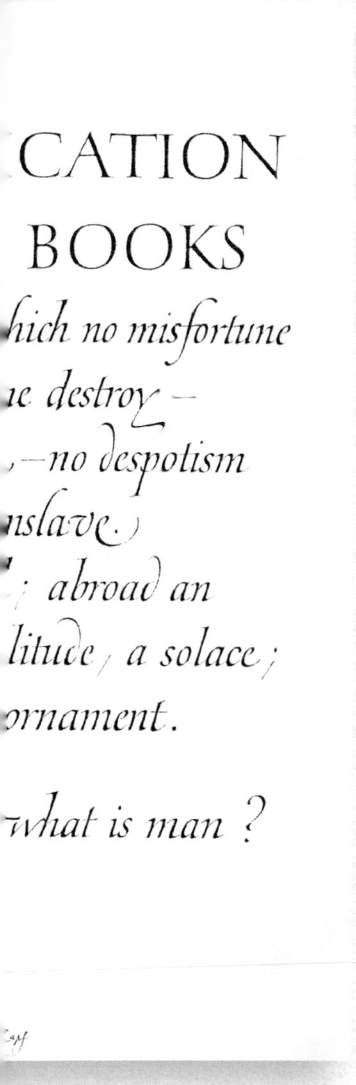
CATION
BOOKS
hich no misfortune
e destroy –
–no despotism
nslave.
; abroad an
litude, a solace;
rnament.
what is man ?

Grabhorn Collection

In 1965, at the instigation of William Holman, the Friends of the Library set up an acquisitions fund and pledged $5,000 that was matched by the library to buy from Robert Grabhorn his personal library, which became the Grabhorn Collection on the History of Printing and the Development of the Book. Grabhorn started to build his collection when rare books were still relatively inexpensive. He bought, for example, a 1502 Aldine edition of Dante's Divine Comedy *in the 1930s for $35. With the assistance of Friends board members Bill Barlow, George Fox, Andrew Hoyem, and Jeffrey Thomas, and the work of dedicated library staff, Grabhorn's original collection of 1,500 books has grown to 9,000 books, 100 journals, and 35,000 pieces of ephemera reflecting the renaissance in book arts that swept the Bay Area beginning in the 1970s and continues to be an important component of its book community.*

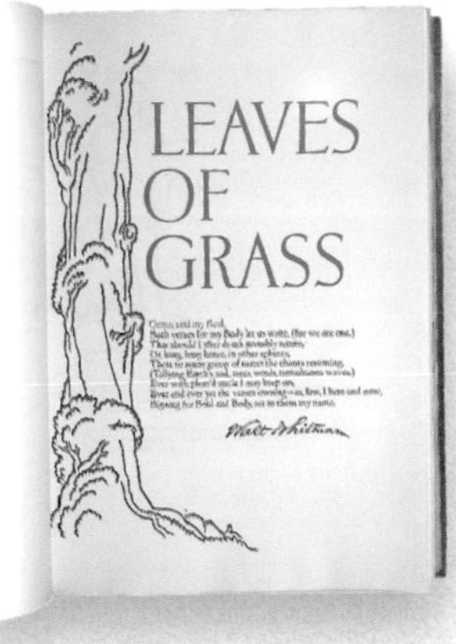
LEAVES
OF
GRASS

Walt Whitman's *Leaves of Grass,* printed by Robert Grabhorn with woodcuts by Valenti Angelo for a limited edition distributed by Random House in 1930.

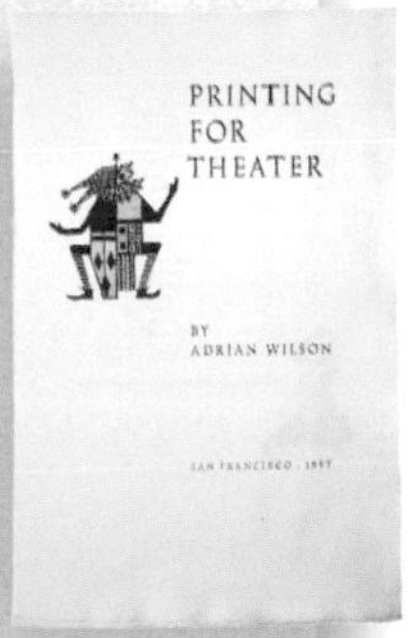
PRINTING
FOR
THEATER
BY
ADRIAN WILSON

Adrian Wilson's *Printing for Theater* (1957), an illustrated essay on the history of the Interplayers theater group.

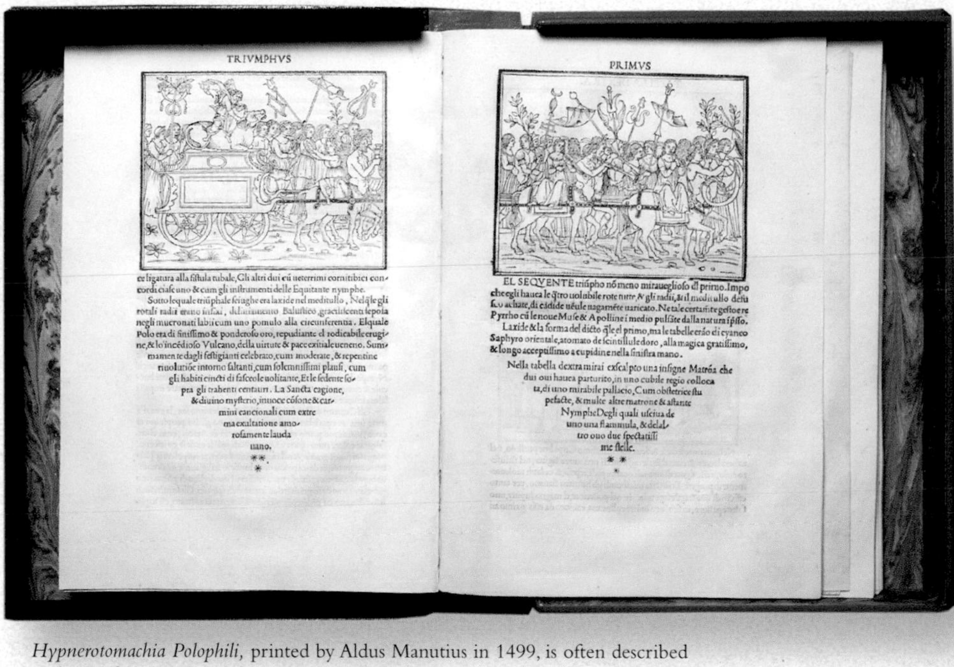
TRIVMPHVS
PRIMVS

Hypnerotomachia Polophili, printed by Aldus Manutius in 1499, is often described as the perfect marriage of typography and illustration.

Shepherded by author Ken Kesey and beat culture hero Neal Cassady, the Merry Pranksters toured the country in their bus, "Further," spreading a vast political-cultural network, with San Francisco as its center. The literature that emerged from this network and other alternative publications of the sixties were collected by the main library.

"WHEN I WAS IN COLLEGE IN DENVER, IN MY MIND YOU HAD THIS PLACE CALLED SAN FRANCISCO, AND WE WERE ALL READING ALAN WATTS AND JACK KEROUAC, DRINKING CHIANTI, READING BY CANDLELIGHT, WRITING POETRY, WEARING BLACK."

✿

Faun McInnis, Manager of Arts and Special Collections for the library

important to reviving the library as a whole and to accommodating the growing book collection. Describing the main as "the most miserable library building in America," Holman at first suggested that the library could share a new building on Marshall Square with the law courts. In this way Holman hoped to head off any conflict over the use of Marshall Square, which had been designated as the site of a new courts building in the 1958 Civic Center master plan. However, Holman's first problem was getting money for a study of the main library, which was repeatedly cut from the budget by the supervisors from the time of the 1958 Greenaway report until the spring of 1962. In that year $20,000 was put in the budget to fund a study by local architect John Bolles, Detroit librarian Ralph Ulveling, and Charles Mohrhardt, his assistant.

The results of their study, which were presented in the spring of 1964, surprised no one. The consultants proposed two alternatives. The first was to remodel the existing Main and build an addition at the corner of Hyde and McAllister, as called for in the original plans for the main library, at a cost of $6.5 million. The second, at $12 million, was to build an entirely new library. The consultants pointed out that it would cost more to build a new library, but that in the long run the city would save money because of the steep costs associated with running a larger, partly nonfunctional Main. "The more I see this," Holman concluded, "I think the only solution ultimately is to have another [main] building."

The library commission supported the Bolles-Mohrhardt-Ulveling report, and Holman, the commission, and the Friends began to prepare for a bond measure in 1966. Their efforts gained momentum when the state library commission started to work on a proposal to designate certain big-city libraries as centers of new regional library systems. The city needed a new main library, explained Friends' president Marjorie Stern during National Library Week in 1966; otherwise Oakland might be designated as the new regional library center for northern California, and San Francisco could lose millions in state and federal funding. Proposals for a New Main began their tortuous passage through the many-layered city bureaucracy.

GOING INTO THE COMMUNITY

Delayed in his attempt to get a new main facility, Holman conferred with his staff about future development plans. The results were a clear response to the forces shaping a new San Francisco. Across the country, the 1960s were an era of ebullient community activism inspired by the civil rights movement, federally funded programs targeting the poor (Lyndon Johnson's Great Society), and urban riots, which devastated Los Angeles' Watts neighborhood in 1965, hit San Francisco's Hunters Point in 1966 and again in 1969, and swept other major cities in 1967 and 1968.

San Francisco, with its long-standing indigenous radicalism and its strong labor movement, quickly became a center of activism and a city known for its heady cultural atmosphere. The decade began with a violent police attack on a City Hall demonstration against the U.S. House of Representatives' Un-American Activities Committee, followed by civil rights demonstrations against the city's auto dealers, who were clustered along Van Ness Avenue. The Free Speech Movement swept the University of California's Berkeley campus in 1964, and hippies flocked to the city's Haight-Ashbury district for the 1966 Human Be-in. Persistent efforts by the San Francisco redevelopment agency to clear poor neighborhoods, such as Japantown and the Western Addition, triggered other oppositional community forces. Many young San Franciscans—whether born here or attracted by the city's liberal atmosphere, as they were from out of town in the thousands—were committed to working, in one way or another, with the new social forces that came to the fore. New neighborhood and ethnically based organizations elbowed their way into politics, overshadowing older organizations tied to the unions, the Democratic Party, and assorted community groups.

In a 1965 memo to the staff, Holman, speaking of "a potentially revolutionary era," stated that "this library now feels that its primary focus must be on reaching out into the community." He described the need for special materials for job training, homemaking, consumer education, and childcare, for the placement of professional librarians at community centers, for door-to-door visits by library personnel to familiarize the public with the library's resources, for sidewalk paperback collections and sidewalk movies. Many of these and a number of other programs would, he hoped, be financed with funds provided by the Economic Opportunity Act, which was passed as a centerpiece of the Great Society programs in August 1964.

The library had already begun to extend its services into the community. In 1963 the Children's Department under Effie Lee Morris sent the bookmobile to Hunters Point, a predominantly African-American neighborhood, to serve as a center for a storytelling program. That summer Morris and her colleagues set up

Anti–Vietnam War demonstration on Fulton Street during the April 15, 1967, Moratorium. Library commissioner William Malone objected to a display of antiwar posters at the library during the Moratorium. Two years later, the Librarians' Guild protested police use of the library as an observation post and staging area during antiwar demonstrations in the Civic Center.

A partially blind man listens to a tape at the Communications Center opened in 1978 at the Presidio branch under the direction of Roberto Esteves. Starting in 1974, the San Francisco library pioneered the establishment of services for the deaf and blind, using new technologies such as videotapes and audiotapes.

a summer reading program for children, which they turned into a fifteen-week television series called *Wake Up and Read,* shown on local television.

Over time the library tried various approaches to the extension of community services. Librarians were sent to community centers and housing projects. New programs, from reading for preschoolers to tie-dyeing and jazz and poetry workshops, were offered in the branches, which saw themselves more than ever as community centers. Free paperback books were distributed to children in targeted neighborhoods. In some cases the library went literally out of doors through its street-corner library service, which provided materials in Spanish, Chinese, and Tagalog. A community room was added to the Chinatown branch, and a Spanish-language book and film program was developed at the Mission branch, which served a predominantly Hispanic neighborhood, with the assistance of the Mission Rebels, a community organization. With funding from the San Francisco Foundation, the Friends joined the fray, assembling a collection of materials and a bibliographic study about African-Americans in the West and California.

With federal funds supplementing the meager library budget, the library played a significant role in job training. The New Careers program, funded by the Economic Opportunity Act, provided training in library skills for the hardcore unemployed. It ultimately produced a number of library technicians and fully trained librarians with library science degrees. Working with the Neighborhood Youth Corp, the library provided dozens of summer jobs for pages in the library. Eventually the library came to rely on federally funded jobholders to replace more professional staff that the city refused to fund. This ultimately created a two-tier workforce—one with low pay and no benefits, the other with excellent pay and benefits—and all the attendant social tensions.

THE IMPACT OF THE BAY AREA REFERENCE CENTER

Despite the lack of a new main library, the state library in 1967 named San Francisco as the pivot of a northern California library system that, for the first time in American library history, would draw on new technology to provide reference materials for an entire region. "There had been studies of library service in California," explained Gil McNamee, a former director of what would become the Bay Area Reference Center, "and they said that librarianship was very backward, and that in many rural areas you didn't have the facilities to get the information and knowledge that you wanted." BARC became the source of last resort for reference questions that could not be answered in other public libraries throughout the nine library systems in northern California. Besides setting up a pioneering information system years before networks were commonly used, BARC

LONERS

A LOT OF PEOPLE, for one reason or another, find themselves alone. I am one of these. We are shy, they tell us, and should make an effort to "get over it," and join the human race. Well, we can't. We'd like to, but we can't. We live alone, and unless we are very rich, we prepare our own meals and clean our own houses. We make our own beds and then we lie in them.

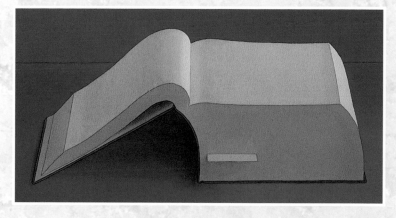

There are different kinds of loners. Some are gregarious, charming, funny, busy, and you only discover their loner status when you try to get close. This is where the loner freezes up, and as much as we would like to invite you into intimacy, a chilling shyness overtakes us, and what might have been a warm friendship dries into acquaintance. Love is very hard for loners, even charismatic loners.

But most loners are not charming. We do not have the gift of gab. We can't unbend to our fellow workers or to anyone else, and whatever we might have to say about ourselves stays unsaid, bottled in shyness. We can go through our day without speaking or without being spoken to, except in perfunctory or official ways. One might ask, what happens to you people? Do you spend your lives in muffled silence? Do you explode?

Loners have their pastimes, of course. Plenty of us are alcoholics and drug addicts. If you've ever had the pleasure of entering a 6 A.M. saloon, then you've seen us, sitting alone at the bar, staring down at our dearest love, that first A.M. drink. We are not without friends. The bartender is our friend. Some of us, myself, for example, have given up on booze and get our morning thrill from coffee or tea, served up warmly in the easy intimacy of a coffeehouse. And we go to the movies in droves, to sit with our contemporaries and beam our love up onto the screen. Lots of us watch television. We even call in and give the world our cranky loner views. And then we watch *Columbo* reruns and the noon news and millions of sporting events. Some of us even spend our long lonely nights watching topless movies. Loners have lots of ways to go.

But the best, the greatest, the most wonderful place for loners is the public library. There you will find us in plethora. We are at the tables and in the stacks. We have the best easy chairs staked out. We know when the new periodicals arrive. The library is our home away from home. And there is a reason for this. The library, you see, is full of BOOKS.

Don Carpenter

In 1970 John Anderson (right), city librarian from 1968 to 1973, accepted an award from the American Institute of Architects, the American Library Association, and the National Book Committee for the design of the Anna E. Waden branch.

employed technologies, such as the teletype machine and a fascinating new device known as the facsimile machine, for the transfer of information. Until funding was cut off in 1988, BARC was an important source of federal funds that not only enhanced regional reference services but permitted BARC to purchase for the San Francisco library books and other services that the city was not willing to support.

In 1967 BARC began publishing *Synergy,* a bibliographic magazine that provided information for librarians on numerous current topics. Some of them, such as the New Left, the New Right, the underground press, feminism, and gay liberation, were considered highly controversial. In time *Synergy* developed a national and even international readership, and for two years in a row it received the H. W. Wilson Library Periodical Award for being "a highly contemporary, off-beat, consistently communicative now-oriented publication."

Synergy became increasingly irreverent, according to its second editor, Celeste West. In 1973 she found a treasure trove of old photographs of Richard Nixon in the photographic files of the *San Francisco News-Call-Bulletin,* some of which, according to West, "made him look really loaded." After West ran one of the photographs in *Synergy,* Ethel Crockett, the state librarian and a Ronald Reagan appointee, cut off *Synergy*'s funding. West and her colleagues organized a national protest, but to no avail. For her efforts, West received a reprimand for unprofessional behavior, which she opposed by threatening to seek a resolution of support at the annual California Library Association meeting. The reprimand was withdrawn, but *Synergy* was finished. Its successor, *BARC Notes,* lacked the vitality and controversial edge of its predecessor.

Despite problems with its funding source, BARC continued to expand its influence, ultimately serving 12 million people. It offered workshops on how to do reference work in a wide range of areas, including art, music, geneaology, and medicine. BARC staff also worked with a diverse group of libraries to extend its reference network by linking up with the University of California, Library of Congress, National Aeronautics and Space Administration, British Museum, and local private libraries at companies such as Bechtel and Standard Oil of California.

This new focus on and experimentation with community outreach programs would influence the future of the library, but without Holman. In July 1967 he resigned to take a job as a tenured professor at the University of Texas with bibliographic assignments at the Humanities Research Center Library. Holman had inherited at the San Francisco Public Library, as the *Examiner* put it, "one of the most infamous cultural fossils in the country" and had somehow breathed life into it, moving it in the direction of becoming a modern library. He had reorganized and professionalized the staff, attracted well-known librarians from outside the city, started to rebuild the book collection, secured much larger budgets, and built a Rare Book and Special Collections Department. Above all he made the library, for the first time in its history, a significant cultural center.

Of course, there were numerous frustrations. He had not overseen the construction of a new main library, whose prospects now seemed remote. Holman had hoped to locate and equip a major downtown business branch, but the efforts of the first Friends president, Bank of America vice president Alan K. Browne, to organize support in the business community had quickly fizzled. There were controversies with the staff over whether the library should pursue the kind of special collections that fascinated Holman or provide resources for a broader public. Holman was backed by the new Friends organization and a number of engaged and influential library commission members, such as John Bransten, Mortimer Fleishhacker Jr., Edward J. Callanan Jr., and William Malone, a powerhouse in the local Democratic Party, who was appointed by Mayor John Shelley. But even this new support was not enough. After seven years Holman concluded he had outstayed his effectiveness. Weary of his numerous administrative tasks, plagued by internal conflicts, and suffering from a facial neuralgia because of the strain, he left for Texas warning that the San Francisco legal establishment still wanted Marshall Square for a new courthouse.

William Ramirez summed up the Holman years best: "It was never enough, of course, because the library had gone without for so many years. It was a long catch-up game during a very difficult time in which to catch up."

A New Librarian Faces a New Austerity

In February 1968, the library commission announced that it was hiring John Anderson, a thirty-nine-year-old Tucson city librarian, as the new city librarian. Anderson, a graduate of Michigan State and the University of Illinois library school, had started his career at the Enoch Pratt Free Library in Baltimore and served as director of the Knoxville, Tennessee, library before going to Tucson. In Tucson, Anderson presided over a rapidly expanding library whose budget had doubled and whose staff had grown by seven times during his tenure.

Anderson, who arrived with a reputation for informality and innovation, described the library as the "worst metropolitan library in the country." Noting that urban centers faced a crisis, he argued that the library should accept "a special responsibility to the people in the changing city who do not have educational and cultural advantages." The watchwords of his administration, Anderson said, would be *experimentation* and *communication.* "I think very definitely, very shortly, the central library [problem]

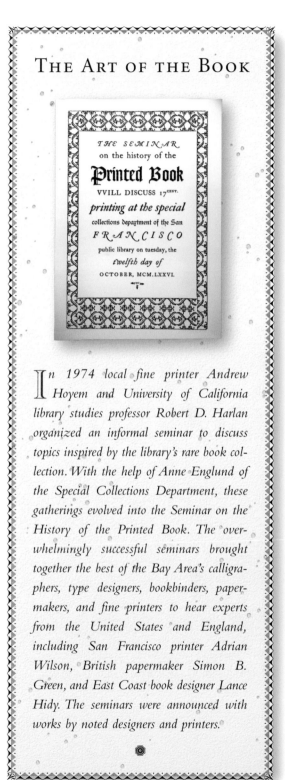

THE ART OF THE BOOK

In 1974 local fine printer Andrew Hoyem and University of California library studies professor Robert D. Harlan organized an informal seminar to discuss topics inspired by the library's rare book collection. With the help of Anne Englund of the Special Collections Department, these gatherings evolved into the Seminar on the History of the Printed Book. The overwhelmingly successful seminars brought together the best of the Bay Area's calligraphers, type designers, bookbinders, papermakers, and fine printers to hear experts from the United States and England, including San Francisco printer Adrian Wilson, British papermaker Simon B. Green, and East Coast book designer Lance Hidy. The seminars were announced with works by noted designers and printers.

In 1970, a year after the formation of the Librarians' Guild as part of the Service Employees International Union, the librarians supported the largest city workers' strike in recent history. The strike led to the guild's increased involvement in the SEIU local and the operation of the library.

has to be settled, probably with a new building." What Anderson did not know was that, with Holman's departure, the momentum that contributed to improvements in the library and toward construction of a New Main was slowly ebbing away. Anderson's arrival coincided with the first year of the mayoralty of Joseph Alioto. Alioto, a nationally known antitrust attorney and former chairman of the redevelopment agency, was selected as a mayoral candidate by real estate interests that wanted to see the city's redevelopment effort back on track. A proponent of the most ambitious plans for San Francisco since the era of Mayor James "Sunny Jim" Rolph, Alioto brought tremendous energy and intelligence to the push for redevelopment in the city's poor neighborhoods, such as the Western Addition and Hunters Point; new efforts to build a downtown convention center (the Moscone Convention Center); high-rise development in the central business district and along the city's publicly owned waterfront; and plans for a new performing arts center in the Civic Center. Alioto, who had a restless mind and was extremely well read, was both a regular user of the library and a supporter of a New Main. With excellent connections in Washington, he helped secure a $115,000 Housing and Urban Development grant for preliminary planning of a new building on Marshall Square. He also appointed Madlyn Day, a local Democratic Party fund-raiser, to the library commission, hoping that she would help build support for a New Main.

In 1970 the HUD study by John Bolles and Arthur D. Little, the consulting firm, joined the growing shelf of studies that condemned the main library as inefficient and grossly inadequate. A New Main twice the size of the present one, plus renovation of the Old Main for other use, would now cost $38.5 million, it was estimated. Noting that the use of the branches had declined by 23.5 percent over the past ten years while use of the Main had increased, the report also called for the closing of ten branches and their consolidation into three new research centers in the northeast, southeast, and western sections of the city. The report warned that the potential failure to get a bond issue approved by the city and supported at the ballot box was very high.

Despite these warnings, supporters of a New Main led by the Friends pressed on, and there were reports that a bond issue would go on the November 1970 ballot with the blessing of both Alioto and the city's powerful chief administrative officer. But in fact the bond proposal was not well received by the citizens' bond review committee, which was chaired by the CAO. The date for the bond measure slipped two years. Unable to leap this final hurdle, the Friends executive committee, at the urging of Friends president Henry Miller Bowles, voted in June 1971 to postpone its campaign for a new bond issue until 1974.

Alioto faced his own problems. Almost a decade of new social programs had expanded city services to an unprecedented degree. Inflation, caused by the escalating costs of United States intervention in Southeast Asia, was eating at the city's budget. In November 1969 the San Francisco electorate voted against raising property taxes to fatten the city's budget. Alioto's response was twofold: First, he tried to limit pay raises for city workers. When that led to a public employees' strike in March 1970, Alioto backed down, but then froze hiring in all city departments in 1971.

In this atmosphere of increasing austerity, the situation at the library began to slip backward. The modernization of library services inched ahead with computerization of the library's periodical list and then ground to a halt when the equipment budget was cut drastically. Staffing levels declined. The book budget was adversely impacted by the rapid increase in book prices, and the number of volumes purchased declined accordingly. The only exceptions to this otherwise depressing picture were federally funded programs, such as BARC and the various job training and employment programs, and even BARC was threatened for a time with closure by Richard Nixon's cuts in federal library funding in 1973. Participants in the library's employment and job training programs were called upon to compensate for the lack of trained staff, while trained librarians were forced to take on more and more clerical work because of staff shortages.

Faced with a stagnating budget, Anderson was compelled to reduce library hours and begin closing branches. After Alioto imposed his hiring freeze in 1971, the library commission voted in February 1972 to close the Ocean View, Portola Valley, and Golden Gate Valley branches as a first step toward closing two more branches. A new library support group immediately protested the closures. For a time the Friends of the Library had recognized that its political and lobbying activities were constrained by the Friends' nonprofit status. Accordingly, Grace Macduff Parker, Mary Louise Stong, Elsa Lane, Sally Brunn, and Billie Pearl-Schuler led the effort to found Keep Libraries Alive!, which undertook the task of lobbying for the library at City Hall and in Sacramento. The immediacy of the public outcry about branch closures, symptomatic of the larger activism that was now a fundamental part of San Francisco politics, led Alioto to come up quickly with federal emergency employment funds, which were used to hire enough staff to keep the branches open.

LIBRARIANS TURN ACTIVISTS

In 1969 city librarians, inspired by a successful organizing drive by Los Angeles librarians and faced with problems in the library, decided to form their own union. There had been a brief scuffle over unions during the Holman years when

To protest cuts in library funding during the Nixon administration, the library dimmed lights throughout the system on April 10, 1974. Supervisor Ronald Pelosi and student Mary Williams watched the lights go down in the catalogue room at the main library.

THE LIBRARY OF EXPERIENCE

My experiences with libraries are both benign and violent. I am a fourth-generation Californian, the first, on one side of the family, to make it not only through college but through high school. My Portuguese grandfather was a cattle buyer; my Spanish grandfather ran a bar and gambling house. Both men had many stories to tell, but told none to me. My first encounter with a library was my Portuguese grandmother. She ran a boardinghouse in a small California farming town. She didn't read or write, but words never failed her. She invented her own vocabulary when the one the world offered went from inadequate to lifeless. She picked off the best bits of the words she liked, spliced parts of other words to them, patterned doughy sounds to round them off, and flipped them high into the air. Word pizzas. They floated down fully clever on the tongue, darting between lips in such a delicious way that she always had a hungry audience surrounding her. She served stories about our world, California in the early 1950s, ripe with promise, hustle, heartbreak, and humorous miracle. I didn't go to the library after school. I went to my grandmother's kitchen.

My grandmother was still alive when I finished my first novel at the age of twenty-two. It was the 1960s. In California, the very cutting edge of the continent, nothing rubbed, everything sliced. One was either for or against: drugs, the Vietnam War, free love. Conspiracy riddled the air, reaction ruled the day. I was teaching creative writing at San Francisco State University. A vicious strike broke out at the university. Us against them, them against us. Those who wanted to change the system, those who administered the system. The strike spilled from the classrooms into the streets, it raced from singular academic concerns to multicultural curricula, it flooded from television screens and screamed disparate viewpoints on op-ed pages. One day, my classes having been canceled because of a bomb threat, I was walking across the grassy commons of the campus. Terrified students came running from all directions. Behind them charged lines of police. The police advanced methodically, bludgeoning students to the ground with riot sticks. Swept up among rushing students, I took refuge in the massive library, its heavy glass doors slamming shut behind, locking the less fortunate out, leaving them to the mercy of the charging police. Heads cracked, screams filled the air, blood flowed down the library steps. I witnessed this while standing amidst thousands of books which teach that when a society devours its youth it will surely perish. I was a writer locked up with books, while outside violence swirled. I belonged to the reality of both these worlds. One cannot exist without the other. I was determined to turn that knowledge into the action of my life.

Thomas Sanchez

he took the library's bindery business to a nonunion shop. Bertha Metro, a library commission member and union official, resigned from the commission in protest. There were also lingering resentments about Holman among certain staff members who welcomed his emphasis on professionalism, but felt that he was not accessible to employees and that key people on the staff, who did not have library degrees, were moving into administrative positions. The immediate impetus for organizing came when a librarian without an accredited library degree sought a promotion to a job that required a library science degree. At the time the library was an open shop, and only a handful of librarians were union members, most of them from families with a history of union membership. But many librarians were upset by the prospect of returning to the days when there were no requirements for a library degree. The librarian who was seeking promotion won the right to take a promotional examination with the support of her union, Local 400 (later Local 790) of the Service Employees International Union. When other SEIU members at the library, including Joan Dillon, Jack Coll, and Dan Tatko, went to the SEIU to argue against the promotion, the SEIU leaders explained that they had supported their member because they were unaware of the attitude and existence of the other SEIU members. As a result, the union activists in the library formed the Librarians' Guild.

In March 1970 the librarians joined other city workers in a four-day strike against Alioto's attempts to restrict wage increases for city workers. "We wanted to counter our image of being meek people who wouldn't stand up for anything," explained Ruth Maginnis, a West Portal branch librarian and former guild president. After playing a prominent role in the strike, the Librarians' Guild affiliated with Local 400. Two of the first presidents of the guild, Joan Dillon and Florence Mitchell, went on to be local presidents.

The guild, which quickly supplanted the moribund Staff Association, began to play a role in library affairs, aiming at first to improve working conditions. Later, after passage of a city referendum in 1988 that permitted collective bargaining among public employees, the guild began negotiating its first contract with the library. By the 1980s San Francisco librarians were among the best paid in the state, and the union had secured a voluntary reduced work week as well as improved benefits.

In July 1973 city librarian John Anderson resigned. From his first meeting with Mayor Alioto, he sensed that he faced a difficult and vastly more complicated political situation than he had in Tucson, where he had the backing of the city manager to build a modern library system. His initial problems in San Francisco came when he encountered the civil service system, which dictated that job vacancies be filled according to seniority and a testing system. "In effect, I was

The library has inspired two novels. Richard Brautigan's The Abortion *(1970) is about a librarian at the Presidio branch and his girlfriend. Brautigan's library accepted and shelved all unpublished manuscripts, leading to a huge influx of manuscripts and many inquiries at the branch. On the book's cover, Brautigan and a young woman are shown on the front steps of the Presidio branch. In 1979 former city librarian Kevin Starr wrote* Land's End*, which weaves a number of complicated plot lines into a roman à clef about the library.*

Russell Hartley, dancer and costume and scenery designer for the San Francisco Ballet, and two of his costume designs. Hartley began collecting material on the history of dance in the Bay Area in the 1940s. In 1975 city librarian Kevin Starr asked Hartley to make his archives a special department of the library, housed at the Presidio branch. The Performing Arts Archive moved out of the library in 1981 and into a new home as the Performing Arts Library and Museum in 1989.

given responsibility as a chief executive officer to do major things in the library," Anderson said, "and I was not given any real authority to appoint the personnel that I thought could get them done."

His second problem was equally systemic. The secretary of the library commission, Robert Figone, a former San Francisco school district employee, and his successor, George Cerasi, a North Beach businessman, were appointees of the mayor. Anderson described the commission secretary as essentially the library's business manager. "I had a business manager," Anderson explained, "who had his loyalty to the political establishment of the time perhaps without having the qualification of a business manager."

As the librarians unionized, Anderson, who prided himself on his consensus-building management style, became enmeshed in an increasingly confrontational situation. The final straw came when the Librarians' Guild sued the city to force the department of public works to make repairs at the library annex at 45 Hyde Street, which was repeatedly flooded during the excavation for the Civic Center BART station. Anderson found himself defending the city's unwillingness to put money for repairs in the library's budget in front of a large crowd of angry librarians at a city hearing.

Anderson was always aware, and often made aware, that he was an outsider attempting to battle powerful political forces in a period of budget cutting. Having taken the job with plans for more outreach and a New Main, he presided over some new programming, particularly for the blind and elderly in the South of Market area, but funding for much of this came from the federal government. Otherwise, he was frustrated in his attempts to maintain the momentum for change that had led to significant reforms in the 1960s.

As the library commission began a search for a new librarian, Alioto suggested in his usually forceful manner that it consider Kevin Starr, a thirty-three-year-old San Francisco historian who was an associate professor at Harvard. Starr had met Alioto when he invited Alioto to address a class on the subject of San Francisco writers. With a sabbatical coming up, Starr asked the mayor for work at City Hall and was answered with a job as an executive aide to Alioto working on cultural assignments. While working in the mayor's office, Starr would make occasional visits to the city librarian's office to suggest changes for the library. At Alioto's persistent urging, the library commission, which normally had full autonomy in the hiring of a new librarian, appointed Starr acting librarian, announcing that it was still planning to undertake a national search for a new librarian.

Many librarians, and particularly the guild, which had been formed to protect the professional status of librarians, were outraged. Starr was getting national recognition as a historian for his *Americans and the California Dream,*

1850–1915, which was nominated for both a Pulitzer Prize and a National Book Award, but he had virtually no experience as a librarian. "I don't think Joe knew the furor it would cause because I didn't have a library degree," Starr recalled. Starr, however, had significant support within the commission, particularly from Bill Malone, and as a condition for taking the job, he agreed to get a library degree at the University of California. Rather than assuaging the librarians, this proved doubly annoying since openings at the University of California library school were limited, and many of the librarians were awaiting admission so they could further their careers.

The Librarians' Guild, threatening a lawsuit, promised a major campaign against Starr's appointment. "We find it outrageous, scandalous, that the commission paid him $24,000 a year while he was earning his degree," said Thomas Fowler, a librarian who was president of the guild, to a reporter. "We need the skillful direction of an experienced administrator, not someone who's learning on the job." The library commission, which never did undertake a search for Starr's replacement, removed his acting status in July 1974. The lawsuit never materialized.

The Fight for Marshall Square

The controversy about Starr's appointment was blown off the front page by a bombshell that seemed to drop from nowhere: the mayor, it turned out, was backing an effort to build a new symphony hall, known as the Performing Arts Center, in Marshall Square, the promised site of a new main library. The library commission found out in April 1974 when Alioto called president Edward Callanan to his office and asked him what he envisioned for Marshall Square.

"Oh, a new main library," Callanan recalled the conversation.

"How much money do you have for a new library?" Alioto asked.

"Well, at present we don't have any money," Callanan answered.

Alioto's response was to introduce him to Samuel B. Stewart, retired vice chairman of the board of Bank of America; R. Gwinn Follis, retired chairman of the Standard Oil Company of California; and Harold Zellerbach, retired Crown-Zellerbach Paper Company board chairman. "Now, these gentlemen have a proposal," Alioto said. "They want to put a new symphony hall in Marshall Square, and they have the money to do it."

Callanan could not have been confronted with a more formidable array of local corporate firepower, but he held his ground, suggesting that the symphony

In a cartoon from the San Francisco Progress, *the Performing Arts Center, represented by a man in a top hat, plays Monopoly with a worried librarian for coveted Marshall Square. The Friends of the Library led a successful fight in 1974 to keep the Performing Arts Center (later Louise M. Davies Symphony Hall) from being built in Marshall Square, long considered the proper site for a new main library.*

In 1975 city librarian Kevin Starr marched the library budget across the Civic Center plaza to City Hall, accompanied by a band from the San Francisco Conservatory of Music dressed as ragged and bloodied minutemen.

might be better suited to a site near the opera in the block bounded by Grove, Van Ness, Hayes, and Franklin, the location of the old Commerce High School athletic field. Alioto continued to back a new main library, but he wanted it somewhere else in the Civic Center area, perhaps at 45 Hyde Street or across the street where the Federal Building is currently located.

It was a classic San Francisco confrontation: downtown business interests and the wealthy supporters of high culture versus the motley crew of artistic and neighborhood groups that were galvanized by the Friends of the Library and Keep Libraries Alive! The first test came before the planning commission in July 1974. The library, despite a large turnout by its supporters, lost by a vote of 7–0. The battleground shifted to the board of supervisors, who the supporters of the Performing Arts Center thought would fall quickly in line. After impassioned pleas by Callanan, Starr, and numerous others, the supervisors put the vote over for several weeks.

"We don't want to be the ones to kill the Performing Arts Center," the library's publicist David Belch told the *Los Angeles Times.* If the city were ever to build a New Main, it would need the support of the people who wanted the PAC in Marshall Square. Behind the scenes, the Friends and Starr were working with attorney William Coblentz on a negotiated settlement. With the help of supervisor Ronald Pelosi, Coblentz crafted a compromise. The board of education turned the Commerce High School athletic field over to the symphony, and the library retained Marshall Square.

Reinvigorated by its victory, the backers of the New Main hoped finally to put a bond measure on the ballot in November 1976. But for the next decade the time was never quite right. George Moscone, who followed Alioto as mayor in 1976, cut funding for preparation of a bond issue. Then the city, in the wake of the passage of Proposition 13 in 1978, which rolled back property taxes and limited future increases, entered an era of perpetual budget crises. Even the Friends pulled back, fearing that if a bond measure ever reached the ballot and was voted down, the library would be crippled for years to come.

It was hoped by many that Starr's friendship with the mayor would help the library at budget time, but Alioto was dealing with the financial consequences of the 1970 city workers' strike, which resulted in higher pay for those already employed, and the library as usual was a low priority. When Starr in his first budget, for 1974–75, asked for additional staff, Alioto's budget director promptly deleted his request. On his first day on the job as regular city librarian, July 3, 1974,

AN ESCAPE INTO AMERICA

❋

MY FIRST LIBRARY WAS IN OAKLAND, near our flat in Chinatown. A few blocks in one direction, and we were at our family restaurant, the New Eastern Cafe, where we, the kids, spent much of our time while our parents worked. A few more blocks in the other direction, and we would be at the three-story white building that housed the Oakland Public Library. One soon became an escape—or at least some relief—from the other.

In those years in the fifties just before Elvis, we juggled chores, American school, and Chinese school. For kids who ached to simply be American, life in Chinatown, at the largely Chinese-populated Lincoln Elementary School, and at the Chinese Community Center was life as ordained by your parents.

But ah, the library. Especially as I moved into junior high and fell increasingly in love with two kinds of writing—humor and baseball—the library was where I found America. Memories come easily, because they're so sensory: shiny marbled tiles and fluorescent lighting and acoustic ceilings; light oak shelves of books; wooden catalogue boxes of index cards more fascinating to me than the similar-looking cabinets of mysterious herbs I'd see in Chinatown shops. Most of all, there was the smell—perhaps of ink on paper, of fabric book jackets and bindings, or of some magical combination of the three. There was also the quietness, interrupted only by the clicks of heels or the shuffling of chair legs, which made the library such a welcome escape from the busyness of the restaurant and a five-children household.

The way a library looks—and smells—and sounds—does make a difference. In San Francisco, I've found it easy to slip into the city's grand old library, although a visit to the Oakland library for my most recent book triggered a rush of nostalgia. It was the same building, the same lighting, the same floors—even the same smell. Only life was different.

The book I wrote was *The Rice Room*, all about growing up and out of Oakland's Chinatown, and into the sixties, into a career that amounts to illusions come true. My mother told me she'd just been to the new Asian branch of the Oakland Public Library, and that she'd learned that *The Rice Room* was stocked there. It was checked out, and she was proud. I hope she'll go back. Since my father's recent death, she is alone, and I believe the library could provide an escape—into America, or back into China, or into any world she chooses.

Ben Fong-Torres

John Frantz presided over the library from 1977 to 1987, one of its most difficult periods—when an attempt to consolidate branches was defeated by a group of neighborhood activists led by supporters of the Noe Valley branch. Frantz was named city department head of the year in 1984 by Mayor Dianne Feinstein and wrote a number of her speeches.

Starr announced a further reduction in branch hours. "I am caught in a positively Darwinian system where each head of each department is fighting, struggling for his chunk of the available money," Starr told the *Bay Guardian.* "The struggle is brutal. . . . I never realized what goes on in city government. I'll never be so naive again."

Talk in the press about the library as a public embarrassment surfaced once again, harking back to the grimmest years in the 1950s. The book-buying budget continued to shrink. The level of theft was alarming, but the library could not get the funds to install a proper security system. "Most San Franciscans really don't care about their library system," proclaimed *Examiner* columnist Guy Wright, who described the main library as "a public urinal with reading rooms attached. . . . Changing that attitude will be Starr's acid test." In November 1974, Alioto came through with federal funding once again, this time from the Comprehensive Education and Training Act. For the first time since 1961, the main library and the branches were opened on Sunday, but only until July 1976, when Sunday hours were cut once again.

Despite his divided staff, Starr, who was known for his brashness (or arrogance depending on one's source), opted for dramatic appeals to the public to get City Hall to focus on the plight of the library. To mark the start of his new budget campaign in January 1975, Starr marched his request for a 50 percent budget increase across the Civic Center to City Hall at the head of a fife and drum corps recruited from the San Francisco Conservatory of Music and dressed like minutemen. The resulting press coverage drew attention to the library, but Starr's effort produced only a 6 percent budget increase.

After receiving a fellowship to work on the sequel to his first book, Starr requested a leave of absence from the library commission in early 1976. His request was denied, and he promptly resigned. Starr was replaced by Dr. Edwin Castagna, the retired director of the Enoch Pratt Free Library, who agreed to accept the job while the library commission undertook a search for a new librarian. In February 1977, John Frantz became San Francisco's new city librarian. Most recently Frantz had been working with the shah of Iran to build a national library. He had served as executive chairman of the National Book Committee, where he had become acquainted with Marjorie Stern. He had also headed the Brooklyn Public Library and worked in the Office of Education in Washington directing programs funded under the Library Services and Construction Act.

A Main Library: Relevant or Not?

John Frantz found a library funded with a budget that was in the middle range of big-city library budgets but had no prospect of significant increases. In fact, with the passage of Proposition 13 in 1978, the budget situation began to deteriorate even further. Frantz directed his attention to the cost of the city's branch system as a possible way to economize. Before Frantz's arrival, the Librarians' Guild, concerned about the number of large branches in the northeastern part of the city and their lack in the lower-income southeast quadrant, had come up with a plan for reducing the number of branches from twenty-six to twelve. The proposal was passed from Castagna to Frantz, who began consolidating branches by turning some of the smaller ones into reading centers in the charge of a library clerk rather than a librarian. In early 1980, Frantz proposed closing ten branches. He knew that closing branches would be unpopular, and when the library commission held its first hearing on Frantz's plan, Frantz and the commissioners were opposed by a rowdy crowd from numerous neighborhood library support organizations. As a result, no branches were closed.

In 1981 the library commission hired Columbia University library expert Lowell Martin to study the branch system. Working with Frantz, Martin prepared a report that recommended closing ten of the smaller branches and using the $825,000 that would be saved to improve the remaining facilities. Seven of the remaining branches would become "supermarket libraries," offering a wide range of services to their patrons. Nine others would be special-purpose libraries. The commission made substantial changes in the Martin proposal by creating a three-tier, rather than two-tier, system that would lead to the closure of only six libraries.

Frantz and Martin took the draft report to Mayor Dianne Feinstein's office. "She was lecturing us on the importance of libraries and on the importance of having all of the branches open all of the time with real librarians," Frantz recalled. "And she got herself into such a froth that she increased our budget for 1982–83 by about 30 percent in order to leave things alone. And I said to Lowell when we left that he was worth his weight in gold." The mayor's dramatic increase continued for two years, but, welcome as it was, in the end it proved to be only a brief reprieve from continuing decline. The threat of branch closures galvanized opposition in the neighborhoods, ultimately convincing the mayor that it was politically dangerous to move on this front.

Frantz's efforts to reform the branch system convinced him that the idea of building a new main library was a mistake. The Feinstein administration was refashioning the master plan for the Civic Center, and in the mayor's thinking the library was central to finishing off the Civic Center. Frantz felt that it would be cheaper to rebuild the Old Main while maintaining its facade on the Civic Center, and more importantly he was convinced "that a large central city library as a repository of books and other services is obsolete." The use of computers meant that

Library commissioner Marjorie Stern cuts a cake at a celebration of the library's one hundredth year in 1979. Stern used the event to call for the establishment of a Business Friends of the Library. After speaking to politicians and wealthy business-people at the Bohemian Club, Stern reported that she could raise only $38,000, a figure reminiscent of the supervisors' parsimonious appropriations in the library's first years.

Chinatown is the traditional heart of the city's Asian community. Today San Francisco has at least two Chinatowns, as well as a vibrant Southeast Asian community in the Tenderloin. The library provides books in ten Asian languages. A significant part of its Asian Interest Collection is housed in the Chinatown branch, the most heavily used branch in the city.

libraries were moving toward "smaller, cheaper, faster, more processing of information" with the end result "a far reduced requirement for physical storage space."

"I thought the new library was excessive, it was grandiose, a throwback to what should have been built in 1917 and wasn't." Frantz's views put him in the opposite corner from the library commission and the Friends, and rather than make a public issue of his views, he chose to resign in March 1987.

Since William Holman's effort to reform the library in the 1960s, the face of the city had changed in ways that were, if anything, more overwhelming than the changes that marked the reconstruction of the city after the earthquake and the early years of the Rolph administration. Plans for the new San Francisco, like the reforms at the library, had been initiated in the immediate postwar years, but did not become apparent until the 1960s. For one, the graceful skyline of the old brick-and-granite downtown business district was barely visible behind the soaring and boxy array of glass-and-steel structures that clustered in the area. *Manhattanization* was the buzzword among the opponents of high-rises, and San Francisco, on a small scale, had become Manhattanized. New freeways reached into the city but, with the exception of the link to the Bay Bridge, abruptly came to an end, stopped in their tracks by neighborhood resistance. BART linked the city to the suburbs, and a new federal building shadowed the Civic Center. The Louise M. Davies Symphony Hall was completed in 1980, a new state office building on the opposite side of the War Memorial complex in 1985. After a prolonged battle, the Moscone Convention Center was finally completed in 1981.

And the people had changed too. Activity along the waterfront died out as containerization and the shift of cargo operations to Oakland cut the heart out of the blue-collar workforce. The hippie hajj and general gathering of free spirits initiated the in-migration of thousands of young white professionals who staffed the downtown high-rises and rebuilt many of the city's picturesque but rundown neighborhoods. Simultaneously the city became a magnet for immigrants. Successive waves of Latinos and Asians—lured as their ancestors had been by jobs or driven from their homes by murderous conflicts in places like Vietnam, Cambodia, Laos, and El Salvador—broke on the city. Typically most of these immigrants entered the workforce at the bottom, and San Francisco became a city where wealthy old families, affluent yuppies, and poor immigrants intermingled, rekindling old social problems and igniting new ones such as homophobia, but showing a striking degree of tolerance for a city so diverse. Having identified itself for at least a century as a capital city of the Pacific Basin, San Francisco became a truly international city.

Mayor Alioto's struggle with the city budget foreshadowed the leaner years that would follow the passage of Proposition 13. Proposition 13 proved to be a disaster from which California has yet to recover. Public institutions, such as schools and libraries, were impacted most noticeably and continue to suffer in 1995 to the detriment of both the private and the public sector. By the middle 1980s the construction of new high-rises in San Francisco began to outstrip the demand for new office space, a development that was exacerbated by the decision of a number of corporations to move all or part of their operations out of the city. In the late 1980s the California economy was struck by a recession, and for the first time in recent memory the state's unemployment rate soared past that of the rest of the country, further limiting public expenditures.

It was not that the city was poor. One needed only to look at the wealth displayed in its finest neighborhoods or its suburbs. Funds, both public and private, could be found for a new symphony hall and a new convention center and later to add to the convention center and build a new museum of modern art. The problem was that public access to wealth was severely limited after the gross redistribution of wealth in favor of large property holders brought about by Proposition 13 and the recession of the late 1980s and early 1990s. Even before the Reagan presidency and the billowing clouds of free enterprise rhetoric, Californians, or at least those Californians who voted, had decided that they would starve the public sector. Essential institutions, such as libraries, which have never been high on the list of public priorities, and public schools, were fed the leanest diet. And this at a time when the library was under pressure to provide services for an increasingly diverse population with a rapidly growing demand for information.

During these years, the library struggled on. Successive city librarians, several young and idealistic, took the job full of enthusiasm and devotion to the institution. They left disillusioned and in some cases embittered. Much of the staff worked diligently despite the library's problems. Because of the strength of the union, many were well paid with good benefits, but with limited resources to serve the public. Even in the darkest days, the leadership of the Friends still held a candle for a New Main, and remarkably its time would come.

Influenced by the great Mexican muralists, young Latino artists began in the 1960s covering the walls of public and private buildings in the Mission District with works such as this mural, A Tribute to Carlos Santana, *at the corner of Twenty-second and South Van Ness. Neighborhood arts were an integral part of neighborhood activism, which inspired the movement to save the branch libraries in the 1980s.*

Chapter Nine

Building the House of the Book

❖

The Campaign for the New Main

"If European cities seemed like beautiful architectural museums," wrote Witold Rybczynski in his study titled *City Life*, "our cities were more like unfinished building sites where each generation was free to try its hand." Approaching the midpoint of its second century, San Francisco in the 1980s was by European standards young, protean, and still

The staff of the Noe Valley branch library from a March 1980 article in the Noe Valley Voice *headlined "Library Makes Last Stand at Budget Battle." Supporters of the Noe Valley branch led the successful fight to prevent the closing of branches in 1982 and 1988.*

Preceding pages: Aerial view of the Civic Center, with the new main library on the right and the Old Main in the center, opposite the City Hall dome. The Old Main will become the Asian Art Museum.

full of building sites. For years starting in the 1960s, the city looked like a vast construction project as Market Street, the city's major artery, was torn up for the Bay Area Rapid Transit system and high-rises sprouted like mushrooms in springtime. In the 1980s there were still plenty of vacant sites, including two in the Civic Center. Directly across the plaza from Mayor Dianne Feinstein's City Hall office window lay Marshall Square, the bitterly contested location for a new main library that no one could find the money to build.

Marshall Square, the Friends of the San Francisco Library believed, had been set aside for the new main library, and with little public support, they pressed on with their plans for the structure. There was virtually no one in the larger library community besides the Friends who would make a commitment to a New Main. When the chips were down, no city librarian had championed the cause. Nor had the library commission. Every politician supported public libraries in principle, but a New Main was hardly a priority in a city beset with numerous financial problems and still bedazzled by bigger, more expensive projects, like a new ballpark for the San Francisco Giants. "So the Friends were pretty much out there on their own," remembered Marilyn Smulyan, the public affairs consultant who became the coordinator of the campaign for a new main library.

In 1977 Smulyan was hired by the Friends to conduct a survey of citizens' attitudes as part of the library's first master plan. What jumped out at Smulyan from the results was the demand for books, books, and more books. She found a strong constituency that supported the branches. She also found a solid basis of support—two-thirds of those surveyed—for a bond issue to build a New Main.

Despite Smulyan's findings, the Friends remained unsure about the sources of funding for a New Main. The situation was further complicated in 1978 by Proposition 13, which precluded the kind of bond measure that the library had been attempting to get on the ballot for twenty years. The city could barely fund its existing library system. And there were limited prospects for state or federal funding. Nor had the library, despite the efforts of the Friends, ever been supported by a community of wealthy donors similar to those who funded the ballet, opera, and symphony. Then came Lowell Martin's 1982 report, which called for branch consolidation and "galvanized the library-using public into action," according to Margaret Mayer, Friends executive director.

NEIGHBORS AND THEIR BRANCHES

In San Francisco there has been a long history of active support for neighborhood branches starting in the 1890s. When the library commission voted to close some branches in 1972, members of the Friends and neighborhood activists formed Keep Libraries Alive! to fight the closures. *Passionate* is the word most often used by neighborhood library advocates when they speak of their support for their branches. And in San Francisco's political climate, which was increasingly characterized both by an intense neighborhood localism and by what one analyst described as "hyperpluralism," it was not surprising that the new and more vigilant neighborhood organizations, which had become revitalized in the 1960s, would take on branch libraries as a major issue.

Indeed, many people had a strong personal investment in the development of their local branch. Branches to them were part library, part community center, part children's room, and part living room, almost an extension of the home. When the rent was doubled on the building occupied by the Glen Park branch, forcing it to seek new quarters in 1977, Bill and Val Tietz personally borrowed money to put up a new building, which they then rented to the library for less than market rate. In Noe Valley, the fountainhead of branch activism, neighbors began working on the Carnegie-funded branch in the early 1970s, building a reading deck and a community room and adding a community garden.

Unwittingly the Martin report struck at the very core of these neighborhood sentiments. "This city is built on seven hills like Rome," said Miriam Blaustein, a Noe Valley activist, about Martin's recommendation that Noe Valley's children's services be consolidated at the Mission branch, "and he didn't take into account that topographically it is not possible to do this with little kids and people walking with a load of books."

Martin's 1982 recommendations were greeted with an unprecedented outpouring of sentiment on behalf of the branches. The atmosphere lightened almost overnight when the mayor responded to the uproar with a dramatic budget increase for the library. The increases continued for the next three years so that by 1985 the library received $16.1 million, its largest budget to date. The prospects for a New Main might be improving. But could these branch partisans be mobilized to support it?

CITY BEAUTIFUL ONCE AGAIN

The problem was how to draw public attention or at least the attention of the mayor, whom the Friends considered generally supportive of the library, to the need for a New Main in a new building. In April 1985, James W. Haas, a member of the Friends board, wrote to Feinstein to suggest working with her on a grand scheme for the completion of the Civic Center. He proposed building the new main library in Marshall Square while moving the Museum of Modern Art to the Old Main. The mayor's

A LIBRARY FRIEND

*S*ally Brunn was one of the library's most effective supporters. A founder of Keep Libraries Alive!, the lobbying arm of the Friends of the Library, she was also a principal organizer of several campaigns that kept the Noe Valley branch from being closed. During the Main Campaign, Brunn lobbied in Sacramento on behalf of the state bond measure passed in 1988 as a companion to the city bond measure that funded the construction of the New Main.

"She was the most unlikely-looking politician you would ever like to meet," remembers Margaret Mayer, longtime Friends director. "She was the most clear-headed, astute, and respected politician in the city. She could call anybody, the mayor, the supervisors, Sacramento officials, and they would see her." After Brunn's death in 1992, her local library was rededicated as the Noe Valley Sally Brunn branch.

response was cautious, but positive. Three weeks later Feinstein met with a delegation from the library, which included city librarian John Frantz, and library commissioners Edward Callanan, Marjorie Stern, and Mary Louise Stong. The mayor immediately asked how the library proposed to pay for a New Main. The group discussed public funding sources. The mayor suggested a major private fund-raising campaign, such as the one that had paid for the symphony hall. The mayor, who was unenthusiastic about vacating the main library, then recommended that the library acquire extra space in a new multipurpose city building in Marshall Square. "The mayor was not as sympathetic or as encouraging as we would have liked," Frantz reported to the library commission, but she left the door open for more planning to solve the library's space needs. The library delegation left the meeting knowing that the mayor ruled out the use of city funds both for library construction and for most of the studies that she needed to publicly back new, but vaguely defined library facilities. Feinstein, as Haas put it, was taking a "show me" attitude. In a more ominous sign, at the end of the year the mayor asked the library commission for two budget requests for 1986–87, at 90 and 100 percent of the present level. The days of the surplus were over, and the library faced difficult financial times.

Meanwhile the mayor and her staff were developing their own reasons for figuring out what to do with the main library. Early in 1986 Feinstein, who was considering what she had to accomplish before she vacated office at the end of 1987, asked deputy mayor Peter Henschel to create a task force that would work with city agencies and the private sector to complete the design of the Civic Center. There were, according to Henschel, "a whole series of dominoes. If we say 'yes' to the New Main, what do we do with the Old Main, about office space, about new courts?" James Haas's "grand scheme" had now become a Feinstein effort to finish planning for the Civic Center, and the library could become a bright star in a larger universe.

The discussions with the Feinstein administration did not get off to a good start. When commissioners Stern and Stong met with Henschel in Marshall Square, "he just really read us the riot act to lay off the new main library and to add to the present one," Stong recalled. The mayor preferred working with the Old Main because it would be cheaper.

A cartoon in the San Francisco Chronicle *of May 26, 1987, captures the Friends of the Library's concern about where Mayor Dianne Feinstein stood on the construction of a new main library in Marshall Square. For a time she appeared to be more interested in building a new baseball stadium for the San Francisco Giants, but she ultimately backed the library.*

MAYOR PROPOSES DESIGN FOR NEW LIBRARY

Anxious but not dismayed, the Friends continued on with the studies that were needed to justify the New Main. In September 1986 a report by Becker and Hayes and the Omni-Group described the Old Main as on the verge of being dysfunctional and enumerated its shortcomings, including the building's compartmentalized design and wasted space, the books flowing out of the stacks onto the floor, fire and safety hazards, and cramped office space. The study concluded that Marshall Square could more than meet the needs of a new library. Henschel responded by asking for another study that would look at whether the new library program could be carried out in the Old Main.

The central problem remained—funding for the New Main wherever it was to be located. First there had to be money for the numerous studies, which was solved during a sustained campaign when the Friends tapped their members and nine local foundations for $230,000. On another front, the library was backing a state senate bill that provided for a $300 million library bond issue but was bogged down in the legislature. Then in a major turn of events, voters in the November 1986 election approved a state ballot measure that revised Proposition 13, allowing local governments to issue general obligation bonds if supported at the ballot box by a two-thirds vote. The door was open to a city bond issue that would pay for construction of the library.

Funds from a city bond measure could not be used, however, to equip the library. To raise this money, the Friends inaugurated a private fund-raising effort on November 17, 1986, with a gala event at the old library. In an inspiring speech, Vartan Gregorian, the president of the New York Public Library and leader of a $34 million campaign to refurbish that venerable institution, quoted Thomas Jefferson: "A nation that expects to be ignorant and free expects what never was and never will be."

At Gregorian's suggestion, the Library Foundation of San Francisco was incorporated soon after the gala. With the possibility of a city bond issue as early as November 1987, the Friends hired Marilyn Smulyan to plan a campaign to build grassroots support, while Sally Brunn, the head of Keep Libraries Alive!, was dispatched to Sacramento to lobby to get the state bond issue out of the legislature and onto the ballot. A Main Committee was formed to connect the campaign to important political constituencies, such as African-Americans (Aileen Hernandez), Chinese-Americans (Joanne Foo), Latino-Americans (Fred Rodriguez), labor (Steve Neuberger from Service Employees International Union Local 790), and gays and lesbians. A speakers bureau was organized, and the fund-raising firm of Marts and Lundy was retained at the urging of Marjorie Stern.

With only a few more months left in her last term, Mayor Feinstein, who was still not committed to a new library in Marshall Square, and her Civic Center

Fire Marshal Lieutenant William Jovick inspecting the library stacks with head building engineer Al Campos in May 1987. In a carefully orchestrated campaign to underscore the shortcomings of the old main library, the Friends called the fire department's attention to the fact that the library was a dangerous fire hazard. The fire department closed the stacks until 100,000 volumes were moved into storage.

task force were running out of time. The mayor was waiting for the completion of the second Becker and Hayes/Omni-Group study and for the results of yet another study by Skidmore Owings Merrill, which was looking at alternative uses of the Old Main if vacated by the library. The results of the second Becker and Hayes study in August 1987 provided several more arguments for a New Main in Marshall Square, while the SOM study found that the best use of the Old Main would be for a museum.

With the Museum of Modern Art planning to move South of Market, Henschel thought that the Asian Art Museum might be a prospect because of serious problems with space at its Golden Gate Park home. In August, when he knew the results of the SOM study, Henschel made a call to Judy Wilbur, who chaired the museum's board. The mayor, he explained, wanted to know if the Asian Art Museum was interested in the Old Main and if the museum could successfully mount a campaign to renovate and move into the Old Main. In two weeks Wilbur called back to say that the Asian Art Museum was definitely interested, a commitment that became official in May 1988.

Finally all the pieces had fallen in place, and only the formalities were left to ensure that the new main library, if it could be funded, would be built in Marshall Square. In October, the mayor, evoking the City Beautiful movement in her state of the city speech, called for the completion of the Civic Center and the construction of a new main library in Marshall Square. In the waning days of 1987, after the election of Art Agnos as the new mayor, Feinstein convinced the board of supervisors to unanimously support her Civic Center proposal.

"I really think without those studies and raising money to pay for them," Mayer concluded, "we would still be working on it [the New Main]. The press kept on saying, 'Not another study,' but in reality each one was a little different, and they built a very solid case. They built it more for the politicians than for the voters because the voters seemed ready to vote for the main library."

THE SEARCH FOR A BUILDER

The voters did seem ready to vote for a new main library, but the library was presented with a new problem when city librarian John Frantz resigned in March 1987. His resignation afforded the library commission and the Friends the opportunity to recruit a librarian who was truly committed to building a New Main.

The library system, outside of the campaign for a New Main, faced numerous challenges. As the budget flattened in the last two years of the Feinstein administration, usage was growing, as was the demand for new services. San Francisco's increasingly diverse population required information in numerous languages. The instability of the job market sent many San

TIME IS TO BE SAVORED NOT SAVED

❋

WHAT I TREASURE MOST ABOUT BOOKS is the gradual, cumulative effect of detail. Reading has much in common with walking. The eye moves from side to side and line to line, in the regular rhythm of a stroll. When you walk, there is no way to get anywhere *before* you get there. The approach is every bit as illuminating and interesting as the destination and, in fact, *is* the destination. A word is a step. A sentence a small meander and soon, word by word, sentence by sentence, one recognizes in reading the similarity to a physical journey: pregnant with promise, anticipation, occasional dry patches, and then redeemed by wonder, fear, or awe.

Something about the *gradualness* with which information in a book accumulates is so essential to its pleasure, and cannot be foreshortened or compressed. Occasionally I will watch MTV with my ten-year-old son. The rapidity with which the jittery collage of images accompanying the song lyrics passes before the eye deprives the viewer of *reflection* and *resonance*—without which life is essentially meaningless; deprives because both require the unmediated passage of time.

The idea of separating time and space is just that: an idea, made possible only by a trick of language. In reality, February 15, 4:30 P.M., *is* the Mediterranean light filtering through the blue gum trees on the east-west spine of Mt. Tamalpais where I live. It is the throb of automobile engines muffled by distance, the cries of children whipped away by breeze and rustling leaves. It is also the *reflections* of all these things in the mind: all that one knows of mountains, children, breezes, and blue gums, similar days and the history of the place where you stand. It is a slurry of imagery, crossing synapses, *resonating* with other junctures of time, place, and memory. Savoring such a moment deepens it, like the experience of a book, gradually.

The world of MTV is a world condemned to first impressions and robbed of history. It is a world severed from the collective history of the species. The world of books pulls the past into the present and dips the present into the hidden streams of the past. We are free to dive into the streams of time where we choose: the February 15 of Cervantes, or Shakespeare, or Jane Austen, or Malcolm X. Once we've picked the point of departure, we set off with our chosen companion, reflecting and resonating, forging a relationship—*gradually.*

A *library* of books is the mind of humanity made tangible, a physical environment where the past, present, and future are available to any and all who seek. There is only one prerequisite for its use: that you take your time.

Peter Coyote

Franciscans to the library looking for assistance. Public schools were shutting down their libraries, and community centers were losing the funds needed to provide day-care and afterschool programming. By the 1980s the Main itself had become a neighborhood branch catering to the large Southeast Asian population in the nearby Tenderloin. As public institutions deteriorated under the impact of Proposition 13 and the Reaganite attack on big government, public libraries were being called on to fill the gaps. A new librarian would have to know how to build a library while understanding the new demands for service and the complex nature of San Francisco's heterogeneous population. That person also had to be adept enough to tread skillfully and lightly through the city's political minefields.

During the summer of 1987 the library commission's search committee decided on Kenneth E. Dowlin, the director of the Pikes Peak County (Colorado) library system. Dowlin, who had supervised the construction of three libraries, was regarded as one of the leading advocates of the high-tech library of the future. Born in eastern Colorado, he graduated from the University of Colorado. While preparing at the university for a career as a Marine Corps officer, he took a part-time job driving a bookmobile for a library in a Denver suburb. Getting married foreclosed a career in the Marine Corps. "Their view was if we wanted you to have a wife, we'd issue you one," Dowlin recalled. Instead Dowlin went to library school at Denver University, at the same time managing the Arvada library outside Denver, where at the age of twenty-three he built his first new library. In 1969 he took the job of library director in Casper, Wyoming, built another library, and set up the first video reference center in the country. From Casper, he moved in 1974 to become director of the Pikes Peak County system centered in Colorado Springs. In his twelve

Drawing of the Civic Center from the October 1987 urban design recommendations by the American Institute of Architects that accompanied Mayor Dianne Feinstein's Civic Center proposal. The AIA study noted that Marshall Square was "the most significant site remaining in the Civic Center." The next month Mayor Feinstein called for a new main library in Marshall Square.

years there he built a new main library and doubled the number of branches. He also oversaw the development of the first public library computer catalogue as part of what the *Library Journal* described as the most sophisticated library automation system in the world. Dowlin's initial response to the San Francisco library's overtures was negative. "Most directors [of public libraries] said this is a snake pit for a director," Dowlin said. After a long deliberation, Dowlin decided to take the job: "Here I felt there was really strong residual support for the library."

As Dowlin was arriving in September 1987, Mayor Feinstein was packing up, leaving the city with the prospect of a $78 million budget deficit for Art Agnos's first year in office. For Dowlin it was headfirst into the snake pit.

The Main Campaign

In April 1988 state senate bill 181 passed the legislature and was placed on the November ballot. At $85 million, the bond measure was disappointingly small. Since there would be very little state money for the San Francisco public library system, the size of the city bond issue became all-important. To demonstrate political support, the Friends asked the board of supervisors to put the city bond measure on the November ballot. First, the measure needed a recommendation from the chairman of the capital improvements advisory committee, who was Rudy Nothenberg, Mayor Agnos's new chief administrative officer. The early estimates indicated that the library would cost approximately $120 million. But there was an unwritten rule of thumb that a bond issue of this magnitude would never get the support of voters. After prolonged negotiations between library officials, Nothenberg, and John Molinari, the chair of the supervisors' powerful finance committee, the amount was whittled down to $109.5 million for a 376,000-square-foot building.

In a move to broaden and shore up the New Main's base of support, $5 million of this would be spent on renovation of certain branches, an amount that, it was hoped, would be supplemented by funds from the state bond measure. The Friends' initial support for the 1982 Martin report had driven a wedge between its membership and the supporters of the branches. As the Main Campaign heated up, Mayor Agnos, facing an enormous deficit, decided to close five branches. Some neighborhood activists began to question why so much money was being spent on a New Main when the branches were once again on the chopping block. The branch supporters had initially called public attention to the plight of the library. They were certainly needed now.

The Main Committee's polling showed that a little over two-thirds of those contacted favored a New Main and that the cost of a new library was not a negative factor. According to Smulyan, when those polled were asked about a

City librarian Kenneth E. Dowlin, who came to San Francisco after building three new libraries. He is an internationally recognized expert on library technology and a spokesperson for the high-tech library of the future.

What the Library Means to Me

By Amy Tan

My name is Amy Tan, 8 years old, a third grader in Matanzas School. It is a brand new school and everything is so nice and pretty. I love school because the many things I learn seem to turn on a light in the little room in my mind. I can see a lot of things I have never seen before. I can read many interesting books by myself now. I love to read. My father takes me to the library every two weeks, and I check five or six books each time. These books seem to open many windows in my little room. I can see many wonderful things outside. I always look forward to go to the library.

Once my father did not take me to the library for a whole month. He said, the library was closed because the building is too old. I missed it like a good friend. It seems a long long time my father took me to the library again just before Christmas. Now it is on the second floor of some stores. I wish we can have a real nice and pretty library like my school. I put 18 cents in the box and signed my name to join Citizens of Santa Rosa Library.

Bay Area author Amy Tan wrote this essay when she was eight years old for a contest sponsored by the Citizens Committee for the Santa Rosa Library. The essay became the theme of a Library Foundation solicitation in 1992.

⸺

more expensive building, they were more likely to vote *for* it! The challenge now was to get out the vote. The Main Committee had hired Dick Pabich to serve as campaign consultant, and Kelly Cullen, a Franciscan brother, neighborhood activist, and member of the Main Committee, to mobilize voters for the "Yes for Libraries" organization, which was backing what was now Proposition A.

Pabich's strategy called for the new committee to secure its natural base of support—in the liberal activist community—through the endorsement of political clubs and other community organizations, but then to focus on the more conservative, often Republican homeowners in the western part of the city, who would be inclined to vote against a bond issue. The campaign organizers took a close look at how precincts voted in a recent school bond election and targeted neighborhoods with a low percentage of support. With one-on-one personal contact being de rigueur in San Francisco's supercharged political atmosphere, the campaign organizers put hundreds of volunteers on the streets, but decided that an effective phone operation was more important. More than 40,000 phone calls were made during a five-week, five-nights-per-week campaign.

A number of the campaign's leaders, including Cullen and Smulyan, were confident that the bond issue would pass. The earliest polls showed that it started with 67 percent support in an election where a two-thirds vote was required. The campaign also was achieving high visibility because of support from Mayor Agnos, who had been elected by a landslide with 70 percent of the vote, and from his wife Sherry, a cochair of the campaign. Others were less sure. They were particularly concerned about a small group of vocal opponents of the library, including State Senator Quentin Kopp, the darling of the conservative westside voters whom the campaign was targeting; former librarian John Frantz; and Gladys Hansen, former city archivist and head of the San Francisco History Room at the library. While virtually all the other newspapers were supporting Proposition A, the *San Francisco Independent* was leading the charge for the opposition.

From early on election eve in November 1988, it was clear that Proposition A would win, which it did by an overwhelming margin of 78 percent. The state bond measure, thanks to the large vote in San Francisco, passed by a narrower margin. Finally, after thirty-five years of campaigning, San Francisco was going to build a new main library.

Choosing a Funding Strategy

With library construction assured, the Library Foundation had to devise a strategy to raise the funds to equip it. Here, too, the challenge would be formidable. Marts and Lundy, the fund-raising consultants hired by the Friends in July 1987, dispatched two researchers to interview sixty-four of the city's elite including people from the city's twelve largest foundations, the two daily newspapers, leading corporations, and unions. The consensus was that the library was a worthy cause, but that it had no history of substantial philanthropic support and that there was considerable competition for donations among the city's top cultural institutions. "Privately supported cultural institutions, close neighbors of the library, are perceived as the causes of choice," a draft of their report explained. "They are more often patronized by such donors, most of whom, while voicing a belief in the importance of libraries, never enter the San Francisco library or its branches." Although three-quarters of those asked said they would give to a campaign, they also offered the opinion that contributions of over $1 million would be hard to secure. Nearly half were unsure about the campaign's $20 million goal. In addition, the library had formidable rivals in the Asian Art Museum and the Museum of Modern Art. To add to the Library Foundation's problems, the California economy after 1989 sank into one of the worst recessions in recent memory.

After the Library Foundation was incorporated, Marjorie Stern, who served as its first president, and Caryl Mezey, a community activist involved with educational issues, had turned to members of Mayor Feinstein's fiscal advisory committee and asked James M. Edgar, a management consultant, and Ben W. Dial, the executive vice president for human resources at Pacific Telesis, to join them on the board. Edgar became the foundation's first chairman and Dial its secretary-treasurer. They were joined by Art Agnos, Steve Coulter, Ken Dowlin, Ann Witter Gillette, Michael Mellor, Ellen Newman, and Martin Paley.

The Library Foundation's first years were difficult and often frustrating. By the end of 1989, the library commission hired the architects for the New Main with foundation money, but the foundation was still slowly organizing. Marjorie Stern recruited Ann G. Getty, who had recently acquired a publishing company and was married to Gordon Getty, a local oil billionaire and major supporter of the city's cultural institutions, as honorary chair, and then signed up John W. Gardner, the founder of Common Cause, to be her cochair. Gardner and Getty gave the foundation a cachet with the city's philanthropic elite. In 1991 Gardner and Getty passed on leadership to Mel and Charlotte Swig. Mel Swig was a well-known hotel and real estate owner—proprietor of Nob Hill's Fairmont Hotel among others—with a long history of philanthropic work. His wife, the city's chief of protocol, was also known for her fund-raising acumen and had "the guts of a burglar when asking for money," according to the foundation newsletter. Mel Swig prevailed upon Martin Paley, the former director of the San Francisco Foundation

In one of the more imaginative demonstrations in support of the library held by Keep Libraries Alive!, people dressed as their favorite storybook characters.

THE SOURCE

❋

I LEARNED ABOUT THE MAIN LIBRARY when I was in the seventh grade. This was in 1972, and our history teacher was a sharp-tongued, ferociously hard-driving man who wore a tie to class and lifted weights. For a final project he made each of us write a report on an African country, and his own ferocious touch was that each of us was required to use at least fifty primary references. Those were the words he used—Primary References—standing before us with his immense biceps crossed over his chest. We were not to use encyclopedias or text-

books or the picture-laden Time-Life send-outs from which we'd copied every other report since we'd been in school.

It was a barbarously tough assignment for a twelve year old, but I was spurred on. That winter I had to take the bus every afternoon down to the main library near Civic Center to try to find my references. I had no idea how to find anything, but our teacher had given us a handout of what to do. Top on it was a book called the *Reader's Guide to Periodical Literature*. There to my amazement I found that somebody had gone through every magazine and journal ever published, and for the benefit of struggling students like me had noted every article in which any particular subject had been even casually mentioned. My country happened to be Burundi, and I saw with glee that in that single, saintly volume there were more than all the references I needed.

All I had to do was find them, and in the weeks that

followed I learned how: I discovered the rudiments of the library's labyrinthine stacks, tracked down obscure journals among its echoing metal shelves, pedaled furiously in the dark microfiche carrels so that the years of newspaper headlines formed a swift blur on the screen and bumped to a stop right near the date I was searching for. I was discovering a world within a world. The stacks smelled of dust and paper, the stairways of cool, damp stone, the reading rooms of wood and the arcane, half-kempt men who sat researching at the long tables.

I wrote my report on Burundi and at the end listed seventy-five references, though today I remember almost nothing from my research. What I do remember well from those days was being startled by two things: one was the extent of human learning, and the other was the vehemence and gratitude with which the grown men and women around me in those quiet rooms seemed to be reading books. Up until then, the library had been a chore for me, but I think that what our teacher was trying to show us, and what I realized one afternoon while standing at the great, light-filled center of the reading room, was that the library was as great an achievement as our culture will ever know.

Ethan Canin

and a Library Foundation board member, to head the foundation staff as director after the first director did not work out. Swig was so enthusiastic that he bumped the foundation's goal from $20 to $25 million and then encouraged Paley to add another $5 million to endow the library.

Paley and the foundation board initially took a conventional approach to fund-raising. Following the traditional idea of a fund-raising pyramid, they went first after the small number of donors at the top of the pyramid who were expected to make the largest donations. Smaller, more labor intensive, and therefore more costly solicitations of lesser donations would come later. The results were disappointing. "Almost everybody we asked gave money," Paley said. "There were very few turndowns, but they gave a lot less than they might have been able to or we expected they would. It was agonizing. . . . There was no excitement. There was no buzz in town."

On July 17, 1991, the foundation officially launched its campaign with the announcement of $10,280,602 in lead gifts. Typically a capital campaign, like the foundation's, is launched when half the funds are collected. But in this instance the foundation had raised only 34 percent of its goal. Key foundations and individuals had come through, but others were holding back because they were either committed to other projects or skeptical of the final outcome.

By April 23, 1992, groundbreaking day for the New Main, a few more gifts had trickled in. Then the stream seemed to dry up. There was another burst of giving, then another sickening pause at $16 million. Marts and Lundy had predicted that the foundation could raise roughly this amount, "and that's where we flattened out," said Sherry Thomas, who joined the foundation as director of development in 1991 and replaced Paley as director in January 1994.

Because of the very nature of past library support, the foundation, like the Friends, was committed to running a broad-based fund-raising campaign during a second phase when smaller gifts would be solicited. The branches had been saved and the 1988 bond issue had passed because thousands of people had joined a citizens' movement that wanted good libraries. How could that be translated into a fund-raising strategy when every professional believed in the pyramid approach?

The inspiration for turning the Library Foundation's commitment to a community-based approach into a funding reality came from Steve Coulter, a vice president at Pacific Bell. Coulter, asked to join the library commission in September 1988 by Art Agnos, immediately became its president. Taking office in the wake of another attempt to close down some of the branches, he tried to address the continuing contention within the library support community between the backers of the New Main and the branch partisans and to find a way to communicate a larger vision of the library as a system. Coulter had toured the

> "WE WANTED THIS TO BE A DEMOCRATIC CAPITAL CAMPAIGN, ONE WHOSE DOORS WERE OPEN TO EVERYONE. WE NEVER IN OUR WILDEST DREAMS IMAGINED HOW THAT WAS GOING TO BECOME A REALITY."
>
> ✿
>
> Charlotte Swig,
> Chair, Main Campaign

These posters are the work of the McCann-Erickson advertising agency, which donated its services to create an award-winning series of ads for the Main Campaign.

main library's Special Collections and also had met with the staff of the Schaumberg Center for Black Culture in New York. He proposed to the commission that the library be presented as a series of collections and services rather than a main library and branches. This approach was very much in line with the strategic plan for the library being developed by city librarian Ken Dowlin.

Coulter took his idea to a group of gay and lesbian activists and philanthropists. There was already a Gay and Lesbian Collection at the Eureka Valley Harvey Milk Memorial Branch. In a meeting at Coulter's house, the group began a discussion of what an expanded gay and lesbian collection with its own room in the New Main would look like and how to fund it. Some members of the foundation's board were nervous about this approach. Segregating donors by social category—gay-lesbian, African-American, etc.—seemed to set a bad precedent. Ultimately they were convinced of the value of this new strategy. A fund-raising committee, with Chuck Forester and Diane Benjamin as cochairs, was set up, and a goal of $1 million for the library as a whole and $600,000 for the Gay and Lesbian Center was established. This approach was to have a profound impact on the fund-raising campaign.

Despite the concerns expressed by some board members, Sherry Thomas and Charles Howland, the consultant from Marts and Lundy, identified other natural constituencies for fund-raising. "That was actually a stroke of genius," Thomas said of Coulter's approach, "because it was hard to get people to give big gifts to the general library when they didn't exactly know what it was going for." In the spring of 1992 the Special Gifts campaign was launched with the idea that the affinity groups, as they were now called, would reach out into the community for general capital gifts, in addition to raising funds for particular collections.

The second affinity group to get off the ground was the African-American. It was proposed by Renée Dorsey Coleman, who cochaired it with her husband, Dr. Arthur Coleman, both foundation board members. Their initial goal was $50,000. Inspired by the gay and lesbian affinity group, the African-American committee set a goal of half a million dollars. Both affinity groups later raised their goals to $2.7 and $1 million, respectively.

A new fund-raising strategy that would eventually become a national model, despite its controversial nature, was born. The Library Foundation quickly scrambled to set up a series of affinity groups: Art and Music, Business, Children's Center, Chinese-American, Filipino-American, Japanese, Latino, Literacy Services, Rare Books, San Francisco History, Wit and Humor. As predicted, the establishment of a large number of affinity groups increased the foundation's community reach. There was an additional payoff: the excitement and notoriety generated by the foundation's new strategy pulled in many large donors, who originally were skeptical. Remarkably, the foundation soared right past its goal of $30 million and was well on its way to reaching $35 million, which would leave the library well equipped, with a wealth of wonderful new and expanded collections, and a healthy endowment for the future. In one six-month period in 1993 the foundation grew from 600 donors to over 17,000. This fund-raising strategy would have a profound impact on the whole library system and would help to reshape the very definition of library service in a diverse community.

DESIGNING THE NEW MAIN

While the foundation searched for a funding strategy, work on the New Main funded by the 1988 library bond began. CAO Rudy Nothenberg, who would oversee construction of the building, formed a selection committee for the architects, and at the instigation of Marjorie Stern, the committee hired Ada Louise Huxtable, the retired *New York Times* architecture critic, as an advisor. In May 1989 the commission announced that Pei Cobb Freed & Partners, in association with the local firm of Simon Martin-Vegue Winkelstein Moris, had been selected.

SMWM had a background in library building that included more than a dozen projects, among them a major addition to the library at the University of California at Davis. Partner Cathy Simon had been tracking the library project since 1987. When Huxtable was retained, Simon knew that the selection committee was thinking of a world-class design. On a visit to New York she met with James Ingo Freed, a partner in the renowned firm founded by I. M. Pei. Freed's most notable recent work was the Holocaust Memorial Museum in Washington, D.C.

When Freed visited San Francisco in 1988, he and Simon began by taking a careful look at the Old Main, noting the L-shaped curtain facade that runs along Larkin and Fulton streets. "That is very fancy, it has the most detail, the thickest granite, it's the most elaborated piece, it has a fancy cornice and so on," Simon explained. The curtain facade is what gives the library its Beaux Arts character, making it an integral part of the larger Civic Center. They walked around the corner to McAllister and noted how "suddenly the expression of the building changes to the expression of the stacks, and the cornice is more simple and the windows are simple." Finally comes the tail, the back of the library toward Hyde Street, with its unfinished look. George Kelham's 1917 design "told us that we needed to do something that mirrored that."

The use of affinity groups, such as the one organized by the Gay and Lesbian Founders Committee pictured here, to raise money in respective parts of the city's diverse community proved to be a major breakthrough in the Library Foundation's Main Campaign. This controversial fund-raising concept has helped redefine modern philanthropy.

Library commissioner Steve Coulter, Mel Swig, Mayor Frank Jordan, Charlotte Swig, and Kenneth Dowlin (left to right) at the groundbreaking ceremony for the new main library on April 23, 1992. In a major loss to the campaign, Mel Swig, who cochaired the Main Campaign with his wife Charlotte, died in April 1993.

Looking westward from Market Street through the United Nations Plaza and then into Fulton Street, Freed and Simon noted that the Federal Building on United Nations Plaza is closer to the center line of Fulton Street while the Old Main is set back to give a sense of opening up into the Civic Center for a grand view of City Hall, the jewel in the Civic Center's crown.

Accordingly the New Main is set back an equivalent distance from Fulton Street, and in what Simon described as an homage to the Bibliothèque Ste. Geneviève in Paris, Freed decided to re-create the spirit of the L-shaped curtain facade in mirror form. Hence the large windows (which in the New Main are square not arched), the small windows above, and the granite facing, which was taken from the quarry in the Sierra Nevada where the stone for the Old Main was cut.

While paying homage to the past—from the Old Main to Beaux Arts Paris to the classical world—the architects were designing a building for the twenty-first century that would house a high-tech library. Thus the Grove and Hyde sides are in a modern style that both reveals the library within—windows aligned with each floor, large windows above the main entrance on Grove Street—and provides a transition to the glass-and-steel structures lining Market Street. They designed a building, Freed said, that reflects "a genuine struggle between competing [architectural] visions of the city."

To sharpen their understanding of library design, Freed and Simon traveled to Europe in January 1990 with Steve Coulter, Ken Dowlin, and Kathy Page, who had been hired by the library as facilities coordinator for the New Main. To get a sense of how libraries that were unique for their time worked, they visited numerous buildings, ranging from the grande dames (the Bibliothèque Ste. Geneviève and the original Bibliothèque Nationale in Paris, pages 60–61) to the new upstarts (the Bibliothèque de France and the Bibliothèque Publique d'Information in Paris, the Centrale Bibliotheek in Rotterdam, and the Staatsbibliothek in Berlin).

The trip provided an opportunity to rummage through the world of European libraries and select what would work well in the New Main while rejecting those design aspects that were less than satisfactory. Freed was struck by the different facades on the Bibliothèque Ste. Geneviève, and both he and Simon were fascinated by the openness and use of natural light in both the old and the new, for instance, the dramatic second-floor reading room in the Bibliothèque Ste. Geneviève and the huge open spaces of the modern Staatsbibliothek. For Dowlin, whose approach to library building after three previous experiences was very practical, the trip was about what worked and what did not work in everything from creating a flexible design that would permit adjustments for technologies still uninvented to the best way to change lightbulbs.

The European tour brought together a team whose members felt comfortable working with each other and were ready to adjust quickly to the very demanding design process that lay ahead. The trip had a significant impact on the design of the library. All of them were struck, even in the dark days of January, by the uses of light and open space. Hence the New Main has a five-story central atrium and grand staircase where light cascades downward into the center of the building, which was influenced by Berlin's Altes Museum, and numerous light wells and two-story rooms. Large, well-lit reading rooms, evoking the grand reading rooms of Europe, are located on the third floor (in the Center for Humanities and General Collections) and the fourth (in the Center for Business and Technology).

Library Foundation executive director Sherry Thomas stands between the architects of the New Main, Cathy Simon of Simon Martin-Vegue Winkelstein Moris and James Ingo Freed of Pei Cobb Freed & Partners.

Dowlin was particularly concerned with openness and flexibility. In a library more than three times the size of the Old Main, he wanted—and needed because of severe budget constraints at the time—a library that could be run by a staff of approximately the same size as the staff for the Old Main. Thus open space meant extended sight lines so a small number of staff members could monitor a larger area. Open space, for Dowlin, also meant the ability to adapt the building to the future demands of technology and emerging book, manuscript, and ephemera collections.

Then there were specific ideas garnered from the European trip and adapted for the New Main. Patrons are directed to the Center for the Blind and Visually Impaired by a red granite strip in the Sierra white granite floor, inspired by a similar feature in the Salle Louis Braille in Paris's Mediathèque. Signs throughout the library have infrared scanners that, when activated, talk to sight-impaired patrons. The High Technology Showcase, which permits a continuous update on emerging technologies, was influenced by a similar showcase in Paris's Bibliothèque Publique d'Information.

The design also has important original elements. Freed and Simon became fascinated with the use of bridges and their metaphoric significance. A bridge from the Larkin Street entrance passes over the large browsing library on a lower floor and connects with the atrium. A second bridge links the Fulton Street entrance with the atrium. The architects see the building itself as a bridge between the city's political home in the Beaux Arts Civic Center and the modern

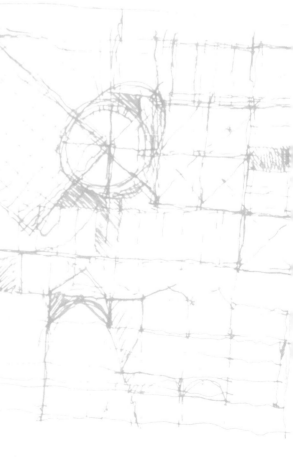

CUBBYHOLES

❊

THE NICE THING ABOUT BEING A WRITER is that you never know who's reading you—or why. My most recent novel, *Maybe the Moon*, involved a dwarf actress living in Hollywood, so last year I found myself addressing the national convention of the Little People of America, where everyone in the audience was less than four feet tall. During the question-and-answer session a man stood up to express his disappointment in my portrayal of a little person. My heroine wasn't believable, he said, because she'd often thought things that he himself would never think. The room got terribly quiet, then a woman shot to her feet and confronted my critic. "That's because you're a man!" she yelled. And all the other women burst into applause.

I love this story because it illustrates how the cubbyholes we build for ourselves are often woefully inadequate. The people in that room had assembled because of their size, but their perception was also shaped by their gender, their upbringing, their race, and an increasingly rare commodity called individuality. Sometimes we humans just can't be pigeonholed. I'm gay, but I find far more to like in Paul Auster than in Jean Genet. I'm Caucasian but I prefer Amy Tan to John Updike. I'm male but I'll always pick Anne Lamott over Norman Mailer. I'm a person, not a publishing market, and I revel in the aberrations that make me that way.

As a writer, I try to reach the part of my readers that isn't gay or straight, black or white, young or old—the part that is simply and vulnerably human. If I succeed at this, I can lead them anywhere, make them feel the sting of any oppression, however alien to their own experience. That's why I cringe a little when I see bookstores restricting some authors to the Gay and Lesbian shelf, or the African-American shelf, or the Feminism shelf, when works by writers who are straight, white, and male are invariably displayed up front as Literature. A bigot browsing through such a store—with all his enemies conveniently segregated—has little chance of stumbling across a book that will open his mind. Literature, in my view, is meant to cross borders, not preach to the choir.

I might have similar misgivings about the new main library's special-interest collections if I didn't fully understand their importance to scholars and readers alike. I also understand the spirit of San Francisco, a place where our similarities are revered just as much as our differences. In this city, at least, we have plenty of straight people secure enough to search for a book in the Gay and Lesbian Center—and white people wise enough to know that a novel from the African-American Center can still speak eloquently to their own secret dreams.

I hope so, anyway.

Armistead Maupin

commercial buildings on Market Street, between what Freed called the heart of the city and its commercial belly, between the library of the past and the library of the future.

The use of new technology is perhaps the most striking aspect of the New Main. Under the guidance of Dowlin, a pioneer in this area, the New Main is at the center of a systemwide network that allows patrons to access the catalogue and electronic databases, and reserve and renew materials from a branch, the Main, or their home. With about six hundred computer terminals for staff use and on-line public access—and custom-designed worktables that permit similar access for personal computers—the library is fully wired for multimedia. To guarantee flexibility for present use and new technologies, there are electrified floor decks that can be rewired at a later date. Through its computers, the library provides access to abstracts and the full text of thousands of journals and periodicals; to various parts of special collections (called the San Francisco Electronic Encyclopedia), including the library's enormous photographic archives; to an image bank of thousands of pictures, drawings, and art reproductions, which can be displayed on high-resolution monitors and reproduced on color laser printers; and to a wealth of government and business information. The Center for the Deaf and Hearing Impaired offers large-screen video viewing; the Jobs and Careers Center, a microcomputer for preparing resumes; and the International Center, multilingual orientation screens and audio and video stations for studying English as a second language. A fully multimedia 247-seat auditorium on the lower floor permits videotaping or screening of previously recorded materials. Via the Telephone Information Project, patrons can call the library with reference questions and speak with technicians who can access information from CDs. TIP also permits non-English-speaking patrons to talk with librarians who know their language. The Children's Electronic Discovery Center allows children to explore and play with new media. While the New Main will be the central server for branches and home use, it will also be an entry point, via the San Francisco Connection through the Internet, to the larger world of networked libraries and information sources, such as the Library of Congress. Using microwave and satellite technology, the library's fully multimedia production studio has the capacity to upload or download to other facilities and provide teleconferencing.

Model of the New Main showing an earlier version of the facades that face Grove (foreground) and Hyde (right) streets. The main entrance is on Grove Street. An atrium and stairwell at the center of the building allow natural light to flow into the interior.

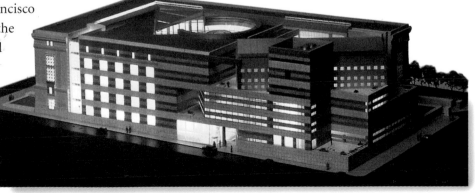

were made due to the January 1994 Northridge earthquake in Los Angeles. The contractor, Huber Hunt Nichols, went through the entire library to reweld the joints where the columns met the beams. The completion of the frame was marked by a topping-out ceremony on May 19, 1994. The building was finally completed in December 1995. All the systems were switched on and tested, and the building was further tested for energy efficiency and indoor air quality. Early in 1996, for the sixth time in its history, the staff packed the enormous collection of books, periodicals, documents, and other materials that now amounted to millions of items and moved them across Fulton Street into the new main library.

SECURING THE FUTURE

From the moment that Ken Dowlin walked in the door in October 1987, he faced a financial crisis at the library. Within a year there would be funding for the construction of a New Main thanks to Proposition A, but the operating budget of the library would be shaped for the next six years by the huge deficits that Mayor Art Agnos inherited from the Feinstein administration and passed on to Mayor Frank Jordan in 1992. The prospects for the library were grim: the city could build a new state-of-the-art library, but would not have sufficient funds to staff and run its library system properly.

The Pioneer Monument was moved in July 1993 from its original location at the corner of Hyde, Grove, and Market streets to a site on Fulton Street between the Old Main and New Main.

Because Agnos was an active supporter of the New Main, Dowlin and the library commission hoped that he would find some way to increase the library budget. But they were in for a rude awakening. When they asked for a 5.1 percent budget increase early in his administration, Agnos responded by asking the commission to prepare a budget at 75 percent of the existing level. When the commission held the line, Agnos proposed closing five branches and reducing library hours including all service on Sundays. The response was predictable: a tremendous outpouring of opposition from neighborhood branch supporters followed by a compromise. The board of supervisors transferred $700,000 from the city courts budget to the library. Only the downtown business branch had to be closed.

A REPOSITORY OF TREASURES

❋

AT THE AGE OF ELEVEN, I was in the seventh grade at Spring Valley School. After school, I walked seven blocks to reach my Chinatown home in a basement where my father's blue-jeans factory operated. I must hurry, for I had to buy the dinner groceries for a family of six and get to Chinese evening school before the bell rang at 5:00 P.M. There I would study until 8:00. But every four days, I squeezed in a pleasure dividend for myself—I would stop at the public branch library (then called "North Beach") at Powell and Jackson on my way home, where I would return the allowed four books and choose four new ones. I read—I devoured a book a day. They were my escape, my easy teacher of the English language in various styles, my window into other worlds. *And they were free!*

This habit was fortified for several years. As a Chinese female teenager hemmed in by cultural interdictions, I found acceptable indulgence in this pleasure. The library became another kind of friend during college years, as a source of references for those endless term papers. It was also an information mine during the forties and fifties, those early years when my husband and I were establishing our own business in manufacturing ceramics and importing.

The time came when we could afford to buy books, but we continued to count on both the main library and the Golden Gate Valley branch as valuable resources for special needs. Did we need a new refrigerator? A new car? A new mattress? We wouldn't dream of choosing an important investment without visiting the reference room of the Main.

Our children grew up familiar with our branch library, only three blocks away. They knew that on Saturdays their dad would accompany them to browse and choose a subject to study in order to frame a presentation for our weekly "show-and-tell" hour before Sunday dinner, when each of the four took his/her turn in front of the fireplace, to speak and answer questions on his/her chosen topic.

San Francisco's public libraries have provided important inspiration and information for my growth and my family's growth. Reading and writing, together with critical thinking, are valued pleasures and disciplines. The New Main will offer present-day technologies, be a repository of treasures, a community center for learning and pleasure. Unlimited choices for self-education and personal development will be available for all ages, races, and religions. Offering a free horizon, the Main takes its place among our democracy's greatest guarantees.

Jade Snow Wong

Jade Snow Wong

The New Main is graced with an outstanding collection of public artwork, including Ann Hamilton and Ann Chamberlain's card wall. Catalogue cards from the old main library are embedded in the wall, preserving the accidental juxtapositions that users of the old system experienced while thumbing through the catalogue. For a $1 donation, San Franciscans were invited to embellish the cards.

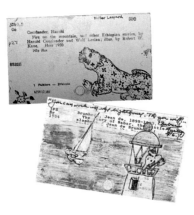

Dowlin moved quickly to head off antagonism between supporters of the New Main and the branches by founding the Council of Neighborhood Libraries. Ultimately the uproar served to publicize the plight of the library and increase support for Proposition A. But the larger problem of funding remained. The library was entering a period that would become all too familiar to students of the past. With a flat budget, service was declining, and staff was being cut. The book budget was stagnant, meaning that the purchase of certain types of books, such as best-sellers, was curtailed, creating longer and longer waiting periods for those who reserved them. "We cut the budget every year I was on the commission," recalled Dale Carlson, who served from 1988 to 1993. "We kept every branch open. We whittled down the hours. We whittled down the book budget. It was a horrible, horrible process."

There were no improvements in the budget situation with the election of Frank Jordan in November 1991, only less sympathy from the mayor's office. Jordan took office facing an even larger deficit. "Jordan thought the commission was motivated by politics, that we were trying to come up with something so draconian that he wouldn't cut our budget," Carlson explained. The library was trapped in a situation from which it seemed almost impossible to escape.

As early as 1988, Mary Louise Stong had suggested that the commission explore a special tax to support the library, an approach that had been tried with varying degrees of success for a number of smaller California libraries. In 1993 the commission started discussions with the Jordan administration on a special property tax that would go directly to the library. The original polling showed that there was support for a parcel tax.

For Jordan, who was elected with substantial backing from the real estate industry, the library was to become a vehicle for his larger, probusiness agenda. Although Jordan disliked the idea, he offered to put a parcel tax for the library on the ballot with the provision that it contain a pass-through measure, which would allow landlords to pass a portion of the tax on to tenants. The pass-through was a lightning rod for tenant organizations, which are a formidable force in a town where the majority of residents are renters. A pass-through was "the kiss of death," according to Friends board president Diane Filippi. "It would divert attention from the real issue—the library." At the very first discussion of a parcel tax with a pass-through, the library commission was confronted by a group of angry and well-organized tenants.

After prolonged negotiations, Jordan refused to remove the pass-through from the initiative. As a result, Filippi and John Whitehurst, the consultant hired by the Friends to manage the anticipated library campaign, went to the supervisors, who immediately agreed to put the parcel tax on the ballot without a pass-through. On the day that Filippi and Whitehurst were to meet with supervisor Kevin Shelley to ask him to take the lead in putting a proposition on the ballot, Dowlin came running up the City Hall steps to say that the library had just received a $4 million windfall for the next year's budget. The windfall made it unnecessary to go to the voters for added funding for the library and saved Jordan from the embarrassment of having the supervisors support a ballot measure that he opposed.

The following year the library was faced with another major cut in its budget, and it became clear that a viable library system could not survive with the anticipated cuts. The Friends conducted a series of "town meetings" at which the attendees voted to support a charter amendment that would provide for a set-aside for the library. The set-aside would require the city to fund the library from existing property taxes at the rate of two and one-half cents for each $100 of assessed valuation for the next fifteen years. The Library Preservation Fund went on the June 1994 ballot as Proposition E. With an impressive support organization left over from the 1988 Proposition A campaign and the New Main now a very visible symbol of the future rising from Marshall Square, the Proposition E campaign quickly churned into gear. In a move that ultimately inspired support-

Maquette of Alice Aycock's sculpture for the New Main. Aycock designed a spiral stairway between the fourth and fifth floors of the glass-enclosed reading room that projects into the great atrium. It is echoed by her sculpture that is suspended from the reading room's support columns and looks like the stairway unfurling.

ers of Proposition E, Jordan, who opposed the set-aside, fired six of the seven library commissioners in February 1994, all of them his own appointees, when they continued to propose branch closures as the best way to deal with the budget shortfall. Among those fired was Steve Coulter, a major leader of the Library Foundation's campaign to fund the New Main.

In June, the library won its second big victory with 70 percent of the vote. The impact of Proposition E was immediately visible. Over its first two years, $9 million was spent for more books, 300 hours per week were added at the main library and its branches, and 250 employees were hired. With their second big victory, library supporters could celebrate the fact that they were well on their way to building a world-class library.

CHAPTER TEN

A HOUSE OF MANY VISIONS

❖

The Library of the future

Even after thirty-five years of relentlessly campaigning for the library, Marjorie Stern, a leader of the campaign to build the New Main, still corrals potential donors and supporters to say, "We have built the New Main, but we still have not built a world-class library. We need you and every San Franciscan to build that library." In a notoriously fractious town, the construction of the New Main

Detail from a doorway of the old main library. Many of the design details of the Old Main evoke the Italian Renaissance.

is a remarkable achievement representing the coming together of an increasingly diverse community around an institution that is sorely needed by all San Franciscans. It reflects a major step toward the completion of the goals of the library's founders, who spoke of a great urban library, and of the vision of James Duval Phelan and his associates, who wanted a great library as part of a larger political-cultural complex that would become the city's Civic Center.

The New Main also marks the literary maturation of the Bay Area. In the past four decades, the city has gradually reclaimed and redefined its reputation as a literary frontier. A writers' haven of international repute, the city is also the center of a heterogeneous book community that includes nationally known bookstores, some of the best practitioners of the book arts, and a thriving and innovative publishing industry. The span of this community's interests is remarkable—from fine printing, papermaking, and binding, with their emphasis on hand craftsmanship, to the electronic frontier, where the book is transformed into something entirely new. Fittingly, the New Main's collections celebrate the full range of these activities, and the city finally has a library consistent with its literary traditions.

The New Main, as its supporters have constantly emphasized, is the outcome of a citizen's movement, the work of thousands of volunteers who eagerly gave their time and money because of their belief that San Francisco deserved something better than the institution that it had long endured. Since the late 1950s the city has undergone a physical remake that has been heavily focused on the plans of the downtown business community and the needs of the city's cultural elite. Community activists have forestalled and reshaped some of these plans, and a motley crew of cultural partisans has built a joyfully unorthodox arts community in dozens of lofts, warehouses, and storefronts. Simultaneously, vital social institutions, particularly the city's school system, have deteriorated dramatically. Against this backdrop, the campaign to build and sustain the New Main as a true people's institution is all the more striking.

BUILDING ON A GREAT ACHIEVEMENT

The library remains a work in progress, a library of many visions that only over time, and if properly supported, will cohere into a world-class library. For example, the library is far from having a great book collection after prolonged periods of inadequate acquisitions and the rampant theft that took place before the installation of a security system. The library owns fine special collections and the beginnings of a series of new special collections housed in centers that reflect the interests and needs of a diverse community, but each requires ongoing and dedicated nurturing to meet its full potential.

Preceding pages: The Fulton Street side of the new main library, showing a portion of the Pioneer Monument.

The library's electronic infrastructure has already extended, in dramatic fashion, the library's informational reach via the Internet and data services. City librarian Kenneth Dowlin and his associates are working on a range of services—such as electronic access to city hall and digital archives where videos of literary events can be stored—that would provide important information in new, more accessible formats. The library is becoming part of a larger informational network, a global network of interconnected libraries. At some time in the future, this network could begin to do justice to the idea of the universal library that inspired the founders of the great library at Alexandria. Using personal computers, patrons can access this system either from home or from a

Supporters of the New Main signing a block of stone that was hoisted into place in the facade of the new library after the topping-out ceremony on May 19, 1994.

branch, thereby redefining library patronage. This system, if properly managed, could be a major step in bridging the gap between the information rich and the information poor, those with access to computers and those without. Along the way, significant problems will need to be addressed: What is the proper balance between books and materials in electronic formats? To what extent can the library seek additional revenues through the commercialization of some part of its research services without compromising its mission as a *free public* source of information?

The nature of the fund-raising campaigns that built the New Main will require a fundamental redefinition of library service. Because of the Library Foundation's innovative approach, the library has a large, diverse constituency of stakeholders who see themselves as having a very direct investment in the operation of the New Main, particularly through the collections their donations are going to build. As a result, many will expect librarians to work willingly and eagerly with the community to develop and utilize the collections. The library's changing information stream, especially the magnitude of its flow, will require a high degree of specialization and training for librarians. The librarian of the future will be called on not only to manage flows of information, but also to provide leadership in working with patrons and volunteers to define the proper role of the library. From the start, the New Main was designed with greater accessibility in mind. Accessibility for the community is a central theme of the strategic plan developed by Dowlin and the library commission. Providing new levels of accessibility will be a major challenge for knowledgeable, service-oriented staff members whose work environment is governed by stultifying civil service requirements.

INSTRUMENTS OF OUR HUMAN ORCHESTRA

LIKE MANY GAY MEN and lesbians born in the 1950s and before, I discovered the first evidence that I was not entirely alone by going to the local library. At that age—my early teens—I was all but overwhelmed with guilt and shame at my attraction to men, and the thin material contained in my small-town library did little to counter that. Still, at the library I learned that words existed to describe what I knew myself to be; and if somewhere someone had named my state of being, then of necessity I could not be alone. I am not overstating the case when I say that this knowledge enabled me to survive until a time when I was better able to understand and appreciate my God-given place in the scheme of things.

I offer this anecdote not as an illustration of an experience unique to gays or lesbians—exactly the opposite. I suspect that all library patrons, present or fallen away, have had some similar experience, in which the library provided a resource for information which turned out to be life-changing. The very universality of that experience underscores the heady power of the written word, our most democratic means of disseminating information, and the magnificent responsibility of the institutions charged with preserving and protecting our access to those words. Books, and by extension libraries, are the foundation of democracy, because they provide now and for the foreseeable future the cheapest, most portable, most accessible, and most enduring means for the exchange of information, ideas, and ideals.

In this much-vaunted Age of Information, I feel I need to make clear my definition of terms. By "books" I mean exactly that—printed words bound between covers. Of course libraries should adapt to and offer new or improved means of gaining access to ideas. But their primary commitment must and should be to words on paper, for among all the means of "getting the word out," books best meet these necessary criteria: cheap, portable, accessible, enduring.

As information becomes increasingly controlled by large international conglomerates, books continue to provide our best means to the end of giving voice to the almost infinite varieties of expression of the human condition. They offer practical and aesthetic advantages which no other means of communication provides. They are the instruments of our human orchestra, whose simplicity and tradition enable the composition of a vast, ongoing, unending symphony, a dialogue between and among peoples. They are our best means of bringing harmony to human endeavor.

Fenton Johnson

The support community, which presently consists of four organizations—the Friends of the Library, Keep Libraries Alive!, the Library Foundation, and the Council of Neighborhood Libraries—is being challenged to sort out and define the role of each organization while increasing efforts to build the library's collections and services. The various aspects of support work, whether serving as a volunteer at the information desk or approaching a major foundation for funding, are all essential to the future of the library. Even with passage of Proposition E in 1994, which guaranteed the library a percentage of the city budget for fifteen years, the library has not been able to isolate itself from the city's larger financial problems, which are likely to worsen before they improve. Indeed, the library's very success in securing a bigger budget may make it a target of opportunity for other city departments that see themselves as less fortunate. These potential conflicts can be offset by the kind of alliances the library is already putting

Drawing by Nancy P. Sun, looking upward at the spiral staircase and central atrium of the New Main. The complex design of the atrium became an emblem of the Library Foundation's Main Campaign.

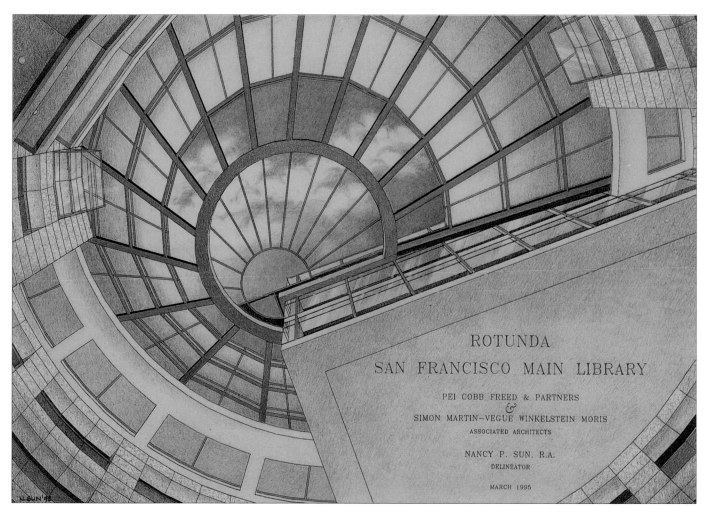

ROTUNDA
SAN FRANCISCO MAIN LIBRARY

PEI COBB FREED & PARTNERS
&
SIMON MARTIN-VEGUE WINKELSTEIN MORIS
ASSOCIATED ARCHITECTS

NANCY P. SUN, R.A.
DELINEATOR

MARCH 1995

The 1917 main library featured exquisite details such as relief work on the card catalogue. The catalogue was replaced by a computerized system in the 1980s, increasing efficiency of use but sacrificing the elegance of handwork.

"SPIRITS OF THE PAST, OF TODAY, OF THE FUTURE; EVENTS, PEOPLE, EMOTIONS, AND STORIES—EVERYTHING IS CONTAINED IN THE NEW LIBRARY."

Isabel Allende

together with other city departments, such as working with health officials to provide medical information.

Since its formation in 1961, the Friends has provided private funding for a wide range of library projects, from acquisitions of books and other material to significant planning and fund-raising work by consultants. With the formation of the Library Foundation, private financial support took a quantum leap as the foundation funded not only the equipping of the new library, but also an endowment. Private funding will continue to play an important role in the future of the library, as library supporters like to point out, by providing the margin of excellence beyond the library's publicly funded budget. There still remains the question raised years ago by the Friends: Does private funding risk offering politicians an excuse to short-circuit public responsibility for a vital city institution?

The opening of the branches in the evenings, which followed the budget increase mandated by Proposition E, alone has brought a stunning increase in library patronage. The New Main will undoubtedly attract even more new patrons. Shaping these potential library supporters into an effective force will be a major undertaking in the next few years.

In the 1982 Bowker Memorial Lecture, Lowell Martin assessed the state of the American public library and described the historical accumulation of library functions from its earliest days. First came adult education followed by children's services, recreational reading, research, community center, community outreach, and multimedia center. Public libraries, Martin warned, suffered from "an overload of good works." With the construction of the New Main, the library has changed from a limited and mediocre institution with a small number of excellent collections and a history of innovation—epitomized by the Bay Area Reference Center and pioneering work with the deaf and blind—into a library that has taken on an ambitious range of new collections and services. The San Francisco Public Library faces the problem of all public libraries: how to focus and maintain its efforts while extending service to those parts of the population that need them most, but are least likely to use them. The educational, recreational, and informational needs of San Francisco's residents are boundless. The library can play a significant role in meeting some, but not all of them.

CARRYING ON VENERABLE TRADITIONS

The role of the first libraries in ancient Sumeria is shrouded in mystery. The nature of the artifacts found at places like Eridu and Uruk indicates that the cities of Mesopotamia were centers of a complex trading society that could no longer master its day-to-day relations without record keeping. Hence the first libraries or archives housed lists of possessions, trading records, marriage and dowry

THE PALACE OF WISDOM

WHAT MAKES A LIBRARY SPECIAL? For one thing, it shaped my life. From the age of seven, when I received my first library card, I buried my nose in a book, as my mother said. Initially proud of my reading and writing skills, which my teachers praised, my mother became critical of this sedentary addiction, prophesying that if I didn't go out and play I'd come to a bad end. She was right; I became a poet, and my first published poem appeared in the *Brooklyn Daily Eagle* when I was nine. Through the library I had chosen my career.

My library card was my driver's license in a magical country, my refuge from home. There I could spend hours beyond the reach of my dysfunctional family, exploring in peace and quiet an inner world. In my teens I was curious about old men nodding over a book or newspaper, as they still do. I wondered whether any of them had known Jack London, who died the year I was born, or Walt Whitman, who died the year my mother was born. I pondered the mysteries of birth and death, of time, hoping to find answers to these giant questions.

I still enter a library not only for literature but for its special ambience. Like the New York main branch, the San Francisco Main has the ancient grandeur of European palaces, with that indefinable patina of age and history that provides the mise-en-scène for time-travel and con-

centration. And since renewal is at the heart of creation, the new main library will acquire a similar majesty.

I also hope my books will be read, as they are now, by the young people of the future. Will they wonder if any of the old men there had known me? With luck, in the next century I may still be sitting across the table from young and old, and will extend my hand in camaraderie to both. My book is the hand I extend to future generations, touching their minds and hearts through the pages.

I believe that a library is the palace of wisdom, that it will always fill a need, and that on-line virtual books, like virtual touch or contact, can't replace it. Books have aesthetic, sentimental reality and, not least, the public library is free whereas the electronic one is not. A library is like a palace of fine arts and sciences; a computer is like a glitzy database for arts and sciences. Each serves a different purpose. It's the difference between a Gideon Bible in a luxury hotel and a visit to St. Patrick's Cathedral. A computer can't provide the experience of awe for architecture, art, and history that a cathedral or library can. But both are indispensable to our progress.

Harold Norse

BEYOND THE BOOK

"ELECTRONIC BOOK"—this hopeful neologism neatly captures the sheer scale of change sweeping through the library world today. The term of course refers to a burgeoning product sector that includes everything from CD-ROM-based textbooks to interactive children's literature, and even digitized versions of popular novels. But there is more to "electronic books" than a mere new medium; the term's currency is a powerful indicator of just how text and electronics will co-evolve, and what surprises the result holds in store for libraries.

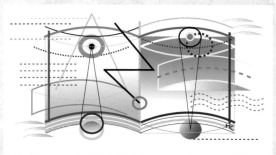

The very inaptness of the term "electronic book" is itself an important indicator. Apart from using text, the electronic books introduced to date are anything but booklike. The quality of the electronic images is horrendous compared with a traditional page, and—more importantly—the experience offered is fundamentally different from anything offered by traditional print. New media will not replace existing media directly; rather, they will penetrate our lives by offering experiences that traditional print does poorly or cannot do at all. Reading *The Tempest* on-screen is pointless and annoying, but imagine an interactive presentation that included seamlessly integrated explanatory notes, historic references, and the opportunity to view video snips of famous Shakespeareans reading or acting out relevant portions of the play.

Of course we will do more than merely revive old greats. The term "electronic book" is misleading because these products are not books at all, but something new. We are living in a moment between two revolutions: one of print, four centuries old and not quite spent, and another of electronics, two decades young and just getting under way. Today's products amount to a bridge between these two revolutions, and the term's historic associations are helping us through a mind-bending shift in much the same way that "horseless carriage" once eased our grandparents into the age of the automobile.

This shift will seem more evolutionary than sudden. Just as practical automobiles lay decades beyond the first horseless carriages, it will be some time before our new electronic books evolve into something that even begin to approach the sophistication and subtleties of traditional print. Traditionalists will howl at the vulgarity of it all, much as fans of manuscript writing shuddered in the late 1400s at the ugly and untrustworthy monochrome works to come off the earliest presses.

And where do libraries fit? In the short run, their role is marginal, for this is a revolution being shaped by individuals and not institutions. But in the long term, the advent of burgeoning digital media will utterly reverse the role of librarians, from that of hoarders of scarce fiber-based information, to filterers and sense-makers of hyperabundant digitally mediated works. Libraries will be all but unrecognizable a few decades from now, but in their new role, they will be even more central to our lives than they are now.

Paul Saffo

agreements, apprenticeship contracts, and other documents of everyday life. But there were also religious works, recipes, encyclopedias, rudimentary histories, multilingual dictionaries, epic poetry—the accumulated knowledge of an urban culture in full flower.

Ashurbanipal, the ruthless warrior, left the earliest known record of a ruler who aspired to accumulate greater knowledge in a library. What intellectual ambition fired Ashurbanipal's curiosity? The great Alexandria library marks the first sustained effort by a group of scholars to collect the books of all the peoples of the world and create a research institution that would further human knowledge. The Romans, emulating the Macedonians and Greeks who founded Alexandria, built structures whose architectural legacy was passed down through the ages to the most modern of American cities. In Rome we find the first evidences of the library as a civic organization defined by an idea of citizen access.

The invention of paper and then the printing press foreshadowed the spread of literacy and the initial stirrings of a nascent democracy. The citizenry came knocking at library doors, so by the early years of the democratic era in the nineteenth century, the great libraries of Europe combined memorialization of the nation-state with the beginnings of the idea of an informed populace. Only with the formation of public libraries in England and the United States, where they flourished, did the venerable institution finally open its doors to everyone— nearly five millennia after its founding.

American libraries, public and private, were one more expression of the "desperate self-reliance," to borrow a phrase from Lowell Martin, that shaped early American democracy. From among a proliferation of library types, civic leaders settled on the public library, most often symbolized by the Boston Public Library, as the library that best served American needs. Through a century and a half of experimentation and repeated identity crises, the public library has risen to great glories and suffered through trying times. Since the 1970s, it has joined the ranks of other underappreciated and misunderstood public institutions that have been grievously weakened by a growing claque of regressive politicians who are unwittingly fixated on a kind of cultural suicide.

How fitting, then, that in San Francisco, with its long tradition of activism, the citizens should reclaim one of its most cherished public institutions. With the construction of the new main library, the American public library system has come full circle. The very act of building a New Main has been a call to arms. It is a plea to every San Franciscan to return to the earliest tradition of American library building, to bring the kind of village involvement—which is the essence of direct democracy and which built the first public libraries—to the shaping of a public library system that will give the citizenry what it needs and deserves.

View of the back of the new main library from United Nations Plaza. The New Main filled the last significant open space in the Civic Center. Future plans call for restoration of the Civic Center Plaza and the construction of a pedestrian mall between the old and new libraries.

A Floor Guide to the New Main

The New Main reflects a successful merging of design, structure, and function to serve the large and diverse communities of the San Francisco Bay Area. The following floor-by-floor tour highlights some of the San Francisco Public Library's special centers and services aiming to meet the multifarious needs of its patrons.

❖

Lower Level

1. Media Production Center
This center houses modern facilities and equipment for library staff to record events and presentations, which can then be distributed throughout the library system and the city.

2. Auditorium
The state-of-the-art auditorium seats up to 260 people for special events and performances, and is fully equipped for audiovisual presentations.

3. Café
The Café offers a variety of beverages and light snacks with seating for up to 50 patrons.

4. Exhibition Gallery
The Exhibition Gallery is environmentally controlled to safeguard the library's collections of rare and valuable artifacts, as well as those on loan from other institutions. The gallery/auditorium/meeting room complex is accessible for receptions and other events even when the library is closed.

5. Latino-Hispanic Community Meeting Room
Sponsored by the Latino community, this space can be divided to accommodate two meetings simultaneously. The room has capacity for 185 people, is audio-visually equipped, and hosts public forums and community group meetings. An attached serving kitchen allows for catered events.

1st Floor

1. Grand Staircase
This begins on the first floor and climbs through the five-story atrium leading to a distinctive skylight.

2. Grove Street Entrance
The library's main entrance from Market Street and public transit lines (BART and MUNI). Automatic sliding glass doors and a ramp entry facilitate access for the physically impaired. Public lockers are also located here.

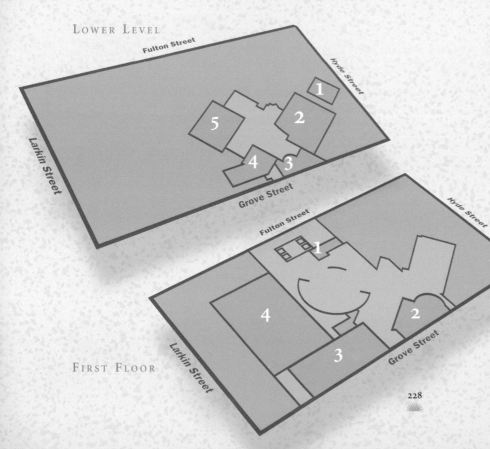

LOWER LEVEL

FIRST FLOOR

3. Center for the Deaf & Hearing Impaired
The center houses book and closed-captioned video collections pertinent to the needs of the hearing impaired community. Patrons have use of TDD (Telecommunications Device for the Deaf) equipment and individual study/video carrels. An adjacent conference room, equipped with large-screen video, is available for group study and video screenings.

4. Browsing Library
In this area, designed especially to encourage exploration, patrons will find new releases, books in popular subjects, new videos, and current daily newspapers.

2nd Floor

1. Center for the Blind & Visually Impaired
The services for the blind and visually impaired in the New Main are a model for libraries across the country. Pathways in contrasting colors enable the visually impaired to utilize the entire building, and transmitter-activated "talking signs" guide blind visitors through the library. The Center for the Blind & Visually Impaired offers text-scanning devices that enlarge print; portable information processing equipment with braille keyboards; speech synthesizers; and electronic reading systems.

3. Grand Staircase

4. Center for Literacy
The Center for Literacy coordinates the library's ongoing literacy programs with its vast team of volunteers, and serves as a location to interview prospective students and tutors.

2, 5. Fulton and Larkin Street Entrances

6. Main Bridge
A suspended "bridge" links the Larkin and Fulton street entrances to the interior of the library. This concourse is an aerial vista point onto the lower level and affords views of the floors above.

7. Children's Center
This is the largest center in the New Main, providing services to children ranging in age from toddlers to junior high school students, as well as to parents and childcare providers. The center has a remarkable collection of children's books in more than 50 languages, audio and video tapes, magazines, and a large multicultural folk and fairy tale collection. The space is furnished with tables and chairs for chess and other games.

Storytelling Room and Early Childhood Collection (7a) Beside the picture book collection is a carpeted area for storytelling sessions.

The Children's Creative Center (7b) accommodates up to 170 children for films, live performances, and craft programs.

The Outdoor Terrace (7c), which is accessible only through the Children's Center, offers one of the few protected open-air spaces for children in the Tenderloin neighborhood.

The Children's Electronic Discovery Center includes multimedia terminals that give children the opportunity to experiment with on-line networking, computer graphics, animation techniques, and learner-initiated educational software.

The Effie Lee Morris Historical & Research Collection of Children's Literature contains some 30,000 volumes, including signed first editions and original manuscripts, which are available to scholars and researchers through Children's Center staff.

8. Friends of the Library Store
The store offers a limited but diverse range of affordable, high-quality merchandise, including items highlighting artwork featured throughout the New Main. All proceeds are channeled back into funding library services.

A hand-colored plate from Walter Crane's Picture Book *(1900), from the* Effie Lee Morris Collection *in the Children's Center.*

SECOND FLOOR

Visitors can make use of an eclectic range of culture-specific resources at the African American Center (above) and the Filipino American Center (top right).

3RD FLOOR

1. AFRICAN AMERICAN CENTER
This center reflects the breadth and depth of past and contemporary African American culture. Its collection includes books, periodicals, photographs, audio- and videotapes, unpublished manuscripts and diaries, and small exhibits, with an emphasis on Bay Area residents and California history.

2. FILIPINO AMERICAN CENTER
Special collections and exhibits in this center spotlight the Filipino American experience, chronicling in printed and audiovisual materials the community's three centuries of struggles, aspirations, and contributions to America—all the while showcasing Filipino history and culture.

3. INTERNATIONAL CENTER
This center focuses on the information needs of people of all ages and nationalities. In addition, it features a comfortable area for reading newspapers and magazines from around the world.

4. CHINESE CENTER
This area houses Chinese language materials and printed and audiovisual resources on all topics related to China and its people. Selected highlights from a collection donated by the Shanghai Library, the Main's sister library, are displayed here.

5. STUDY ROOM
A room designed specifically for individual or small group study. Study rooms are situated on the third, fourth, and fifth floors.

6. TEEN CENTER
The brightly decorated Teen Center is a place young adults can call their own. Catering specifically to the 13–17 age group, the center houses an eclectic collection of books, tapes, magazines, and compact discs.

7. CENTER FOR HUMANITIES & GENERAL COLLECTIONS
This center offers information services in subjects ranging from history to literature. It includes reference and circulating materials in philosophy, religion, psychology, sociology, education, linguistics, science, literature, history, and biography. Within the center is a study area that offers students of all ages a concentrated collection of materials to support their work, including reference materials on the ethnic diversity of San Francisco.

8. JAMES C. HORMEL GAY & LESBIAN CENTER
The Gay & Lesbian Center is specifically devoted to the documentation of gay and lesbian history and culture—the first to be housed in a public library. Its comprehensive collection of books, journals, audio-visual media, and archival materials reflects the lives and history of the gay and lesbian community of San Francisco. The collection also includes works by national and international gay and lesbian authors.

9. AUDIOVISUAL ROOM
Listening and viewing stations for accessing information on audio- and videotapes can be found on the third, fourth, and fifth floors.

THIRD FLOOR

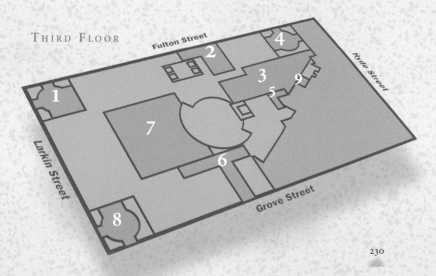

4th Floor

1. Center for Business & Technology
This center provides comprehensive reference services to all facets of the business community. Its resources include a 170,000-volume book collection. Financial services and business periodical indexes are available in both print and electronic formats. On-line catalogs and CD-ROM terminals provide access to the latest U.S. census data, as well as citations and full-text articles from thousands of current business and trade journals and newspapers.

2, 3. Center for Art & Music
The Center for Art & Music offers scholars, musicians, artists, performers, and other interested patrons a complete research department devoted to the visual and performing arts.

The Art Collection, designed to support in-depth research in the visual and performing arts, comprises an extensive art book collection and a separate room for art folios and photographs.

The Music Collection offers facilities for the study and enjoyment of orchestral, popular, folk, and jazz music. Patrons may review scores and listen to compositions. The collection includes books, sheet music, complete scores, and song anthologies. An extensive compact disc and audiotape collection is housed in the adjacent Audiovisual Center.

The Center for Art & Music is also home to one of the foremost musical score anthologies, the *Dorothy Starr Collection*, which contains some 300,000 pieces of sheet music for classical and modern music.

4. Study Room

5. The Audiovisual Center
This center houses a substantial collection of audio- and videotapes and compact discs for circulation, and for listening and viewing at the center's audio and video stations. The collection encompasses music, speeches, plays, feature films, documentaries, and instructional and educational materials.

6. Jobs & Careers Center
The Jobs & Careers Center provides public access computer terminals for individuals seeking jobs, career changes, or career advancement. Users may consult job announcements and peruse test preparation manuals for jobs in a broad array of occupations and professions. A career guidance service helps prospective college students assess institutions of higher learning, their curricula, and costs.

7. International Trade Center
A comprehensive collection of trade journals, directories and import-export business guides is offered to the international business researcher.

8. Audiovisual Room

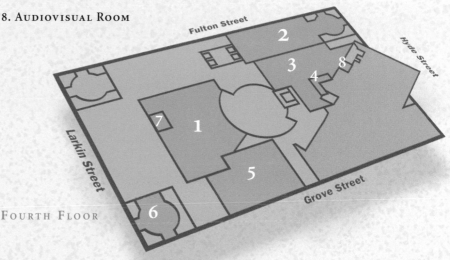

FOURTH FLOOR

The Music Collection offers a breathtaking array of sheet music from a diverse spectrum of musical styles and genres.

5th Floor

1. Wallace Stegner Environmental Center

Named for noted environmentalist and author Wallace Stegner, the center is a gateway to the library's extensive range of materials relating to conservation and the environment. One of the first of its kind in the country, the center provides access to the most current information and a broad range of media, including CD-ROM databases. An on-line catalog system connects it to other libraries, both locally and internationally, and the library's automated network will ultimately provide terminals in San Francisco schools and off-site access by modem to personal computers in homes and offices.

2. Periodicals Reading Room & Periodicals Collection

This two-story, glass-enclosed space, with views from the main floor to the roof, provides open shelving for bound, current-issue volumes, storage space for microfilm, on-line public access catalog terminals, and CD-ROM periodical indexes. The New Main offers 150 current newspapers, 7,500 periodical subscriptions, and a collection of several hundred thousand periodical backfiles in both bound volumes and microfilm.

3. Government Information Center

This center serves patrons seeking legal or government information, and provides access to government-published data on a wealth of topics such as public administration, environmental issues, health and occupational safety, foreign policy, contracts, trade statistics, and demographics. Resources include a comprehensive census data collection.

4. Patent & Trademark Center

In this center, patent researchers are able to search the entire collection of U.S. patents and trademarks from 1790 to the present.

5. Study Room

6. High Technology Showcase

This space is used for displaying and demonstrating the latest in technology hardware and software. The showcase functions primarily as a laboratory for developers to interact with the public to create relevant new products.

7. Audiovisual Room

A souvenir booklet commemorating the building of the old main library in 1916, from the Center for San Francisco History.

Two gems (below right) from the Schmulowitz Collection of Wit and Humor, including Joe Miller's Jests, *which has been described as the most popular joke book ever published.*

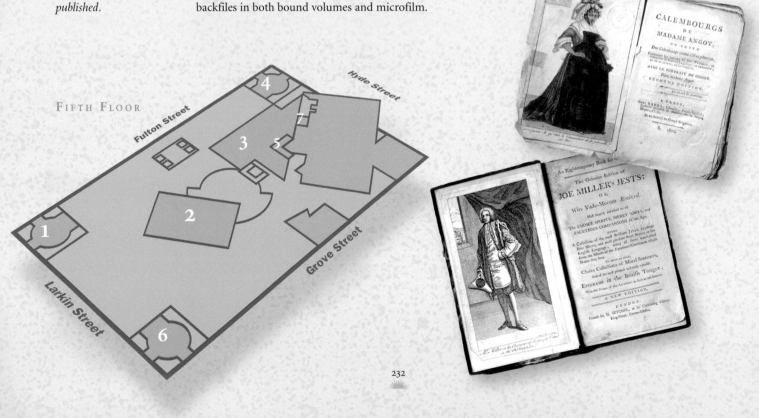

FIFTH FLOOR

232

6th Floor

1. The Main Gallery
This 6,500-square-foot display area features a variety of exhibits from the Main's collections, as well as those on loan from other institutions.

2. Roof Garden & Terrace
Atop the New Main is a rooftop garden and terrace that is open to the sky and fresh air.

3. Closed Stacks
Some of the library's special collections are kept in these closed storage areas.

4. Four Scholar Rooms
Self-contained study carrels provide a quiet work space for researchers and authors.

5. Book Arts Center & Special Collections
This dramatically located area on the top floor celebrates the art of the book and showcases the library's outstanding special collections of books, manuscripts, and archival material.

The environment-controlled Book Arts Center ensures the preservation and accessibility of the library's most cherished treasures, allowing visitors to browse through open shelving and examine books and manuscripts stored in closed stacks. Amongst its prized collections are: the *Robert Grabhorn Collection on the History of Printing and the Development of the Book*; the *Max J. Kuhl Collection* of early and rare printing; the *Richard Harrison Collection of Calligraphy and Lettering*; the *Schmulowitz Collection of Wit and Humor*; and the *Robert Frost Collection*.

6. Center for San Francisco History
This center captures the essence of San Francisco's life and heritage through comprehensive collections of books, old newspapers, historic photographs, memoirs and diaries, and official archives and records. In addition, the center houses a collection of movies and works of literature set in San Francisco, neighborhood newspapers and maps, and oral history tapes and videos.

7. Historic Photographs Collection
This collection was founded with the photo "morgue" of the late *San Francisco News-Call-Bulletin* and includes the *Examiner*'s clippings stock. Its 300,000 images have been culled from the library's larger permanent collection of 3 million images. Access to the collection is made via the photo curator in the Center for San Francisco History. Photographs are available for reproduction for a small fee, by prior arrangement.

8. Elevator Lobby

Diderot's monumental Encyclopédie *of 1751 is one of the treasures in the Book Arts Center.*

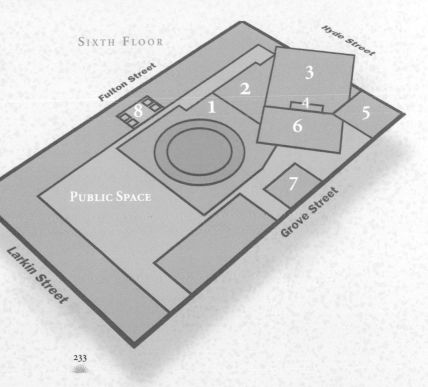

233

Page 69

Blair Fuller is the author of two novels, *A Far Place* (1957) and *Zebina's Mountain* (1975), and a collection of short stories, *A Butterfly Net and a Kingdom* (1989). A longtime editor of the *Paris Review,* he cofounded the Squaw Valley Community of Writers. He is a user of the main library.

Lucy Puls is a sculptor and a professor of art at the University of California at Davis.

Page 73

Marilyn Sachs has written more than thirty books for children and young adults, including *A Pocket Full of Seeds* (1973), *Thirteen Going on Seven* (1993), and *Ghosts in the Family* (1995). She is an enthusiastic user of the Anza and Richmond branches.

Wendy Schwartz is a graphic artist also known for her landscape paintings of rural Northern California, where she has lived since 1983.

Page 86

Jewelle Gomez is the author of *Forty Three Septembers* (1993), a collection of essays; *The Gilda Stories* (1991), a novel; and *Oral Tradition: Poems Old and New* (1995). An expanded version of her essay in this book was delivered as the keynote speech for a fall 1993 fundraising

dinner benefiting the Gay and Lesbian Center of the new library.

John Mattos is a San Francisco–based illustrator whose clients include national publications and major corporations.

Page 100

Ruthanne Lum McCunn is the author of seven books on the Chinese-American experience, including the novels *Thousand Pieces of Gold* (1981), *Sole Survivor* (1985), and *Wooden Fish Songs* (1995). She has had a San Francisco Public Library card since 1968.

Dugald Stermer, illustrator and magazine designer, is the author of Vanishing Flora *(1995) and* Birds & Bees *(1995).*

Page 108

Molly Giles, who teaches creative writing at San Francisco State University, has trained her family, friends, and students to enter public libraries with reverent swiftness and silence, to slip into the G section, to take her book, *Rough Translations,* down from the shelf, and to reposition it in the shelf marked Librarian's Choice. If other writers are wondering: This works.

Jill McElmurry has worked as an illustrator in the United States and Germany since 1978. Her clients include the San Francisco Opera, Random House, and Pentagram Design.

Page 114

Floyd Salas is the author of *Tattoo the Wicked Cross* (1967), *What Now My Love* (1970), *Lay My Body on the Line* (1978), *Buffalo Nickel* (1992), and *State of Emergency* (1996), as well as numerous essays, poems, and short stories. The San Francisco library has supported him and his work over the years.

Bud Peen has been enjoying making all kinds of art ever since gripping his first pencil. He works and lives in Oakland, California.

Page 127

Don Herron has led the Dashiell Hammett Tour in San Francisco since 1977. His published works include two guidebooks, *The Literary World of San Francisco* (1985) and *The Dashiell Hammett Tour* (1991). He first stepped into the main library in 1974.

Earl Thollander, artist and world traveler, has authored and illustrated many books, including Back Roads of California *(1971) and* Earl Thollander's San Francisco *(1987).*

Page 133

Dorothy Bryant has written ten novels, including *Miss Giardino* (1978) and *The Test* (1991). Her *Confessions of Madame*

Psyche was the 1987 winner of the American Book Award. The San Francisco Public Library is still her second home.

Mercedes McDonald's illustrations, primarily in the medium of pastel, have appeared in national magazines and corporate advertising campaigns.

Page 137

Martin Cruz Smith's novels include *Nightwing* (1977), *Gorky Park* (1981), *Stallion Gate* (1986), *Polar Star* (1989), and *Red Square* (1992). He has only one book overdue at the Mill Valley Library.

Dorothy Remington, a painter, printmaker, and graphic artist, is a partner in the San Francisco design studio Akagi Remington.

Page 140

Herbert Gold is the author of more than two dozen novels and collections of stories and essays, including *Travels in San Francisco* (1990), *Best Nightmare on Earth: A Life in Haiti* (1991), and *Bohemia: Where Art, Angst, Love & Strong Coffee Meet* (1992). Some of the pages in these books were written at the North Beach branch.

Debbie Drechsler's illustrations have appeared in numerous publications, including the Boston Globe, Child *magazine, and* Women's Sports & Fitness.

Page 148

Gerald W. Haslam has published eleven collections of essays and short fiction, a novel, four nonfiction works, and five anthologies. He won a Josephine Miles Award from PEN in 1990 for *That Constant Coyote: California Stories.*

Karen Barbour is the author and illustrator of Little Nino's Pizzeria *(1987),* Nancy *(1990), and* Mr. Bowtie *(1991). Her short stories and paintings have been included in many anthologies.*

Page 153

Anne Lamott is the author of *Hard Laughter* (1980), *Rosie* (1983), *Joe Jones* (1985), *All New People* (1989), *Operating Instructions* (1993), and *Bird by Bird* (1994).

Gary Bukovnik, a twenty-year resident of San Francisco, is a fine artist who specializes in watercolor renderings of flora.

Page 156

Bill Barich is the author of *Laughing in the Hills* (1980), *Hard To Be Good* (1988), and *Big Dreams: Into the Heart of California* (1994), among other books. He received a good part of his education at the San Francisco Public Library.

Harvey Hacker is an architect who obtained his first San Francisco library card in 1969. In 1984 he founded Harvey Hacker Architects.

———

Page 159

Michael McClure has published fifteen books of poetry, two novels, and three books of essays. His plays include *The Beard* (1965) and *Josephine the Mouse Singer* (1980). His song "Mercedes Benz" was popularized by Janis Joplin. McClure performs his poetry with Ray Manzarek on piano.

Lawrence Ferlinghetti is a poet, playwright, publisher, and painter who founded City Lights Books in San Francisco in 1953.

———

Page 168

Jessica Mitford is widely known for her 1963 book, *The American Way of Death*. Her other books include *Poison Penmanship: The Gentle Art of Muckraking* (1979) and *The American Way of Birth* (1992).

David Lance Goines is an artist and writer who has worked as a printer and graphic designer for thirty years.

———

Page 177

Don Carpenter's works include the novels *Hard Rain Falling* (1965) and *A Couple of Comedians* (1979) and the screenplay for the 1973 film *Payday*. He died in July 1995.

Mark Adams, who has created numerous tapestries and other large-scale designs for architectural projects, has worked in the watercolor medium for the past two decades.

Page 182

Thomas Sanchez is the author of three novels, *Rabbit Boss* (1973), *Zoot Suit Murders* (1978), and *Mile Zero* (1989).

Joseph Goldyne's paintings, drawings, and prints, offering intimate views of objects and scenes from everyday life, have been exhibited in galleries and museums around the world.

Page 187

Ben Fong-Torres is the author of *Hickory Wind: The Life and Times of Gram Parsons* (1991) and *The Rice Room: From Number Two Son to Rock and Roll* (1993). He is managing editor of *Gavin*, a magazine about the radio and recording industry, and has been a card-carrying member of the San Francisco Public Library for twenty-five years.

Bill Russell has illustrated novels and travel guides. His work has also appeared in Esquire, Outside, *and other magazines.*

Page 199

Peter Coyote, writer, actor, and director, has appeared in numerous films, including *E.T.* (1982), *Cross Creek* (1983), *Jagged Edge* (1985), *Outrageous Fortune* (1987), and *Bitter Moon* (1992).

James Stagg is a painter whose work has appeared in Focus *magazine and* Communication Arts.

Page 204

Ethan Canin is a physician and writer who spent a good part of his childhood in San Francisco. His works of fiction include *Emperor of the Air* (1988), *Blue River* (1991), and *The Palace Thief* (1994).

Manuel Neri, professor of art at the University of California at Davis, is internationally known for his figurative sculpture.

Page 210

Armistead Maupin is the author of the six-volume *Tales of the City* series (1978–89) and *Maybe the Moon* (1992). A PBS miniseries based on *Tales of the City* received a Peabody Award in 1995.

Rik Olson specializes in the time-honored skills of wood engraving, woodcuts, scratch-board illustration, and letter-press printing.

Page 215

Jade Snow Wong is a writer, artist, and travel consultant whose books include *Fifth Chinese Daughter* (1950) and *No Chinese Stranger* (1974). She has carried a library card for more than sixty years.

Cynthia Fitting is a designer and illustrator who creates corporate logos, packaging, and paintings.

Page 222

Fenton Johnson is the author of two novels, *Crossing the River* (1989) and *Scissors, Paper, Rock* (1993), and a memoir, *Lucky Fellows* (1996). He has haunted the Mission and Eureka Valley branches since 1978.

Ward Schumaker's illustrated books include All My Best Friends are Animals *(1991),* Let's Do It! *(1993), and* Mouse Chase *(1995). He is the author and illustrator of* Dance! *(1996).*

———

Page 225

Harold Norse has published several collections of poems and a novel, *Beat Hotel* (1983). His autobiography, *Memoirs of a Bastard Angel*, appeared in 1989. It is available at the San Francisco Public Library, of which he has been a member for twenty-four years.

Stephen Haines Hall, a painter, designer, and illustrator, has created posters for museums, performing arts organizations, restaurants, and wineries.

Page 226

Paul Saffo is a director at the Institute for the Future in Menlo Park. His essays on information and media trends have appeared in publications including *Wired*, the *Los Angeles Times*, the *New York Times*, and *Fortune* magazine.

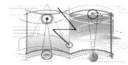

Michael Cronan is president of San Francisco–based Cronan Design, founded in 1980. He is also the creative director of Cronan Artefact, a product development company.

———

The idea for this book originated in 1990 in a conversation between John Owen, the president of Weldon Owen Publishing, and Library Foundation founding president Marjorie Stern, to whom John had been introduced by a mutual friend, Wash SyCip, an Asian businessman with strong links to San Francisco. When John discovered that no book was planned to commemorate the opening of the New Main, he offered to produce one and donate the royalties to the Library Foundation. The editorial structure of the book was outlined by Weldon Owen publisher Roger Smoothy, who then found the author and commissioned the project team.

In writing a history like this, the author must first acknowledge the enormous contributions made by hundreds of anonymous librarians, who built the library and nurtured its collections while fulfilling the role of public servant in the finest sense.

The author would like to thank Peter Ginsberg, who helped him negotiate his contract with Weldon Owen; his research assistants, Sue West, Kathleen O'Brien, Mariska van Aalst, Tom Downs, and Stuart Odom; and the Weldon Owen publishing team of John Owen, Roger Smoothy, Laurie Wertz, John Bull, Lindsay Kefauver, Judith Dunham, and Liz Marken. They brought enthusiasm, tolerance, and great professional skill to the project. He would also like to thank those who have shared their writing and their thoughts about the library with him: Joseph Augustino, Jack Coll, Gray Brechin, Steve Coulter, Ken Dowlin, James Haas, Bill Ramirez, Cathy Simon, Marilyn Smulyan, Bernadette Dominique Soter, and Joe Sugg.

The author would like to especially thank Faun McInnis and the staff of the San Francisco History Room and the Special Collections department, who went out of their way to be helpful: Pat Akre, Stan Carroll, Susan Goldstein, Andrea Grimes, Michael Sherrod-Flores, and Susie Taylor. The Friends' staff, Margie O'Driscoll, Steven Hanks, Janice Winchester, and Cindy Stierman, helped the author wade through their archives, while Margaret Culver and Donna Marion helped with library commission records.

Numerous other people shared their memories, their knowledge, and their files, including John Anderson, Bill Barlow, Malcolm Barker, Anthony Bernheim, Miriam Blaustein, Cathy Bremer, John Brunn, Edward Callanan, Dale Carlson, George Christopher, Kelly Cullen, Joan Dillon, Roberto Esteves, Jerry Flamm, Chuck Forester, John Frantz, Linda Geislinger, Vivian Goodwin, Mark Hall, Gladys Hansen, Peter Henschel, William Holman, Andrew Hoyem, Ann Kincaid, Sandy Kwan, Michael Lampen, William Mackey, Ruth Maginnis, Malcolm Margolin, Harold Martelle, Michael McCone, Gil McNamee, Caryl Mezey, Florence Mitchell, Effie Lee Morris, Nancy Musser, Rudy Nothenberg, Kathy Page, Martin Paley, Allen Pastron, John Philbrook, Diane Filippi, Jack Pollatsek, Rosie Scott, David Schwabe, Marcia Schneider, Eleanor Shapiro, Albert Shumate, Nancy Snyder, Kevin Starr, Carol Steiman, Kirsten Tanaka, Sherry Thomas, Bill Tietz, Val Tietz, Rich Walsh, Celeste West, George Williams, Jane Winslow, and Helen Witsenhausen.

Margaret Mayer, Marjorie Stern, Mary Louise Stong, and Sherry Thomas offered inspiration, detailed criticism, and their willingness, particularly toward the end of the project, to answer a stream of minute questions. Finally, many thanks to Jim Clark and Carol Field, who joined Marjorie Stern as editorial advisors.

The publisher wishes to thank the special contributors to this book—the writers and artists who donated their time and talents to benefit the library. In the end we received more essays than we could accommodate; we apologize again to those who could not be included. A special thank-you is extended to Publishers Group West, who are distributing this book pro bono.

In addition, the publisher would like to acknowledge the following people for their valuable assistance during the creation of *A Free Library in this City*: Pat Akre, Beverly Anderson, Larry Banka, Anthony Bernheim, Desne Border, Brynn Breuner, Amy Brown, Beatrice Burgess, Susan Coerr (indexer), Karen Cornell, Nadia Czap, Sara Deseran, Elena Engel, Roberto Esteves, Mark Fantone, Greg Gaar, Ruth Ann Gonzales, Celia Graterol, Liza Gregory, Andrea Grimes, Lisa E. Halle, Heather Hendrickson, Olive James, Dana Jones, Anne Kohs, Laura Lent, Faun McInnis, Stephen Mietelski, Ruth Mordokowicz, Mark Ouimet, Marguerite Ozburn, Tina Schmitz, David Schwabe, Eleanor Shapiro, Lu Sierra, Karla Simmons, Albert Troskin, Werner Wandelmaier, Darren Ward, Charlie Winton, and Stephen Wirtz.

Grateful acknowledgment is made for permission to publish the following copyrighted material: *This Quiet Hall* © 1995 by Dorothy Bryant; *The Source* © 1995 by Ethan Canin; *The Narrow Temple* © 1995 by Jewelle L. Gomez; *What Horton Hatched* © 1995 by Gerald Haslam; *The Place to Be* © 1995 by Don Herron; *Instruments of the Human Orchestra* © 1995 by Fenton Johnson; *Signs of Life* © 1995 by Anne Lamott; *The Palace of Wisdom* © 1995 by Harold Norse; *The Library of Experience* © 1995 by Thomas Sanchez. All other essays © 1995 by Weldon Owen Inc.

WELDON OWEN INC.

Since its founding in 1984 in Australia, Weldon Owen Publishing has secured a major international reputation for creating high-quality, award-winning illustrated titles for home reference in the categories of cooking, nature, history, gardening, and children's books. San Francisco has been a benevolent host to Weldon Owen's American offices since 1989, and the company is pleased to have had the opportunity to create this book as a gift to the city.

PUBLISHERS GROUP WEST INC.

Publishers Group West occupies a unique position in the publishing industry. Established in 1976 to support and develop independent publishing, it is the preeminent marketing and distribution company in the United States. Headquartered in Emeryville, Publishers Group West currently employs more than 200 people with sales offices in New York City and Toronto, and a primary distribution center in Hayward.

THE LIBRARY FOUNDATION OF SAN FRANCISCO

The Library Foundation of San Francisco was created in 1988 to raise capital funds for the new main library. A 1988 bond measure was overwhelmingly approved, making $104.5 million available for construction of the New Main, and $5 million available for renovation of the branch libraries. The Library Foundation launched the Main Campaign in 1990 as a means of raising private funds to furnish and equip the New Main. During this process, the Library Foundation's work with diverse affinity groups and the philanthropic sector has led to a strong constituent base. This has allowed the foundation to chart a permanent course with the San Francisco Public Library as partners in designing a library system for the twenty-first century.

Thanks are also due to you for buying this book. Royalties from the sale benefit the Main Campaign of The Library Foundation. If you would like to continue supporting the library, please contact the Library Foundation of San Francisco, San Francisco Public Library, Civic Center, San Francisco, CA 94102.

Augustino, Joseph C. "San Francisco Public Library: A Case Study in Librarianship, Politics, and the Public Library." Master's thesis, San Jose State University, 1976.

Bailey, Anne Lowrey. "A Library's Appeal: Not by the Book," *Journal of Philanthropy*, July 12, 1994.

Berelson, Bernard. *The Library's Public*. New York: Columbia University Press, 1949.

Bottero, Jean. *Mesopotamia: Writing, Reasoning, and the Gods*. Chicago: University of Chicago, 1992.

Brautigan, Richard. *The Abortion: An Historical Romance 1966*. New York: Simon & Schuster, 1970.

Canfora, Lucien. *The Vanished Library: A Wonder of the Ancient World*. Berkeley: University of California Press, 1990.

Coll, John. "My Thirty-five Years at San Francisco Public Library." June 1994, unpublished manuscript in the author's possession.

Dickson, Paul. *The Library in America: A Celebration in Words and Pictures*. New York and Oxford: Facts on File, 1986.

Ditzion, Sidney H. *Arsenals of a Democratic Culture*. Chicago: American Library Association, 1947.

Dowlin, Kenneth E. *The Electronic Library: The Promise and the Process*. New York: Neal-Schuman Publishers, 1984.

DuMont, Rosemary. *Reform and Reaction: The Big City Public Library in American Life*. Westport, Conn.: Greenwood Press, 1977.

Eisenstein, Elizabeth L. *The Printing Press as an Agent of Change: Communications and Cultural Transformations in Early Western Europe*. Cambridge: Cambridge University Press, 1979.

Englund, Anne Elizabeth. *Taylor & Taylor, San Francisco Printers: The Early Period, 1896–1911*. Ph.D. diss., University of California, Berkeley, 1978.

Ferguson, Jane. *A History of the San Francisco Public Library*. Nevada City, Calif.: Harold Berliner, 1985.

Ferlinghetti, Lawrence, and Nancy J. Peters. *Literary San Francisco: A Pictorial History from Its Beginnings to the Present Day*. San Francisco: City Lights Books and Harper & Row, 1980.

Fry, James. "The Library Services Act and The Library Services Construction Act, 1956–73: A Legislative History." *Library Trends* 24 (July 1975).

Garrison, Dee. *Apostles of Change: The Public Librarian and American Society, 1876–1929*. New York: Free Press, 1979.

Geller, Evelyn. *Forbidden Books in American Public Libraries, 1876–1939*. Westport, Conn.: Greenwood Press, 1984.

Gleason, Eliza Atkins. *The Southern Negro and the Public Library*. Chicago: Chicago University Press, 1941.

Grabhorn, Robert. *A Printer's Library: An Introduction to the Robert Grabhorn Collection on the History of Printing and the Development of the Book*. San Francisco: Andrew Hoyem, n.d.

Harris, Michael H. *History of Libraries in the Western World*. Metuchen, N.J.: Scarecrow Press, 1984.

———. "The Role of the Public Library in American Life: A Speculative Essay." University of Illinois, Graduate School of Library Science, Occasional Paper no. 117 (1975).

Hart, James D. *Fine Printing: The San Francisco Tradition*. Washington, D.C.: Library of Congress, 1985.

Held, Ray E. *The Rise of Public Libraries in California*. Chicago: American Library Association, 1973.

Helling, Madelyn. "History of the San Francisco Public Library, 1906–1917." University of California, 1966, unpublished manuscript in San Francisco Public Library.

Hobson, Anthony. *Great Libraries*. New York: G. P. Putnam's Sons, 1970.

Johnson, Alastair. "The Robert Grabhorn Collection on the History of Printing and

Development of the Book at San Francisco Public Library," *Bookways*, nos. 15 and 16 (Summer 1995).

Josey, E. J. *What Black Librarians are Saying*. Metuchen, N.J.: Scarecrow Press, 1972.

Kahn, Judd. *Imperial San Francisco: Politics and Planning in an American City, 1897–1902*. Lincoln, Nebr.: University of Nebraska Press, 1979.

Leigh, Robert D. *The Public Library in the United States*. New York: Columbia University Press, 1950.

Lichtenstein, Joy. "Recollections of the Early San Francisco Library," *California Library Bulletin* 11 (June 1950).

Mackensen, R. S. "Four Great Libraries of Medieval Baghdad," *Library Quarterly* 2 (July 1932).

Marshall, D. N. *The History of Libraries: Ancient and Medieval*. New Delhi: Oxford University Press, 1983.

Martin, Lowell. "The Public Library: Middle-Age Crisis or Old Age?" *Library Journal*, January 1, 1983.

Mood, Fulmer. "Andrew Hallidie and Librarianship in San Francisco," *Library Quarterly* 16 (July 1946).

Moon, Eric. *Book Selection and Censorship in the Sixties*. New York: R. R. Bowker, 1969.

Prestianni, John. "A Scribe's Treasure: Calligraphy in the San Francisco Public Library," *Calligraphy Review* (Summer 1993).

Ramirez, William, and Deanna Gumina. "The San Francisco Public Library: A History," *Encyclopedia of Library and Information Science*. New York: M. Dekker, 1968.

Reichmann, Felix. "The Book Trade at the Time of the Roman Empire," *Library Quarterly* 8 (January 1938).

Ring, Daniel F., ed. *Studies in Creative Partnership: Federal Aid to Public Libraries during the New Deal*. Metuchen, N.J.: Scarecrow Press, 1980.

Simon, Cathy. "A Civic Library in San Francisco." *Representations*, no. 42 (Spring 1993).

Starr, Kevin. *Land's End*. New York: McGraw-Hill Book Company, 1979.

Sugg, Espert. "The San Francisco Public Library, 1917–1929," MLS, University of California, Berkeley, 1966.

Thompson, James Westfall. *Ancient Libraries*. Berkeley: University of California Press, 1940.

———. *The Medieval Library*. 1957.

Walker, Franklin. *San Francisco's Literary Frontier*. Seattle: University of Washington Press, 1970.

Wall, Joseph Frazier. *Andrew Carnegie*. New York: Oxford University Press, 1970.

West, Celeste, et al. *Revolting Librarians*. San Francisco: Booklegger Press, 1972.

Whitehill, Walter M. *The Boston Public Library*. Cambridge: Harvard University Press, 1956.

Williams, Patrick. *The American Public Library and the Problem of Purpose*. New York: Greenwood Press, 1988.

Wong, William Shen, "The Development of Archives and Libraries in China: A Historical Sketch," *Libri* 26 (June 1976).

A NOTE ON SOURCES

In a history of this sort, the author is necessarily dependent on numerous secondary sources. Unfortunately space does not permit either footnotes or a complete bibliography. Readers may write the author care of the publisher for a complete bibliography. The primary sources for this history are located in the Center for San Francisco History at the new main library. They include an extensive but very uneven collection of library documents, several volumes of newspaper clippings about the library, the annual reports of the library's board of trustees, the library commission, and city librarians, photographs, and numerous consultants' reports beginning in 1928. The Friends of the Library has its own collection of documents, reports, and newspaper clippings. The minutes of library commission meetings are in the office of the secretary of the library commission. The author has deposited transcripts of the interviews conducted for this history and a small amount of additional documentation in the collection in the Center for San Francisco History.